PENGUIN CLASSICS

THE PSYCHOLOGY OF LOVE

SIGMUND FREUD was born in 1856 in Moravia; between the ages of four and eighty-two his home was in Vienna: in 1938 Hitler's invasion of Austria forced him to seek asylum in London, where he died in the following year. His career began with several years of brilliant work on the anatomy and physiology of the nervous system. He was almost thirty when, after a period of study under Charcot in paris, his interests first turned to psychology; and after ten years of clinical work in Vienna (at first in collaboration with Breuer, an older colleague) he invented what was to become psychoanalysis. This began simply as a method of treating neurotic patients through talking, but it quickly grew into an accumulation of knowledge about the workings of the mind in general. Freud was thus able to demonstrate the development of the sexual instinct in childhood and, largely on the basis of an examination of dreams, arrived at his fundamental discovery of the unconscious forces that influence our everyday thoughts and actions. Freud's life was uneventful, but his ideas have shaped not only many specialist disciplines, but also the whole intellectual climate of the twentieth century.

JERI JOHNSON is a Fellow in English at Exeter College, Oxford. She has written on textual theory, feminist literary theory, Virginia Wolf, and James Joyce, and has also edited Joyce's *Ulysses*.

SHAUN WHITESIDE was educated at the Royal School, Dungannon, and King's College, Cambridge, where he graduated with a First in Modern Languages. His translations from French, German, Dutch, and Italian include Nietzsche's *The Birth of Tragedy*, *Beatrice and Her Son* by Arthur Schnitzler, and *The Confusions of Young Törless* by Robert Musil, all of which have been published by Penguin.

ADAM PHILLIPS was formerly Principal Child Psychotherapist at Charing Cross Hospital in London. He is the author of several books on psychoanalysis including *On Kissing, Tickling and Being Bored, Darwin's Worms, Promises, Promises* and *Houdini's Box*.

SIGMUND FREUD

The Psychology of Love

Translated by SHAUN WHITESIDE
with an Introduction by JERI JOHNSON

PENGUIN BOOKS

PENGUIN BOOKS
Published by the Penguin Group
Penguin Group (USA) Inc., 375 Hudson Street, New York, New York 10014, U.S.A.
Penguin Group (Canada), 90 Eglinton Avenue East, Suite 700, Toronto,
Ontario, Canada M4P 2Y3 (a division of Pearson Penguin Canada Inc.)
Penguin Books Ltd, 80 Strand, London WC2R 0RL, England
Penguin Ireland, 25 St Stephen's Green, Dublin 2, Ireland (a division of Penguin Books Ltd)
Penguin Group (Australia), 250 Camberwell Road, Camberwell,
Victoria 3124, Australia (a division of Pearson Australia Group Pty Ltd)
Penguin Books India Pvt Ltd, 11 Community Centre, Panchsheel Park, New Delhi – 110 017, India
Penguin Group (NZ), 67 Apollo Drive, Mairangi Bay, Auckland 1311,
New Zealand (a division of Pearson New Zealand Ltd)
Penguin Books (South Africa) (Pty) Ltd, 24 Sturdee Avenue, Rosebank, Johannesburg 2196, South Africa

Penguin Books Ltd, Registered Offices: 80 Strand, London WC2R 0RL, England

This translation published in Penguin Classics (UK) 2006
Published in Penguin Books (USA) 2007

3 5 7 9 10 8 6 4 2

"Bruchstück einer Hysterie-Analyse" first published in 1905 (Basle)
in *Monatschrift für Psychiatrie und Neurologie*

Drei Abhandlungen zur Sexualtheorie first published in 1905 (Leipzig, Vienna)

"Über infantile Sexualtheorien" first published in 1908
(Frankfurt-am-Main) in *Sexual-Probleme (Mutterschutz)*

"Über einen besonderen Typus der Objektwahl beim Manne" first published in 1910
(Leipzipg, Vienna) in *Jahrbuch für psychoanalytische und psychopathologische Forschungen*

"Über die allgemenste Erniedrigung des Liebeslebens" first published in 1912 (Leipzig, Vienna)
in *Janrbuch für psychoanalytische und psychopathologische Forschungen*

"Das Tabu der Virginität" first published in 1918 (Leipzig) in Sigmund Freud,
Sammlung kleiner Schriften zur Neurosenlehre

"'Ein Kind wird geschlagen': Beitrag zur Kenntnis der Entstellung sexueller Perversionen" first
published in 1919 (Leipzig) in *Internationale Zeitschrift für ärztliche Psychoanalyse*

"Über die weibliche Sexualität" first published in 1931 (Leipzig) in
Internationale Zeitschrift für ärztliche Psychoanalyse

ISBN 978-0-14-243746-9
CIP data available

Printed in the United States of America

Contents

Introduction

Everyone knows that Freud changed everything. Freud changed everything by making everything about sex. Like the serpent urging the apple on Eve, Sigmund Freud brought sex to a world until then innocent, Edenic. When Freud published his theories, the era into which he wrote, having convinced itself publically at least of its own piety, could now publically declare itself scandalized, incapable ever after of unlearning what Freud had taught. Just as Eve's apple, fruit of the tree of knowledge, yoked sex and knowledge irrevocably.[1] Freud's theories plunged everyone into a lamentable, seemingly inescapable state of knowing. Or so (not just) popular wisdom has it.

When in 1924 Virginia Woolf staked her claim that modern fiction differed substantively from that of previous generations, she suggested a reason: her contemporaries *knew* more than their parents, and *knowing more* meant knowing Freud: 'If you read Freud you know in ten minutes some facts – or at least some possibilities – which one's parents could not possibly have guessed for themselves.'[2] To read Freud was to come to know something that even scrupulous scrutiny could not divine.

But what, post-Freud, did they know? A few racy sexual facts ('or at least some possibilities')? Were their minds coloured by 'Freud' as clear water by a drop of dye: was seeing now seeing always through the tincture of innuendo? Henceforth did all erect monuments connote penises, all undulant mounds breasts? Surely not. As Mary Ellmann quips, 'a person who points out breasts, thighs et al, in the contours of a landscape is asked to leave the average car'.[3] Such mind-numbing banality reduces everything to relentless sameness, and Woolf's modern fiction would have died at birth. Even Freud insisted that sometimes a cigar is just a cigar. Yet this – the irredeemable fall into saucy, seaside-postcard innuendo – is exactly the kind of lost innocence for which popular wisdom holds Freud responsible.

But if for the common reader Freud has made the modern world legible only as a reductive dirty joke, in academia, in consulting rooms, in places where psychoanalysis is analysed or adhered to, Freud's theories have become serious required reading when the knowledge sought is sexual. 'Psychoanalysis is the official discourse of sexuality,'[4] wrote the French feminist theorist Monique Wittig, intending the remark to sting. For Wittig, 'official discourses' coerced, constrained, co-opted, and none more than psychoanalysis, and no one more than women.

These days it's hard to countenance 'official' and 'Freud' in the same sentence. Science and philosophy guffaw at Freud's 'unconscious mind', the former accepting only that there are purely nonconscious processes in the brain but insisting that these are entirely neurological in nature, the latter snorting at the idea that 'mind' after Descartes could be anything but 'conscious'; the oxymoron remains unprovable for one group, pure nonsense to the other. As for sexuality, and its correlate 'gender', every day seems to bring a new discovery in genetics which purports, like the 'gay gene', to prove a biological source for yet another aspect of 'sexual identity', of gender. And while Freud yearned to be 'scientific', psychoanalysis can hardly claim to satisfy Karl Popper's qualifying test for science: no conditions for its 'falsifiability' can be drawn. Similarly, every day brings a new attack on Freud: for his ideas being reductive (those undulant mounds) or abstruse (who can begin to understand the intricacies of his theories, the precise meanings of his terms? Entire schools have developed to translate, gloss, parse and enforce orthodoxy); for his being a liar (remember his false claims to have cured a morphine addict by administering cocaine) or not dissembling enough (how *could* he talk straight about sex to his young woman analysands); for being a bully one moment (he must have coerced his patients into accepting his readings of their memories, dreams, childhoods, lives) or too submissive the next (how could he not see his – at least complicity with – malpractice when Fliess, his beloved Wilhelm, left surgical gauze in Emma Eckstein's nose and Freud read her subsequent bleeding as a plea for him to come to her bedside); a thief (it was Anna O. who invented the 'talking cure') or an exaggerator (and it didn't work anyway, at least on her). More Fraud than Freud, at once shaman and sham, and none more denunciatory than those once enamoured themselves. With such a catalogue it's hard to see what anyone sees in him or his writings.

So what is there left now to know of Freud and sex? What knowledge worth having? What is it exactly that one knows when one knows Freud? What (or how?) has sex to do with knowing? And what has any of this to do with 'the psychology of love'?

Freud himself postulated that 'knowing' is like sex . . . and not just because Adam *knew* Eve. The drive to know, he claimed, emerges in childhood at the same time as what he had already radically and momentously denoted childhood *sexual* instincts or, more precisely, drives. For Freud, the child is not pre-sexual, or asexual. Instead, children are little 'polymorphously perverse' bundles, somatic fields traversed by intense urges. As physiological creatures, they take in and put out; they eat and evacuate; both orally and anally, as stimulus follows response, they experience satisfaction, pleasure. Such impulses – to suckle, to defecate – begin in animal need, but the infant's urge to suck when no need for food exists Freud saw as specifically sexual, its presence marking the oral stage of development. It shares with the explicitly genital sexual drive a stimulus in an erogenous zone (e.g., the urge to suckle / the mouth), an aim for satisfaction (or release of tension), and an object (or part-object, such as a body part) through which that aim can be accomplished (e.g., the breast). The three dominant erogenous zones gave their names to the three principal stages through which Freud claimed infants develop – so, the oral, the anal and the genital (what in strictly infantile sexuality Freud called the 'phallic'[5]) stages – but he insisted the zones' number should be increased to include any region of the skin or mucous membrane capable of sexual excitation. Beyond these drives so specifically erotogenically attached arise other drives – to be cruel, or to look or be looked at, for example – which involve other people. Gradually all fall under the sway of genital sexuality.

But for Freud, all of them, severally and distinctly, made up the explicitly sexual components (or partial drives) which in later adult life might, just might, be integrated into full adult sexuality; any one might also become hypertrophied, over-developed into a sticking point to which adults might sexually return again and again. Adult sexuality takes many and varied forms, selects from a seemingly infinite range of options;[6] collectively, the libido ('the dynamic manifestation of [the sexual drive] in mental life'[7]) is whimsical and inventive even if individually recursive to particular aims and objects. That adult practices and fixations could be so variable, so plastic, led Freud to account for the deviations from 'normalcy', the perversions, as explicable only if infantile sexual drives were several and multivalent. As he drew his increasingly detailed schema, Freud came to think that at any point anything could happen in the early life of the child to cause a particular arrest, fixation or added intensity to attach to any of the erogenous zones or developmental stages he proposed. These fixations would manifest themselves as adult sexual preferences or practices. And despite a recurrent swerve, like a premagnetized compass needle, back to heterosexuality as norm, Freud repeatedly maintained that there is nothing to be 'cured' in homosexuals, nor are they to be judged pathological: 'to undertake to convert a fully developed homosexual into a heterosexual does not offer much more prospect of success than the reverse, except that for good practical reasons the latter is never attempted'.[8] Their predilection results from particular histories that are not to be undone. For Freud, then, the child exists as biological, emotional, mental amalgam which comes slowly to maturity with an individual history unfolding in – and being formed in interaction with – an idiosyncratic familial and social context. No two kids are alike; each adult comprises the interwoven details of a complex, unique history of becoming. But if this suggests forward unfolding, Freud himself construed his theory of infantile sexuality in a reverse movement, analeptically, as a back formation, a hypothesized antecedent, a precondition derived to account for actual adult sexuality. He construed infancy from adulthood, 'normalcy' from perversion.

Freud began not by wanting to account for human sexual variation, nor to find a disturbing theory of infantile sexuality; he began with the desire to explain the disturbing symptoms of his distressed and hysterical patients, symptoms he was convinced were somehow sexual in nature. His (and Breuer's[9]) first theoretical leaps consisted in thinking that their patients' symptoms had their origins in psychical trauma, and that the trauma was sexual in nature. In 1896 Freud added his own 'discovery': these traumas related to actual events experienced in childhood. In short, the daughter was seduced.

None of this could be verified, and when in April 1896 Freud presented to the Viennese Society for Psychiatry and Neurology his theory that his hysterical patients had each suffered actual sexual abuse at some early stage of childhood – '*these sexual traumas must have occurred in early childhood (before puberty), and their content must consist of an actual irritation of the genitals (of processes resembling copulation)*'[10] – and that the father was the agent of abuse, he was met with Richard von Krafft-Ebing's rebuff, 'It sounds like a scientific fairy tale'.[11] Or as James Joyce had it in *Finnegans Wake:*

> we grisly old Sykos who have done our unsmiling bit on 'alices, when they were yung and easily freudened, in the penumbra of the procuring room . . . could (did we care to sell our feebought silence *in camera*) tell . . . that *father* in such virgated contexts is not always that undemonstrative relative . . . who settles our hashbill for us . . . and . . . what a neurasthene nympholept . . . with a prepossessing drauma present in her past and a priapic urge for congress with agnates before cognates fundamentally is feeling for under her lubricitous meiosis when she refers with liking to some feeler she fancie's face. And Mm. We could. Yet what need to say? 'Tis as human a little story as paper could well carry, in affect.[12]

Writing in the condensed, portmanteau language of dreams, Joyce provides a pithy precis *and* implied critique: as Freud, inventor and arch practitioner of 'Sykos . . . on 'alices', listened to his patients, as they talked of their lives, their memories, their dreams, and as their symptoms manifested themselves in shades at once muted ('meiotic': understated) and technicolour ('lubricitous': lubricious and solicitous), he noted their recurrent recourse to 'prepossessing drauma present in [their] pasts' ('drauma': drama, trauma, and from the German *Traum*: dream; and 'prepossessing': possessing them before the fact, preoccupying, both prejudicing and attractive). The cause or source? '*Father* in virgated contexts' (variegated, and Latin *vir*. man, i.e., in all his male variations). For his female patients, Freud read in their symptoms, 'prepossessing' daddies who were 'not always undemonstrative relative(s)'. Joyce, writing later, generously applies litotes – 'not always undemonstrative'. Freud in 1896 thought his patients' fathers too, too demonstrative: they had 'seduced' (now there's a euphemism) their daughters.

In this, his now infamous 'seduction theory', Freud proposed that his patients' belated (adult) neurotic symptoms could be traced to actual early (childhood) experiences of being 'seduced'. Early the empiricist, Freud assumed that adult illness arose from childhood event and that its evidence lay in the tics, paralyses, coughs, catatonias, and in the tangled memories, dreams and fantasies, of the women who came to him for relief. The symptoms were the somatic indicators of events too wretched for conscious recall, the markers of a now forgotten prior injury returning from the realms of repression. Insisting that the childhood assault was actual, Freud puzzled over the precise reasons for its delayed effects, its subsequent irruption in illness. He reasoned that the child could have the experience but not, strictly, know it, for the child has the capacity neither for understanding the experience as sexual, nor for a sexual response not available until puberty. The event as experienced could carry no *sexual* affect. A memory would remain of events which only later could be understood and felt as sexual. What released the affect, and converted the memory into a repression, was a pubertal event (itself often innocent) carrying associations (through elements in themselves usually innocuous) which stirred the earlier memory and made available for the first time an 'unpleasurable' sexual response and an unbearable understanding. In hysteria, said Freud, 'a memory is repressed which has only become a trauma by *deferred action*'.[13]

In general, Freud used 'deferred action' to signify the after-the-fact, retrospective reordering and reconfiguring of, the providing of significance to, experiences or feelings, memories or memory traces, not originally so invested with this (now new) meaning. Individuals' idiosyncratic histories of becoming are repeatedly reread and revised, or as Freud put it 'retranscribed', in 'accordance with new circumstances'.[14] For the retranscription to be traumatic, the initial transcription to which it refers must have been of an event which ought to have been traumatic but which could not be experienced as such, an event the full meaning of which, and the appropriate affective response to which, is *necessarily* unavailable to the child. In short, a *sexual* event which the child could neither understand nor somatically respond to as such. Cognitive sexual understanding and pubertal physiological development are the necessary preconditions for such response. So only post-pubertal associations, which stir the memory and allow it finally to be understood and experienced as sexual, allow the initial event to be, only now, traumatic. As the trauma results from benign associations fixed to a previously benign memory, the usual mechanisms used to avoid actually perceived threat or danger are not available; instead the now intolerable memory and the associated trauma are repressed into the 'unconscious': 'What determines pathological defence (repression) . . . is *the sexual nature of the event and its occurrence in an earlier phase*';[15] '*The traumas of childhood operate in a deferred fashion as though they were fresh experiences; but they do so unconsciously*.'[16] And what is repressed as intolerable will return as illness. His patients' memories 'almost always' involved the father.[17] QED: hysterics suffered from having been sexually abused as children. Or so Freud believed in 1896.

By September 1897 he had changed his mind. As he wrote to Fliess, 'I no longer believe in my *neurotica*' [theory of the neuroses].[18] In the preceding May he had confessed to Fliess of dreaming of having 'overaffectionate feelings' for his eldest daughter. As he interpreted the elements of his dream, he concluded it showed the fulfilment of his 'wish to catch a *Pater* as the originator of neurosis'.[19]

Freud knew he hadn't seduced his daughter; in what sense then could 'the father' originate neurosis? Within four months, he'd abandoned the 'seduction theory' (though it was only with *Three Essays on Sexual Theory* (1905) that he publically parted company from it). His justifications? Hysteria was widespread. Were all these hysterics' fathers molesters? 'Such widespread perversions against children are not very probable,' he reasoned. But perhaps most significantly for the future of psychoanalysis, he declared that 'there are no indications of reality in the unconscious, so that one cannot distinguish between truth and fiction that has been cathected with affect'.[20] Now, he realized, he could not say that his patients' 'memories' were not fantasies.[21] Nor could he claim that all their fathers were 'not undemonstrative relatives'. But if some, perhaps most, such 'memories' were fantasies, to what did they testify?

Later he claimed that his abandonment of the seduction theory marked a crucial moment in the history of psychoanalysis: 'If hysterical subjects trace back their symptoms to traumas that are fictitious, then the new fact which emerges is precisely that they create such scenes in *phantasy*, and this psychical reality requires to be taken into account alongside practical reality. [. . .] And now, from behind the phantasies, the whole range of a child's sexual life came to light.'[22] Slowly his theory of infantile sexuality began to take shape, an infantile sexual life psychical as well as physiological. At the time, he was engaged in a radical selfanalysis. He now scrutinized the riddles presented in his own dreams, his own memories of childhood, what he described as his own 'hysteria', as relentlessly as he did those offered in his patients' symptoms, dreams and memories. In September 1897, he wrote again to Fliess declaring that he had found what he called an 'idea of real value':

I have found, in my own case too, [the phenomenon of] being in love with my mother and jealous of my father, and I now consider it a universal event in early childhood . . . If this is so, we can understand the gripping power of *Oedipus Rex* . . . the Greek legend seizes upon a compulsion which everyone recognizes because he senses its existence within himself. Everyone in the audience was once a budding Oedipus in fantasy and each recoils in horror from the dream fulfillment here transplanted into reality, with the full quality of repression that separates his infantile state from his present one. Fleetingly the thought passed through my head that the same thing might be at the bottom of *Hamlet* as well.[23]

Here Freud first offers the name he will assign to the 'universal event' at the heart of the 'kernel complex' of early childhood: Oedipus. For Freud, every infant – subject to physiological, emotional, mental needs but not yet possessed of understanding, or the capacity to fend for itself – is locked in relationships with parents whose love – and power – it both resents and craves. Central to that early life, he realized, lay the more-or-less successful (but always necessary) wrestling with, and attempted resolution of, that intense tangle of love, power and desire that is the (at first dyadic, then triadic) parent–child relationship. This relation he saw as of paramount – and sexual – significance, even if it took him years to see it without blinkered male bias. Later, in *Interpretation of Dreams* (1900), he was to credit this discovery, too, to his observation of psychoneurotics: 'We learn from them that a child's sexual wishes – if in their embryonic stage they deserve to be so described – awaken very early, and that a girl's first affection is for her father and a boy's first childish desires are for his mother. Accordingly, the father becomes a disturbing rival to the boy and the mother to the girl.'[24] It took him twenty years to recognize that far more likely was that *both* infants began life attached to the mother, that this created an asymmetry, and meant that the path to such heterosexually oriented 'childish desires' was necessarily more complex for girls than for boys.[25]

But of real and shocking significance in Freud's account of the Oedipus complex was his insistence that the child's first, infantile, desires were sexual *and* incestuous. It was to the early psychical reality of these desires, now occluded or repressed, that his hysterical patients' fantasies referred. Caught up into this scenario is the child's burgeoning recognition that not everyone possesses the organ so very evident in the case of one, so very missing in the case of the other. He imagines that his might be taken away; she that hers has been (her own genitalia, so little susceptible to visual self-scrutiny, are imagined by Freud to play no part in this most scopic of scenes). Sexual difference in the child's fantasy consists in being or not being castrated. *He* fears castration, convinced that this is the ultimate punishment lying behind the paternal threat with which his sexual activities, his desire for Mummy, have been met. *She* imagines herself castrated, perhaps for some unaccountable felony, and seeks to find what she has had taken away; envying the penis, she turns to Daddy to provide one; this too is banned; she must make do with an alternative, which she imagines a gift from him, a child. *His* castration complex concludes his infantile Oedipal desires; he now enters sexual latency and, in an ideal world, will eventually satisfy himself with a mother substitute, a wife, and identify with his father, aiming thereby to acquire the power he so clearly commands. *Her* castration complex inaugurates her Oedipal phase, and in her search for the penis she envies, she turns away from desiring mother to desiring father. Her complex will resolve itself with her accommodation to her 'loss', and only when she rests content that she can make do with a phallic substitute (in accepting the child offered by her father substitute). If, indeed, this can be called a resolution; Freud never quite managed to provide a wholly plausible explanation for why, having spurned her mother, she would turn back to identify with her, in a final, necessary turn. Nor did he ever quite satisfactorily account for why she would turn from her early, active, clitoral genitality to one which he saw as ultimately necessary, passive, vaginal. The path Freud described for her from at first polymorphous, then to clitorally active, and finally to vaginally passive heterosexual adult is tortuous and precarious. His analysis here was, he admitted, incomplete: 'We know less about the sexual life of little girls than of boys. But we need not feel ashamed of this distinction; after all, the sexual life of adult women is a "dark continent" for psychology'.[26] Still, the incompleteness galled him, as the contradictions of 'On Female Sexuality' attest: 'our statement about the Oedipus complex only applies, strictly speaking, to the male child'; 'In fact, it is barely possible to produce an account that is universally applicable'; yet, 'we cannot avoid making a certain judgement about femininity as a whole'.[27]

These admissions and denials mark strongly Freud's own resistance, his inability – quite – to accept that he could not fully describe, and exhaustively delineate, a holistic system which at least anticipated every variation, every deviation. His drive was towards what his biographer Peter Gay has called 'the ideal of simplicity; the reduction of apparently dissimilar mental events to a few well-defined categories was his aim in scientific research'.[28] But the drive to *this* scientific research seized him passionately. He described it to Fliess as 'a hobbyhorse', 'a consuming passion', 'in Schiller's words – a tyrant – . . . in (whose) service I know no limits. It is psychology'.[29] And with psychology, specifically what he preferred to call '*psychosexuality*',[30] he thought he had found the answer to more than the 'riddle of the Sphinx'.[31] Tempting as it may have been, though, he never became a 'pansexualist', attributing every motive, cause or drive to sexuality. But he did repeatedly insist that psychoanalysis 'extended the concept of what is sexual far beyond its usual range . . . [It] comprises far more; it goes lower and also higher than its popular sense'.[32] It goes 'higher' when its redirection, its sublimation, feeds the drive to create, to discover, to know.

For, yes, the drive to know *is* akin to the sexual drive. Remember Freud's claim that, coincident with the infantile sexual drives, with a distinct but equivalent force, the desire to know first stirs. It too seeks satisfaction, mastery; its initiating quest is unmistakably sexual information. The first grand question of life – and what are questions but manifestations of the desire to know – is, claimed Freud confidently, a sexual question . . . or rather two questions; he vacillated between two variants: 'What is the difference between boys and girls?' and 'Where do babies come from?'[33] The whole future of our intellectual life, he declared, hangs on the parental reply. Censoriousness ('Put that away!' or 'Stop fiddling') and dissembling ('storks' or 'cabbage patches') produce little cynics, or at best sceptics, who have learned only not to trust adults when the answer really matters. In the face of such evasions, if children are going to know, they will have to proceed secretly. Henceforth, like little Sherlock Holmeses, they pursue their research. Tiny empiricists, relentlessly logical, their now secret questions lead them inexorably on: 'There's a baby in there?! How did it get there? And how, pray tell, is it going to get out?' Only their inability to *see* (or their naive insistence that what can be seen locally must be ubiquitous) hampers them. What they cannot see is that the way in and the way out are the same way; what they refuse to acknowledge is that not everyone is like them. (Freud's model child, being male, puts a very high premium on his penis; he is perhaps most childlike in his insistence that everyone must have – or will come to have or, at last and most terrifyingly, once had – this marvellous organ.) Their researches stymied, they turn to theory, to hypotheses based on observed fact, yes, but also to fantasies rested on beliefs tenaciously held despite the evidence of the senses. Their theories may be wrong – for they lack the crucial information that would put them right (women have vaginas) or cannot accept what is patently true (boys alone have penises) – but each bears the marks of logical extrapolation from the known: 'babies come out like poo' and if this is so then 'boys can have babies too'. In the quest, in its intensity and frustration, in the openness or resistance offered by adults, the seeds of later intellectual life are sown. If adults want to stifle early a child's capacity for independent thought, there is no better way than to dissemble or censor when confronted by the child's drive to know about sex.

For Freud, the implications of this scenario reached far beyond the satisfactions or frustrations of the individual child's desire for sexual answers. In the turn to theory when observation offers no evidence, children most resemble, he claimed, those adults who attempt 'to solve universal problems beyond human understanding'.[34] 'Those adults like me', one imagines him thinking. When his first public outing for his nascent theory of infantile sexuality in its first redaction as 'seduction theory' met with Krafft-Ebing's riposte 'Scientific fairy tale', Freud remarked indignantly, 'And this, after one has demonstrated to them the solution of a more-than-thousand-year-old problem, a source of the Nile! They can go to hell, euphemistically expressed.'[35] What he hoped for, and thought he'd found, was the answer to 'a universal problem beyond human understanding'. What he most shared with his little detectives was the need to theorize in the absence of empirically observed fact. While he could have studied young children and deduced from their behaviour some facts ('or at least some possibilities'), he could never have arrived at his theory of infantile sexuality *that* way. Then too, remember, the evidence offered him came not from children, but from adults, from the manifest symptoms of his adult hysterical patients. The scientist in him assumed an antecedent cause. The theorist extrapolated from the empirically known to the empirically unknowable and, in so doing, became a theorist extraordinaire, the author of a grand narrative, the necessary components of which were only inferrable through the observable after-effects of their own unobservable 'causes'.

Freud the scientist is found everywhere in his writings on sexuality: in his urge to analyse, to schematize, to build a grand theory from his observations in the consulting room, and to nail down all its variations and particularities. But Freud the philosopher, Freud the theorist, Freud the poet, Freud the Modernist, pervades and provokes, unties the knots the scientist strives to make fast. And at his most provocative, as in his reading of sexuality, the knowledge which he derived accounted precisely for its own impossible wholeness. Repeatedly he insisted that becoming (adult, feminine, masculine, heterosexual, homosexual, omnisexual, celibate, the list can only proliferate) was not teleological, however much he felt pressed to account for a pervasive, if diffuse, heterosexuality. No end is ever quite arrived at (or as Joyce, that other Modernist *provocateur*, has it, 'nought nowhere was never reached'[36]). Instead, Freud's temporality opened up the relentlessness of 'retranscription'. His recognition of 'deferred action' made sexuality the cause of its own prior effects. The variability, multiplicity, attachability and detachability of the component sexual drives, assigned and reassigned, gathered and unloosed, in histories which could be, were, endlessly revisable, made sexuality a palimpsest of its own becoming.

In the essays that follow, the preceding narrative comes slowly together, in texts as generically heterogenous as Freud's theories lead us to expect. We have here Freud's writings on sexuality – and following Freud's own prescription, 'we use the word "sexuality" in the same comprehensive sense as that in which the German language uses the word *lieben* ("to love")'.[37] In the first, his inaugural case study, *Fragment of an Analysis of Hysteria (Dora)* (1905), Freud unfolds a narrative of love, desire, deceit and entanglement as intricate, and sordid, as Arthur Schnitzler's *La Ronde*, that other, exactly contemporary, Viennese minuet of promiscuity. No work of Freud has so incited, or enticed, feminists to rage, to defence, or to intrigued elaboration,[38] as this, marked as it is at points by a brisk, if Victorian, patriarchal peremptoriness (as when Freud refuses to believe that a healthy fifteen-year-old girl would not respond favourably – and in kind – to the pressure on her groin of her father's lover's husband's unsolicited erection). He also listens, and believes her tale, though he misses some central, salient facts in his reading of her symptoms, dreams and recounted history. (Most notably, as he admits: 'I failed to guess in time, and to inform the patient, that her homosexual (gynaecophilic) feelings of love for Frau K. were the strongest of the unconscious currents in her mental life' (p. 109, below). He imagined the study a supplement to, and further validation of, the interpretative techniques he displayed in *Interpretation of Dreams*, and his teasing of psychosexual implications from the verbal, and pictographic, clues her two dreams contain prove him, here as ever, interpretatively ingenious. Then, too, first in listening, next in retelling, he had to master the unruly elements of Dora's disjointed account (narrative disorder and incompletion being, he asserts, the unmistakable indicators that the narrator is hysterical, unreliable). No wonder then his comparisons of the case history with a long, short story. Dora, however, responded to his therapeutic demands with her own brisk pre-emptiveness: she gave him notice, and departed a fortnight later, leaving Freud astonished but, as he admits, now offered a chance to write up what otherwise might have become too unwieldy and complex a history to capture in his first foray into sustained narrative.

Next, his 'scientific' treatise on sexuality: *Three Essays on Sexual Theory* (1905). Here Freud explicates 'the sexual deviations', 'infantile sexuality', and 'the transformations of puberty'. But if it is a treatise, it is also a historical palimpsest which found its final form only after Freud interlarded its second, third, fourth and sixth redactions with revisions and elaborations, its weight shifting, and the whole rebalancing as it appeared and reappeared over the succeeding twenty years. It forms the bedrock, the substrata of Freud's radical theories of sexuality. We find, too, 'On the Sexual Theories of Children' (1908), an essay seemingly preceded, but actually succeeded, by the section in *Three Essays*, 'Infantile Sexual Research', which Freud added to that work in 1915. Both insist on the sexual significance of the child's drive for knowledge, a significance made apparent to him with his analysis of the five-year-old phobic Little Hans, whose case history he published between the two.[39] In 'Sexual Theories', Freud recreates the child's world as an extraordinary conflux of empirical investigation, cognitive reasoning and fantasy. Here he first mentions directly the castration complex, and penis envy, as he marks the child's swerve into fantasy and theory when faced with frustrations arising from its lack of, and inability to get, real facts.

The next three essays form Freud's efforts to address 'the psychology of love': 'Contributions to the Psychology of Erotic Life' (German: *Liebeslebens*, strictly 'love-life), a subject which until now, he admits, has been left to creative writers. But novelists and poets must aim at 'intellectual and aesthetic pleasure' and 'certain emotional effects'. Not so the scientist who must 'produce the stuff of reality unaltered'. In stating here, that 'Science is, in fact, the most complete renunciation of the pleasure principle of which our psychical work is capable' (p. 241), Freud reveals his own remarkable, if occasional, blindness to his own pleasure, a pleasure which elsewhere he so eloquently elaborates, a pleasure that comes from satisfying the drive to knowledge. Further, he fails to recognize how much these essays share with the work of novelists and poets. In them Freud offers possible answers to perplexing, counter-intuitive yet regular occurrences in adult sexual life: why some people can only desire those who are unavailable (e.g., the married, or affianced), or some men only women who have 'a bad sexual reputation' (e.g., prostitutes); why some men place their beloveds on such high pedestals that they will inevitably be disappointed by them, and so need to move on, again and again, to other women who they then so place; or why they need always to imagine themselves the one man who can 'rescue' his woman from otherwise moral degradation; why so many men suffer from psychical impotence; why many women are frigid. Freud's answers return to, and read the consequences of, the origins of sexuality in infancy (and the Oedipus complex) and its vicissitudes and frustrations in puberty. Society, religion, culture enhance and mitigate the part played by parents in the psychosexual life of infants and adolescents, though Freud insists on the adult's repeated return to the psychodrama of infancy, often with unexpected results.

In 'A Child is Being Beaten' (1919), subtitled a 'Contribution to the Understanding of the Origin of Sexual Perversions', Freud offers an extraordinary tale of fantasy, scripted, rescripted and transformed, and yet another theoretical investigation into sexual difference, this time with hypotheses on the differing mechanisms of repression operating in boys and girls, men and women. If we look closely, we can see him beginning to revise his previously 'universal' template of the Oedipus complex (here asserted to be 'the core complex of neurosis' (p. 305)), to accommodate what he sees as the very different fantasies produced by boys and by girls. Significant, too, in the essay is Freud's insistent drawing of our attention to the distinction between fantasy and reality. The fantasies involve 'a child being beaten'; through them, the child fantasists clearly experience pleasure, a pleasure, he asserts, no child would experience in viewing a real beating. Here, like Oscar Wilde in the 'Preface to *Dorian Gray*', Freud insists that life and fantasy, like life and literature, differ categorically from one another. The pleasure derived from – and the ethics and morality of – the former could only by the most damaging of confusions be said to maintain in the latter. One can do all kinds of things in fantasy, in film, in novels and poems, that one could not, and often most certainly should not, do in life. But for Freud, what it is we like 'doing' in fantasy will always tell us a great deal more about ourselves than we might be willing to admit.

Finally, in 'On Female Sexuality' (1931), Freud offers a confession: he had never, it seems, paid enough attention to that most pressing of childhood questions: 'what is the difference between boys and girls?' Now he had to admit that his model child was definitely a boy, and that girls were different from boys. The will to knowledge finally triumphed over the effects of conditioning, however belatedly. Fittingly, given his repeated characterization of girls and women, with his final turn to them he has also to admit the inevitability that his theories are, still, incomplete, and perhaps in their very nature impossible of completion.

Freud's theories of sexuality, his psychology of love, have a history, one told in the pages of the pieces here, one more evolving than arrived at. The pages come packed with evidence of Freud's genius: his capacity for creating a *seeming* systemic completeness, frequently subverted by the restless intelligence which drew him to narrative complexity, to multifarious and recalcitrant detail, to the dark, contradictory places and temporality of the unconscious, and by his talent for finding error, deviation, perversion, mistake the most fruitful of grounds for investigation. These pages bear witness to Freud's own passionate drive to knowledge. Finally, then, a return: What does one know when one knows Freud? That knowing has *everything* to do with sex.

Jeri Johnson, 2006

Notes

1. As Sarah Kofman, teasing out Freud's sexual knowledge, reminds us, in the Jewish tradition of the *Zohar*, the word *binah* means at once 'maternal nudity' and 'knowledge, understanding: the word *binah* is used to say "Adam *knew* Eve"'. And what Adam knew when Adam knew Eve was most assuredly sexual (Sarah Kofman, *The Enigma of Woman: Woman in Freud's Writings*, trans. Catherine Porter (Ithaca, NY: Cornell University Press, 1985), p. 95).

2. Virginia Woolf, 'Character in Fiction' (1924), *The Essays of Virginia Woolf*, ed. Andrew McNeillie (London: Hogarth Press, 1988), vol. III, Appendix III, p. 504.

3. Mary Ellmann, *Thinking about Women* (1968), (London: Virago, 1979), p. 7.

4. Monique Wittig, 'Paradigm' (1979) in *Homosexualities and French Literature*, ed. George Stambolian and Elaine Marks (Ithaca: Cornell University Press, 1979), pp. 114–21.

5. In Freud's theory of infantile sexuality, only one genital organ matters – the penis, or phallus – around which the psychic drama of the castration complex is played out: 'a genital organization of a sort is established; but only the male genitals play a part in it, and the female ones remain undiscovered. (I have described this as the period of *phallic* primacy.)' Sigmund Freud, 'An Autobiographical Study', *The Standard Edition of the Complete Psychological Works of Sigmund Freud*, trans. James Strachey (London: Hogarth Press, 1955–74), vol. XX, p. 37. Henceforth cited as *SE*.

6. And as that dogged empiricist, Richard von Krafft-Ebing, amply documented in his *Psychopathia Sexualis* (1886), it did so even before Freud. Or as one participant in Alfred Kinsey's 1940's survey of sexual practice put it when asked what she'd learned from the experience, 'I learned that if you can ask the question, "Do people really *do* that?" the answer is "Yes!"'.

7. Sigmund Freud, 'Two Encyclopaedia Articles' (1923), *SE*, vol. XVIII, p. 244.

8. Sigmund Freud, 'The Psychogenesis of a Case of Female Homosexuality in a Woman' (1920), *SE*, vol. XVIII, pp. 145–72, 151.

9. Josef Breuer and Sigmund Freud, *Studies in Hysteria* (1895), trans. James and Alix Strachey, *SE*, vol. II; *Studies in Hysteria*, trans. Nicola Luckhurst (London: Penguin, 2004).

10. Sigmund Freud, 'Further Remarks on the Neuro-Psychoses of Defence' (1896), *SE*, vol. III, p. 163. (In italics in the original.)

11. Sigmund Freud to Wilhelm Fliess, 26 April 1896, *The Complete Letters of Sigmund Freud to Wilhelm Fliess, 1887–1904*, ed. and trans. Jeffrey Moussaieff Masson (Cambridge: Harvard/Belknap Press, 1985), p. 184; henceforth *Letters of Freud to Fliess*.

12. James Joyce, *Finnegans Wake* (London: Faber and Faber, 1939), p. 115, lines 21–32.

13. Sigmund Freud, 'Project for a Scientific Psychology II: Psychopathology' ([1895] 1966), *SE*, vol. I, p. 356.

14. 'I am working on the assumption that our psychic mechanism has come into being by a process of stratification: the material present in the form of memory traces being subjected from time to time to a *rearrangement* in accordance with fresh circumstances – to a *retranscription* . . . Memory is present not once but several times over.' (Freud to Fliess, 6 December 1896, *Letters of Freud to Fliess*, p. 207).

15. Freud to Fliess, 6 December 1896, *Letters of Freud to Fliess*, p. 209.

16. Freud, 'Further Remarks on the Neuro-Psychoses of Defence', *SE*, vol. III, p. 167, note 2. (In Italics in the original.)
17. Freud, 'An Autobiographical Study', *SE*, vol. XX, p. 34.
18. Freud to Fliess, 21 September 1897, *Letters of Freud to Fliess*, p. 264.
19. Freud to Fliess, 31 May 1897, *Letters of Freud Fliess*, p. 249.
20. Freud to Fliess, 21 September 1897, *Letters of Freud to Fliess*, p. 264; 'cathected', from 'cathexis', James Strachey's translation of the German *Besetzung*: 'occupation' (as of a country by military troops), 'casting' (of actors in a play); psychoanalytically, the term means an idea, object, body part, e.g., has been invested with an emotional charge, or psychical energy. See also Translator's Preface below, p. xxviii.
21. Though that they could be fantasies, or fantasmal reconstructions, did not mean that all were, nor did Freud ever suggest that childhood sexual abuse did not exist. He *did* suggest that fantasy plays a critical role in the formation of adult sexuality.
22. Freud, 'On the History of the Psychoanalytic Movement' (1914), *SE*, vol. XIV pp. 17–18; cf. 'An Autobiographical Study', *SE*, vol. XX, p. 34.
23. Freud to Fliess, 15 October 1897, *Letters of Freud to Fliess*, p. 272.
24. Sigmund Freud, *The Interpretation of Dreams* (1900), *SE*, vol. IV, p. 257.
25. He acknowledged this finally in 'Some Psychical Consequences of Anatomical Distinctions between the Sexes' (1925), *SE*, vol. XIX, pp. 248–58, and in the final essay below, 'On Female Sexuality' (1931).
26. Sigmund Freud, 'The Question of Lay Analysis' (1926), *SE*, vol. XX, p. 212.
27. Sigmund Freud, 'Female Sexuality' (1931), below, pp. 312, 317, 322–3.
28. Peter Gay, *Freud: A Life for Our Time* (1988; London: Norton, 1998), p. 91. Note, however, that Gay also credits Freud with a capacity for complexity: 'Throughout his life, Freud's theoretical thinking oscillated fruitfully between complexity and simplicity . . . The recognition of complexity did justice to the stunning multifariousness of human experience, richer by far than psychologists concentrating on the conscious mind could ever know.'
29. Freud to Fliess, 25 May 1895, *Letters of Freud to Fliess*, p. 129.
30. Sigmund Freud, 'Wild Psychoanalysis' (1910), *SE*, vol. XI, pp. 222–3: 'We prefer to speak of *psychosexuality*, thus laying stress on the point that the mental factor in sexual life should not be overlooked or underestimated.'
31. Freud, 'An Autobiographical Study', *SE*, vol. XX, p. 37: 'the problems of sexual life (the riddle of the Sphinx – that is, the question of where babies come from)'.

32. Freud, 'Wild Psychoanalysis', *SE*, vol. XI, p. 222. See Maud Ellmann, 'Introduction', *Psychoanalytic Literary Criticism* (London: Longman, 1994), p. 12. For Freud's account of what sexual sublimation might achieve, see his *Leonardo da Vinci and a Memory of his Childhood* (1910), *SE*, vol. XI.

33. See Sigmund Freud, 'The Sexual Enlightenment of Children' (1907), *SE*, vol. IX, p. 135, note 2.

34. Sigmund Freud, 'On the Sexual Theories of Children' (1908), p. 228, below.

35. Freud to Fliess, 26 April 1896, *Letters of Freud to Fliess*, p. 184; Freud actually wrote '*a caput Nili*'.

36. James Joyce, *Ulysses* (1922), ed. Jeri Johnson (Oxford: Oxford University Press, 1993), p. 652.

37. Freud, 'Wild Psychoanalysis', *SE*, vol. XI, p. 223.

38. See, for example, the superb anthology, *In Dora's Case: Freud – Hysteria – Feminism*, ed. Charles Bernheimer and Clare Kahane (London: Virago, 1985).

39. Sigmund Freud, 'Analysis of a Phobia in a Five-Year-Old Boy' (1909), *SE*, vol. XIV.

Translator's Preface

Embarking on a fresh translation of Freud means reconsidering something one might imagine fixed and immutable: a terminology apparently set in stone. James Strachey's monumental *Standard Edition* is of course an extraordinary feat. In John Forrester's words, the 'erudition, exactitude and uniform care . . . on every page' are 'incalculable', and any subsequent English translator will be very much in Strachey's shadow. So naturalized has the vocabulary of the *Standard Edition* become in English that one might easily mistake it for what Freud actually wrote, as he wrote it. But translation is – of course – not a simple transposition of ideas from one idiom to another, and it acquires certain nuances and meanings on the way, while inevitably shedding others. So it is possible to call some of Strachey's decisions into question, despite the fact that, with the spread of psychoanalytical ideas in the English-speaking world – and not only in the discipline of psychoanalysis itself, but in philosophy, literary and artistic criticism and everyday speech – they may have taken up permanent residence in the English language. The new translator will obviously wish to leave a mark, but must clearly guard against making changes for change's sake – akin to re-inventing the seven times table, or, just as an experiment, relocating Vienna to the Baltic coast. The task is to strip the language of its accretions, with a view to understanding what Freud meant when he said it; laying the original German as bare as possible without sacrificing cadence or intelligibility.

Approaching Freud's work as literature and translating it accordingly, one was not necessarily constrained, as an analytic specialist might have been, by the development of psychoanalytical vocabulary over the past century or so. This freedom also throws up some potential difficulties: there is the possibility that the reader will be alienated by unfamiliar terms where familiar ones are expected. A useful starting-point was Bruno Bettelheim's bracing, and sometimes wrong-headed, polemical essay, *Freud and Man's Soul.*[1] Bettelheim argues that on his journey into English, and more specifically, across the Atlantic, Freud's work has been effectively mechanized, and stripped of qualities of introspection most purely exemplified in his use of the word '*Seele*', or 'soul', which is too often rendered into English as 'mind'. I have translated the word variously as 'soul', 'mind' or 'psyche', according to context. But it should perhaps be borne in mind that the related adjective and adverb, '*seelisch*', whatever it might have meant over the centuries, now has the predominant connotation of 'mental' – as in '*seelisch gestört*' – mentally disturbed – or '*seelische Gesundheit*' – mental health. In such phrases the notion of 'soul' is a distant echo, lingering just as the Greek '*psyche*' does in 'psychology', 'psychiatry' and, not least, in 'psychoanalysis'. The shift from soul to mind seems to me to be the result of a cultural transition over time, rather than a wilful linguistic deformation.

But where it is difficult to disagree with him is in his suggestion – perhaps insistence would be a better word – that in the *Standard Edition* Strachey introduces neologisms which render Freud's language unnecessarily opaque, distancing it from 'normal' writing. To take an example: unlike Bettelheim, I can remember hearing the word 'cathexis' used in conversation, although I suspect the speaker may have been joking. But Bettelheim is quite correct in his insistence that '*Besetzung*', although used in a new and specific sense in the Freudian context, is a quite common colloquial term meaning 'occupation' or 'investment'. To travel through Greek etymology to the neologism 'cathexis', from the Greek '*katechein*' – to hold or grasp – is really to travel further from conventional locutions than the German demands. After hovering for a long time between 'occupation' and 'investment', I eventually fell into line with the French, Spanish and Italians, and opted for 'investment'.

Of the works in this volume, the *Three Essays on Sexual Theory* throw up great technical difficulties for the translator, and Strachey was himself aware of these. In his 'Notes on some technical terms whose translation calls for comment', added to the General Preface in the first volume of the *Standard Edition*, Strachey defends his translation of the German word '*Trieb*' as 'instinct', although he does observe: 'My choice of this rendering has been attacked in some quarters with considerable, but, I think, mistaken severity.' He argues that 'drive', at least in this particular sense, is not an English word, and that Freud employed '*Trieb*' to cover 'a variety of different concepts'. 'It requires [. . .]' he continues, 'a very brave man seriously to argue that rendering Freud's "*Trieb*" by "drive" clears up the situation.'

I was not setting out to be particularly brave, but again, 'drive' seemed the better option, despite being less versatile by virtue of its refusal to be used in an adjectival form. Referring to the essay 'Triebe und Triebschicksale', translated as 'Instincts and their Vicissitudes', in Volume XIV of the *Standard Edition*, Strachey justifies his chosen term by saying that 'the only rational thing to do [. . .] seems to me to be to choose an obviously vague and indeterminate word and stick to it'. Yet as Freud develops his theory, it seems quite compellingly that he does not quite conceive of the '*Trieb*' as something 'vague and indeterminate', but as something akin to a physical force, always operating in a particular direction. Life is perhaps made easier for us by the fact that the word 'drive', used in this manner, does now exist in English in a way that it may not have done in the past, and it does not seem impossible that Freud himself may be at least partially responsible for this. What is interesting, though, is that in this instance the word – as in phrases such as 'death drive' or 'sex drive' (or in this volume 'sexual drive') – seems to have developed a life of its own, independent of the *Standard Edition*.

The intricacies of 'drive theory' are such that one must constantly be on one's guard against confusing the different component parts of the mechanism. There is an intricate relationship between *Regung* (in the end it can only mean 'impulse', although the word also has an appealing suggestion of 'stirring'), *Erregung* ('excitement', although 'excitation' would be equally possible), *Reiz* ('stimulus') and *Reizung* ('stimulation'), and *Trieb* ('drive', as above). Freud's French translators make no distinction between *Erregung* and *Reiz*, although Freud clearly does, and so does the *Standard Edition*. It may not be irrelevant that at one point in the exposition of 'drive theory', the words for 'current' (*Strömung*) and 'impulse' (*Regung*) prove to be interchangeable.

And what about 'love'? Surely such a fundamental term, and one so central to this collection, must be quite straightforward? Well, sadly no, not really. The phrase '*sie liebten sich*' clearly means 'they loved each other'. But '*sie liebten sich mehrmals in einer Nacht*' or *sie liebten sich im Auto*' means simply that they had sex with each other, several times in the course of a night, or in the car. And a similar issue arises with Freud's use of the word '*Liebesleben*', which features in the title of three of the papers included here. Strachey renders the word as 'love', but while that solution combines simplicity and elegance, it is not as direct as I believe Freud intended his meaning to be. '*Liebesleben*', literally 'love-life', refers primarily to sexual activity, as in '*das Liebesleben der Flusspferde*' (to take an example found at random), best translated as 'the mating habits of hippopotami'. I regret the loss of the romantic resonance, but opted for 'the erotic life', retaining the notion of 'Eros' as a kind of love, if not the only kind.

Inevitably, the greatest pleasure for the literary translator was to be had from the 'Fragment of an Analysis of Hysteria', more commonly known as 'Dora'. Here Freud has introduced two distinct narrative voices, the colloquial, almost breathless one that tells Dora's story, and the sober, technical one, part of whose function seems to be to ensure that we don't get carried away with the excitements of the plot. Here, as in much of Freud's writing, a great deal hangs on the interpretation of individual German words and pairs of words (*Zimmer/Frauenzimmer*, meaning 'room' and 'woman', *vermögend/unvermögend*, meaning 'wealthy' or 'capable' and 'incapable' or 'impotent'). While translating this text, though, I was very struck by one detail that must have escaped me when reading 'Dora' in the past. In an early conversation with Freud,

Dora's father uses the phrase '*Ich habe nichts an meiner eigenen Frau*', meaning 'I get nothing from my own wife'. Later, in the scene by the lake, Herr K., Dora's suitor, repeats the words, telling Dora '*Ich habe nichts an meiner Frau*'. It is true that Freud acknowledges this in a footnote, but it seems to me to merit more than this. The phrase is not a common one, yet it is used by both of the most important adult males in Dora's life. Could it be that Freud himself has accidentally conflated father and suitor? Impossible to say, of course, but it would add a fresh dimension to the analysis if it were the case. No one involved in the narration of a story such as Dora's is entirely dependable – this applies not least to the analyst, determined to the last to defend the probity of a man who makes a pass at a fourteen-year-old girl in a shop and then sleeps with his children's governess. I found myself thinking often of the famously unreliable narrator of Ford Madox Ford's novel *The Good Soldier*, published ten years later, and the character of the cad, Teddy Ashburnham. Did Ford know his Freud?

A small note concerning a key piece of terminology: Jean Laplanche and Jean-Bertrand Pontalis's indispensable *The Language of Psychoanalysis*[2] – which is itself, almost unbelievably, translated from the French – adopts a stern line on the exclusive latinization of '*das Ich*', literally 'the I', rendered (of course) by Strachey as 'the ego'. Regretting a complexity that is lost if one insists on choosing 'a different word for every shade of meaning', Laplanche and Pontalis rightly suggest that 'ego' restricts the resonance of '*Ich*', which is used by Freud both as noun and pronoun. There are good grounds for both 'I' and 'ego'. Both also have a sound history in translations into English of such German idealist philosophers as Kant and Fichte. In this volume, however, any references to '*das Ich*' (the ego) and '*das Über-Ich*' (the super-ego) are introduced so much in passing that to reinvent the terms would have been both quixotic on the translator's part and baffling to the reader. In the end, I can't help feeling that Strachey's decision is, by and large, the right one. I should say, though, that had the terms been more central to the texts I might have been bolder, bearing in mind that the German '*Ich*' has a flexibility that the English 'ego' lacks.

I am indebted for their help and suggestions to Adam Phillips, Simon Winder, John Forrester, Sebastian Gardner, Sue Wiseman, Tim Armstrong, John Stevens and my keen-eyed copy-editor, Jane Robertson. All mistakes are, of course, my own.

The translation is dedicated, as ever, to Georgina Morley and Charlie Whiteside.

Notes

1. Bruno Bettelheim, *Freud and Man's Soul* (London, 1991).
2. Jean Laplanche and Jean-Bertrand Pontalis, *The Language of Psychoanalysis*, trans. Donald Nicholson-Smith (London, 1988).

The Psychology of Love

Fragment of an Analysis of Hysteria (Dora)

Foreword

If, after a considerable interval, I am seeking to substantiate the assertions I made in 1895 and 1896 concerning the pathogenesis of hysterical symptoms and the psychical processes at work in hysteria, by publishing a detailed account of the history of an illness and its treatment, I cannot omit the writing of this foreword, which will justify certain of my actions while at the same time returning the expectations that readers may have of it to an appropriate level.

It was certainly awkward for me to have to publish the results of my research, especially results so surprising and uncompromising, when they had not been subjected to the necessary examination by colleagues in my field. But it is hardly any less awkward for me now to begin to submit to general judgement some of the material from which I gleaned those results. I will not escape that reproach – if it was formerly said that I revealed nothing about my patients, I will now be accused of communicating things about them that should not be communicated. I hope that those who change the pretext for their accusation in this manner will be the same people as before, and from the outset I shall make no attempt to deprive them of their accusation.

I still consider the publication of my case histories a problem that is difficult for me to resolve, even if I am not in the slightest concerned about those uncomprehending and malicious individuals. The difficulties are partly technical in nature, although at the same time they arise out of the very essence of the circumstances. If it is correct to say that the cause of hysterical illnesses is to be located in the intimacies of the patient's psychosexual life, and that hysterical symptoms are the expression of her most secret repressed desires, the elucidation of a case of hysteria will inevitably reveal those intimacies and betray those secrets. It is certain that my patients would never have spoken if they had imagined the possibility that their confessions might be scientifically evaluated, and equally certain that it would be utterly futile to ask their permission to publish. Sensitive people, and probably timid ones, would in such circumstances stress the obligation of medical discretion, and regret that they could not serve science in this respect by providing it with information. But it is my opinion that the doctor has duties not only to the individual patient, but to science as well. To science – essentially this means to the many other patients who suffer from, or who will suffer from, the same illness. Publishing what one believes one knows about the causes and structure of hysteria becomes a matter of duty, while neglecting to do so becomes an act of contemptible cowardice, as long as one can avoid doing direct personal damage to the individual patient. I believe I have done everything I can to avoid damage of this kind. I have chosen a person whose destinies were played out not in Vienna but in a distant small town, and hence someone whose personal relationships must be effectively unknown; I have so carefully preserved the secret of the treatment from the very first that only one entirely trustworthy colleague could know that the girl had been my patient. I waited for four years after the conclusion of the treatment until I heard of another change in my patient's life, which led me to assume that her own interest in the events and mental processes narrated here might have faded by now. Obviously no names have been left in that might have put a reader from lay circles on to the trail; publication in a strictly scientific specialist journal was, incidentally, supposed to be a protection against such unskilled readers. Of course I cannot keep the patient herself from feeling embarrassed if the story of her own illness were to fall into her hands. But she will learn nothing from it that she does not already know, and may wonder who else might be able to learn from it that it is about her.

I know that, in this city at least, there are certain doctors who – repellently enough – would choose to read a case history of this kind not as a contribution to the psychopathology of neuroses, but as a *roman à clef* written for their own amusement. I assure this breed of reader that any future case histories will be protected against their sharp perceptions by similar guarantees of secrecy, although the use of my material will be restricted to a quite extraordinary degree as a result.

In this one case history that I have so far been able to free from the restrictions of medical discretion and the unfavourable circumstances of the situation, sexual relations are discussed freely, the sexual organs and functions are named by their proper names, and the pure-minded reader will be able to come away from my account of events convinced that I have not shied away from talking with a young girl about such subjects in such language. So, should I defend myself against this reproach as well? I simply claim the rights of the gynaecologist – or rather rights much more modest than those. It would be a sign of perverse and strange salaciousness to assume that such conversations were a good way of arousing or satisfying sexual desires. I am also inclined to express my judgement on the matter in someone else's words:

> It is lamentable to have to grant space to such claims and assertions in a scientific work, but let no one reproach me for that. Let them rather level their accusations at the spirit of the age, which has brought us to the happy situation whereby no serious book can any longer be certain of surviving.[1]

I shall now reveal how I overcame the technical difficulties involved in the writing of this case history. These difficulties are considerable for a doctor, who has to carry out six or eight such psychotherapeutic treatments every day, and who cannot make notes during the session with the patient himself because in doing so he would arouse the patient's mistrust and obstruct his own understanding of the material being presented to him. The question of how a lengthy course of treatment might be recorded for the purposes of communication is another problem to which I have found no solution. In the present case, two circumstances came to my aid: first, that the duration of the treatment was not longer than three months, secondly, that the elucidations were based around two dreams –

related in the middle and at the end of the cure – which were written down verbatim immediately after the session, and which provided a secure foundation for the subsequent web of interpretations and memories. I wrote down the case history itself from memory only after the cure had come to an end, while my memory was still fresh and sharpened by my interest in publication. For that reason the transcript is not absolutely – phonographically – faithful, but it can claim a high level of dependability. Nothing essential has been changed within it, except, in some places, the order of elucidations, a change undertaken for the sake of the context.

I should like to stress what will be found in this account and what will be missed out. The essay originally bore the title 'Dream and Hysteria' because it struck me as especially well suited to showing how dream interpretation weaves its way into the story of the treatment, and how, with its help, gaps in the memory can be filled and symptoms elucidated. In 1900, not without good reason, I published a painstaking and penetrating study of dreams in advance of my planned publications on the psychology of neuroses,[2] although its reception demonstrated how little understanding my colleagues still had for such efforts. In this case the objection, that my observations were not verifiably convincing because I had withheld my material, was not justified, because anyone can subject his own dreams to analytical examination, and the technique of dream interpretation is easy to learn according to the instructions and examples I give. Now, as then, I must stress that immersion in the problems of the dream is an indispensable precondition for an understanding of the psychological processes involved in hysteria and the other psychoneuroses, and that no one who wishes to spare himself that preparatory work will be able to advance even a few steps into this field. So, since this case history assumes a knowledge of dream interpretation, it will make extremely unsatisfactory reading for anyone who does not have that knowledge. Such a reader will be disturbed where he expected to be enlightened, and will surely be inclined to project the cause of his disturbance on to the author, declaring him to be a fantasist. In fact, this capacity to disturb is inherent in the phenomena of the neurosis itself; but it is masked from us by our medical habits, and only reappears when we attempt to explain it. It could only be averted completely if we were able fully to deduce neurosis from elements already known to us. But it appears highly likely that, on the contrary, the study of neurosis will spur us on to accept much that is new, and will then gradually become the object of certain knowledge. Novelty has always provoked confusion and resistance.

It would be wrong for anyone to imagine that dreams and their interpretation occupy such a prominent position in all instances of psychoanalysis as they do in this example.

If the present case history appears to receive preferential treatment in terms of the use of dreams, in other areas it is poorer than I would have wished. But its shortcomings have to do with precisely those conditions that make its publication possible. I said above that I could not fully master the material of a case history lasting about a year. This one, which lasted only three months, can be grasped as a whole and remembered; but its results remained incomplete in more than one respect. The treatment was not continued to its planned goal, but interrupted at the wishes of the patient once a certain point had been reached. By that time some mysteries in the patient's illness had still not been dealt with, and others illuminated only very imperfectly, while the continuation of the work would certainly have advanced in all areas to the final elucidation. So here I can offer only the fragment of an analysis.

Perhaps a reader familiar with the techniques demonstrated in the *Studies in Hysteria* will be surprised that it did not become possible, in three months, to provide a definitive solution at least for those symptoms that had been tackled. But this will become understandable if I mention that psychoanalytic techniques have undergone a fundamental revolution since the *Studies* were written. Back then, the work arose out of the symptoms, and their solution advanced sequentially towards its goal. I have since abandoned that technique, finding it utterly unsuited to the more delicate structure of neurosis. Now I allow the patient to determine the subject of our daily work himself, and take as my starting point whatever surface the unconscious happens to have brought to his attention. Then, though, I obtain what is required for the solution of a symptom in fragments, woven into various different contexts and scattered over very different periods of time. Despite this apparent disadvantage the new technique is far superior to the old, and without fear of contradiction it is the only possible one.

Given the incompleteness of my analytical results I had no other choice but to follow the example of those researchers who are so happy to bring the inestimable, though mutilated, remains of antiquity to light after their long burial. Using the best models known to me from other analyses, I have completed that which was incomplete, but, like a conscientious archaeologist, I have taken care, in each case, to reveal where my construction added to the authentic parts.

I myself have deliberately introduced incompleteness of another kind. I have not generally described the interpretative work that had to be undertaken on the patient's ideas and statements, but only its results. So the technique of analytical work, dreams aside, has only been revealed at a very few points. In this case history I was concerned to demonstrate the determination of symptoms and the intimate construction of neurotic illness; it would only have caused irresolvable confusion had I attempted to carry out the other task at the same time. In order to account for the technical rules, which are generally found empirically, one would have had to bring together material from many different case histories. At the same time, however, it should not be supposed that the abbreviation resulting from the omission of the technique was particularly great in this case. The most difficult piece of technical work did not arise with this patient, as the element of 'transference' that comes into play at the end of a case history did not occur during this brief treatment.

Neither patient nor author is responsible for a third kind of incompleteness in this account. Rather, it is obvious that a single patient's story, even if it were complete and not dubious, cannot provide an answer to all the questions arising out of the problem of hysteria. It cannot teach us about all types of illness, all formations of the internal structure of the neurosis, all possible kinds of connection between the psychic and the somatic. One might not reasonably demand more from a single case than that case is able to provide. A person who has not previously wished to believe in the general and universal validity of the psychosexual aetiology of hysteria will not be convinced of it by a single case history, but will at best defer his judgement until he has won the right, through his own work, of forming his own personal conviction.[3]

Notes

1. Richard Schmidt, *Beiträge zur indischen Erotik* [*Contributions to Indian Erotica*], [Leipzig] 1902, Foreword.

2. *Die Traumdeutung* [*The Interpretation of Dreams*], Vienna, 1900.

3. [*Addition 1923*:] The treatment recounted here was interrupted on 31 December 1899 [in fact: 1900], and the report on it written over the following two weeks, but not published until 1905. We can hardly expect that more than two decades of continued work should have changed nothing in the conception and representation of such a case of illness, but it would obviously be absurd to bring this patient's story 'up to date' and adapt it to the current state of our knowledge. So I have left it broadly untouched, and only corrected certain errors and inexactitudes to which my excellent English translators, Mr and Mrs James Strachey, have drawn my attention. As regards critical observations that have struck me as justified, I have included these in the notes appended to this case history. Consequently the reader will be aware that I continue to maintain the opinions set out in the text to this day, if he finds no contradiction of them in the notes. The problem of medical discretion which preoccupies me in this foreword does not apply to other stories of patients in this volume [Volume VIII of the *Gesammelte Werke*, which contained four further case histories], for three of these have been published with the express permission of the patients, and in the case of little Hans with the permission of his father, and in one case (Schreber) the object of analysis is not actually a person but a book which that person had written. In the case of Dora, the secret has been kept until this year. I heard recently that the woman in question, of whom I had lost sight for a long time, had recently revealed to her doctor, after falling ill for other reasons, that as a girl she had received analytic treatment from me. That revelation made it easy for my colleague to recognize her as the Dora of 1899. If the three months of that treatment did nothing more than

resolve that conflict, if they could not provide protection against illnesses arising subsequently, no fair-minded person would reproach analytic therapy for this.

I

The Clinical Picture

Having shown in my *Interpretation of Dreams*, published in 1900, that dreams can generally be interpreted, and that once the task of interpretation has been accomplished they can be replaced by irreproachable thoughts which can be inserted at a particular place in the psychical context, in the pages below I should like to give an example of the one practical application that the art of dream-interpretation seems to permit. In that book[1] I have mentioned how I came to the problem of dreams. I encountered it along the way as I was attempting to heal psychoneuroses by means of a particular process of psychotherapy, when my patients told me – amongst other events from their mental life – their dreams, which seemed to demand interpolation in the long connection leading from the morbid symptom to the pathogenic idea. Then I learned how to translate, without further assistance, from dream language into the immediately comprehensible language in which we express our thoughts. This knowledge, I should stress, is indispensable for the psychoanalyst, because the dream is one of the ways in which psychical material can reach consciousness when it has, because of the resistance that its content provokes, been excluded from consciousness, and become repressed and thus pathogenic. The dream is, to put it more succinctly, one of the *detours around repression*, one of the chief means of so-called indirect representation in the psychical sphere. This fragment from the history of the treatment of a hysterical girl is intended to show how dream interpretation intervenes in the work of analysis. At the same time it should give me my first public opportunity to represent my views concerning the psychical processes and organic conditions of hysteria in a manner detailed enough to avoid further misunderstanding. I shall not apologize for this degree of detail, since it is now known that one cannot match the great demands that hysteria places upon the doctor and researcher by responding with affected disdain, but only by immersing ourselves affectionately in the subject.

Nicht Kunst und Wissenschaft allein,
Geduld will bei dem Werke sein!

[Art and science alone won't do, a little patience is needed, too!]

To begin with a complete and rounded case history would be to place the reader in quite different conditions from those of the medical observer from the very first. In general, the account provided by the patient's relatives – in this case the eighteen-year-old girl's father – gives a most unrecognizable picture of the course of the illness. I do begin the treatment by asking the patient to tell me the whole story of her life and illness, but what I hear is still not enough to provide the bearings I require. This first story is comparable to an unnavigable river whose bed is now obstructed by masses of rock, now broken and made shallow by sandbanks. I can only marvel at the way in which some authors have managed to achieve precise and consistent case histories of hysterics. Certainly, they can adequately and coherently inform the doctor about one part or other of their lives, but then there will be another occasion when their information dries up, leaving gaps and mysteries, and at yet another time one will come across periods of complete darkness, unilluminated by any usable information. Connections, even obvious ones, are generally fragmented, the sequence of different events uncertain; during the narration itself, the patient will correct a piece of information, a date, perhaps, before, after lengthy vacillation, returning more or less to her original statement. The patient's inability to give an ordered depiction of her life history, in so far as it coincides with the case history, is not only characteristic of neurosis,[2] it is also of great theoretical significance. This lack, in fact, has the following causes: first of all, the patient is consciously and deliberately holding back a part of something that is very well known to her, something that she knows she should tell, for the motives, not yet overcome, of shyness and modesty (discretion when other people are involved); that is the portion of deliberate dishonesty. Secondly, part of the anamnestic knowledge that the patient still has at her disposal is left out when she tells her story, although she does not consciously intend this reticence; that is the portion of unconscious dishonesty. Thirdly, there is never a shortage of genuine amnesias, gaps in the memory into which not only old memories but even quite recent ones have fallen, and of inaccurate memories, which have been formed secondarily to fill those gaps.[3] Where the events themselves have been preserved in the memory, the intention underlying the amnesia will be achieved just as surely by abolishing a connection, and that connection will most certainly be severed if the sequence of the events is altered. That sequence always proves to be the most vulnerable component of the memory hoard, and the one most often subjected to repression. We come across some memories in what we might call a first stage of repression, and they are charged with doubt. Some time later that doubt is replaced by forgetfulness or errors of memory.[4]

Theory requires us to see this state of memories relating to the case history as the necessary correlative of the hysterical symptoms. In the course of treatment, the patient will repeat what he has been holding back, or that which has not occurred to him, despite the fact that he has always known it. His misrememberings prove to be untenable, and the gaps in the memory are filled. Only towards the end of the treatment can one have a general view of an internally consistent, comprehensible and complete case history. If the practical goal of the treatment lies in the abolition of all possible symptoms, and their replacement with conscious thoughts, one other theoretical goal might be the task of healing all the damage done to the patient's memory. The two goals coincide: once the former has been achieved, so has the latter; the same route leads to both.

From the nature of the things that form the material of psychoanalysis, it follows that in our case histories we owe as much to the patient's purely human and social relations as we do to the somatic data and the hysterical symptoms. Above all, we will direct our interest towards the patient's family relationships out of considerations which, as we shall see, do not have to do with the examination of heredity alone.

Apart from herself, the family circle of this eighteen-year-old patient consisted of her parents and a brother one and a half years older. The dominant figure was her father, both because of his intelligence and his character traits and because of the circumstances of his life, which provided the framework for the story of the patient's childhood and her case history. When I began treating the girl he was in his late forties, a man of rather uncommon sensitivity and talent, a well-to-do industrialist. His daughter held him in particularly tender affection, and her prematurely awoken critical sense was all the more repelled by some of his actions and idiosyncrasies.

In addition, the tenderness of her affection was intensified by the many serious illnesses to which her father had succumbed since her sixth year. Then, a tubercular illness had been the reason for the family's move to a small, climatically favourable town in our southern provinces; his pulmonary complaint quickly improved there, but in order to avoid a recurrence of the illness, that place, which I shall refer to as B., became the main home of both the children and the parents for about the next ten years. When the girl's father was well he was often absent, visiting his factories; in high summer he went to a spa in the mountains.

When the girl was about ten years old, her father needed a darkness cure for a detached retina. This illness caused lasting impairment of his vision. The most serious illness occurred about two years later; it consisted of an attack of confusion, accompanied by fits of paralysis and minor psychical disorders. A friend of the sick man, whose role we shall later examine, had persuaded him, when he was still not greatly recovered, to travel with his doctor to Vienna to seek my advice. I hesitated for a while about whether I should assume he was suffering from a tabetic paralysis, but then opted to diagnose diffuse vascular infection and, after a specific infection before the patient's marriage was admitted, to undertake a vigorous anti-syphilitic cure, in consequence of which all those disorders which were still present subsided. It was probably because of this fortunate intervention that four years later the father introduced me to his daughter, who had clearly become neurotic, and another two years after that he handed her over to me for psychotherapeutic treatment.

In Vienna, meanwhile, I had met a slightly older sister of the father, who manifested a serious form of psychoneurosis, without characteristic hysterical symptoms. After an unhappy married life, this woman died of rapidly progressing malnutrition, which was never fully explained.

Another brother of my male patient, whom I met occasionally, was a hypochondriac bachelor.

The girl, who became my patient at the age of eighteen, had always stressed her sympathetic relations with her father's side of the family and, since she had fallen ill, had taken the aforementioned aunt as her model. Neither had I any doubt that she belonged, with her gifts and her intellectual precocity, as well as her innate tendency towards illness, to that family. I never met her mother. Judging by the statements of the father and the girl, I received the impression that she was an ill-educated, but more importantly an unintelligent woman, who had concentrated all her interests on the household since her husband's illness and the estrangement that followed from it, and thus developed what we might call 'housewife psychosis'. Without any understanding of her children's active interests, she spent the whole day cleaning the apartment, the furniture and appliances, so much so that using and enjoying them became almost impossible. It is hard to avoid comparing this condition, of which I find hints often enough in normal housewives, with compulsive washing and other forms of compulsive cleanliness; but among these women, and indeed in our patient's mother, we note a complete lack of awareness of the illness and thus of a significant characteristic of 'compulsive neurosis'. Relations between mother and daughter had been very unfriendly for years. The daughter ignored her mother, criticized her severely and had fully escaped her influence.[5]

The girl's only brother, one and a half years older than the girl herself, had in her earlier years been the model that her ambition had striven to emulate. Relations between the siblings had become more distant over recent years. The young man tried to stay out of family disputes as best he could; when he had to take sides, he sided with the mother. So the usual sexual attraction had brought both father and daughter and mother and son closer together.

Our patient, whom I shall from now on call Dora, showed nervous symptoms from the age of eight. At that time she had suffered from a chronic respiratory illness with occasional violent aggravations. This illness first appeared after a little trip into the mountains and was therefore put down to over-exertion. The condition slowly subsided over a period of six months, after a rest cure was imposed upon her. The family doctor does not seem to have wavered for a moment from his diagnosis of a purely nervous disorder, ruling out an organic cause of the dyspnoea, but he apparently considered this diagnosis compatible with the aetiology of over-exertion.[6]

The little girl passed through the usual infectious childhood illnesses without suffering any lasting harm. As she told me (with symbolic intent!), it was her brother who usually had the illnesses first, although in a mild form, whereupon she followed with more serious symptoms. She began to suffer unilateral migraine headaches and she had attacks of nervous coughing from the age of about twelve. At first the two symptoms always occurred together, before separating and developing in different ways. The migraine became rarer, and by the age of sixteen it had disappeared. The attacks of tussis nervosa, probably caused by common catarrh, never went away. By the time she came to me for treatment at the age of eighteen, she was coughing again in a characteristic way. The number of these attacks could not be established: they lasted from three to five weeks, and on one occasion several months. At least in recent years, during the first half of one attack, the most irritating painful symptom had been a complete loss of her voice. This had been diagnosed as another nervous attack a considerable time previously. The many usual treatments, including hydrotherapy and local electric shocks, were unsuccessful. The girl, who had, in these circumstances, grown to be mature and independent in her judgements, became used to mocking the efforts of doctors and finally giving up on medical help. She had, incidentally, always been reluctant to ask the doctor for his advice, although she had nothing against her family doctor personally. Any suggestion that she should consult a new doctor encountered resistance on her part, and indeed it was only on her father's orders that she had come to me.

I first saw her in the early summer of her sixteenth year, when she was suffering from coughing and hoarseness. Even at that time I suggested a psychical cure, which was rejected, and this longer-lasting attack passed spontaneously. In the winter of the next year, after the death of her beloved aunt, she had stayed in Vienna at the home of her uncle and his daughters, and had there suffered from a feverish condition which was diagnosed as appendicitis.[7] The following autumn, the family finally left the spa town of B., as the father's health seemed to permit this, and settled first in the town where the father's factory was, and barely a year later in Vienna.

By now Dora had blossomed into a girl with intelligent and agreeable facial features, although she caused her parents grave concern. The main sign of her illness had become mood swings and character changes. By now she was clearly no longer happy either with herself or with her family, she was unfriendly towards her father and could no longer bear the company of her mother, who constantly tried to involve her in the housework. She tried to avoid contact with anyone; in so far as the fatigue and lack of concentration of which she complained allowed, she kept herself busy by attending public lectures, and devoted herself seriously to her studies. One day her parents were shocked by a letter that they found on or in the girl's desk, in which she bade them farewell because her life had become unbearable.[8] Her father's not inconsiderable insight led him to the view that the girl was not seriously planning to commit suicide, but he was horrified none the less, and when one day, after a small exchange between father and daughter, she fell into her first fit of unconsciousness,[9] also involving amnesia, it was decided despite all her protests that she should embark on my treatment.

The case history that I have outlined so far probably does not seem, on the whole, worth communicating. '*Petite hystérie*', with the most common somatic and psychical symptoms: dyspnoea, tussis nervosa, aphonia, along with migraines, mood swings, hysterical irascibility and a taedium vitae that is probably not to be taken seriously. Certainly, more interesting case histories of hysterics have been published, and often more carefully recorded, and in what follows the reader will find nothing concerning the stigmata of sensitive skin, restriction of the field of vision and so on. I shall merely allow myself to observe that all the collections of strange and astonishing phenomena arising from hysteria have not advanced us much in our understanding of that still puzzling illness. What we need is precisely the explanation of the most ordinary cases, and the most frequent, typical symptoms of those cases. I should be satisfied if circumstances had enabled me to give a complete explanation of this case of small-scale hysteria. On the basis of my experiences with other patients I have no doubt that my analytical means would have been adequate to the purpose.

In 1896, shortly after the publication of my *Studies in Hysteria* with Dr J. Breuer, I asked an eminent colleague in my field for his assessment of the psychological theory of hysteria put forward in that book. He answered frankly that he considered it to be an unjustified universalization of conclusions, which might apply to a small number of cases. I have seen many cases of hysteria since then; I have devoted days, weeks or years to each case, and in no single case have I failed to find the psychical conditions postulated in the *Studies*, the psychical trauma, conflict of the affects, and as I have added in later publications, a disturbance in the sexual sphere. Where we are dealing with things that have become pathogenic in their effort to conceal themselves, we cannot, of course, expect patients to want to present them to their doctor; neither can one abandon the treatment after the first 'no' in response to examination.[10]

In the case of my patient Dora, it was thanks to her father's intelligence, which I have mentioned several times, that I myself did not need to seek the source, at least of the final form of the illness. The father told me that in the town of B. he and his family had enjoyed a close friendship with a couple who lived there. During his serious illness Frau K. had looked after him and thus made a lasting claim upon his gratitude. Herr K. had always been very kind to his daughter Dora, taking walks with her when he was in B., giving her little presents, but no one had seen any harm in that. Dora had taken the greatest care of Herr and Frau K.'s two little children, almost adopting a maternal role with them. When father and daughter came to see me in the summer two years ago, they had been stopping off on the way to see Herr and Frau K., who had taken a summer residence by one of our alpine lakes. Dora was to spend several weeks in the K. household, and her father planned to travel home after a few days. Herr K. was also present at this time. But when her father prepared to set off, the girl suddenly announced very resolutely that she was going with him, and she had done just that. It was only some days later that she gave an explanation for her curious behaviour, asking her mother to inform her father that while they were walking to the lake to take a boat trip, Herr K. had been so bold as to make a declaration of love to her. The accused man, confronted at their next meeting by the girl's father and uncle, most expressly denied any move on his part that would have merited such an interpretation, and began to suspect the girl, who, according to Frau K., was interested only in sexual matters and who, in their house by the lake, had even been reading Mantegazza's *Physiology of Love*, and similar books. In all likelihood, inflamed by such reading material, she had 'imagined' the whole scene that she had recounted.

'I do not doubt,' said the father, 'that this event was responsible for Dora's moodiness, irritability and notions of suicide. She demands that I sever any contact with Herr K., and, particularly, with Frau K., whom she had practically worshipped until then. But I cannot do this, for in the first place I consider Dora's story of the man's immoral impertinence to be a fantasy that has sprung into her mind, and secondly I am bound to Frau K. by an honest friendship and can do nothing to hurt her. The poor lady is very unhappy with her husband, of whom I do not, incidentally, have the best opinion; she herself has suffered very badly from her nerves, and I am her sole support. In view of my own state of health I probably do not need to assure you that there is nothing forbidden in our relationship.

We are two poor human beings comforting one another as best we can with friendship and sympathy. You know that I get nothing from my own wife. But Dora, who has inherited my own stubborn demeanour, cannot be diverted from her hatred for Herr and Frau K. Her last attack followed a conversation in which she demanded the same thing from me once again. Please try now to put her on a better track.'

It does not quite accord with these revelations that in other speeches the father tried to place most of the guilt for his daughter's unbearable character on the shoulders of her mother, whose peculiarities spoiled life in the house for everyone. But I had decided long since to defer my judgement about the true state of affairs until I heard the other side.

The experience with Herr K. – the declaration of love followed by an affront to the girl's honour – was supposed to have caused our patient Dora the psychical trauma which Breuer and I had previously postulated as a necessary precondition for the origin of a hysterical illness. But this new case manifested all the difficulties which have led me since then to go beyond that theory,[11] and also presented a new difficulty of a particular kind. The trauma in Dora's life with which we are familiar is, as so often in the case histories of hysterics, incapable of explaining or determining the peculiarity of the symptoms; equally, we would understand the connections just as much or as little if symptoms other than tussis nervosa, aphonia, moodiness and taedium vitae had been the consequence of the trauma. But now there is the additional fact that some of these symptoms – the coughing and the mood swings – had been manifested by the patient years before the trauma, and that they first appeared during childhood, since they had occurred when the girl was seven years old. So we must, if we are not to abandon the trauma theory, return to her childhood to seek influences or impressions that might work analogously to a trauma; and in that case it is quite remarkable that the investigation of cases whose first symptoms did not begin in childhood has also stimulated me to pursue the patient's life history back into the first years of childhood.[12]

After the first difficulties of the cure had been overcome, Dora told me of an earlier experience with Herr K., which was even more apt to act as a sexual trauma. She was fourteen years old at the time. Herr K. had arranged with Dora and his wife that the ladies should come to his shop in the main square of B. in the afternoon to watch a religious ceremony from the building. But he persuaded his wife to stay at home, dismissed his assistant and was on his own when the girl entered the shop. As the time of the procession approached he asked the girl to wait for him by the door which opened on to the staircase leading to the upper floor, as he lowered the awning. He then came back, and instead of walking through the open door, he suddenly pulled the girl to him and pressed a kiss on her lips. That was surely a situation that should have produced a clear sensation of sexual excitement in a fourteen-year-old girl who had never been touched by a man. But at that moment Dora felt a violent revulsion, pulled away and dashed past him to the stairs and from there to the front door. After this, contact with Herr K. none the less continued; neither of them ever mentioned this little scene, and Dora claims to have kept it a secret even at confession at the spa. After that, incidentally, she avoided any opportunity to be alone with Herr K. Both Herr and Frau K. had at that time arranged to go on an outing lasting several days, and Dora was to go along. After the kiss in the shop she declined to go, giving no reasons.

In this second scene, chronologically the first, the behaviour of the fourteen-year-old child is already thoroughly hysterical. Anyone in whom an occasion for sexual excitement provokes predominantly or exclusively feelings of displeasure I would without hesitation identify as a hysteric, whether or not she is capable of producing somatic symptoms. Explaining the mechanism of this *affective reversal* remains one of the most important and at the same time one of the most difficult tasks of the psychology of neurosis. In my opinion I am still a good way away from having achieved that goal; in the context of this communication, however, I shall only be able to present a part of the small amount that I know.

The case of our patient Dora is not yet sufficiently characterized by the emphasis on emotional reversal; in addition, we would have to say that a *displacement* of sensation has taken place. Rather than the genital sensation that would certainly not have been absent from a healthy girl in such circumstances,[13] she feels the sensation of displeasure proper to the mucous tract at the entrance to the alimentary canal: disgust. Certainly, this localization is influenced by the excitement of the lips by the kiss; but I also think I can see another element at work.[14]

The disgust that Dora felt did not become a lasting symptom, and even during the treatment it was only potentially present, as we might say. She had difficulty eating and admitted a slight aversion to food. On the other hand, that scene had produced another effect, a sensory hallucination, which recurred from time to time even when she was delivering her account. She said she could still feel the pressure of that embrace on her upper body. According to certain rules of symptom formation which I have learned to recognize, along with other, otherwise inexplicable particularities of the patient, who would not, for example, walk past a man whom she saw standing in animated or affectionate conversation with a lady, I have made the following reconstruction of the events involved in this scene. I think that during this passionate embrace she felt not only the kiss on her lips but also the pushing of the erect member against her body. This – to her – repellent perception was excised from memory, repressed and replaced by the harmless sensation of pressure on the thorax, which draws its excessive intensity from its repressed source. A new displacement, then, from the lower to the upper body.[15] The compulsive nature of Dora's behaviour, on the other hand, is formed as though prompted by an unaltered memory. She cannot walk past a man she believes to be in a state of sexual excitement because she does not want to see the somatic sign of that state again.

It is remarkable here how three symptoms – disgust, the sensation of pressure on the upper body and a fear of men in affectionate conversation – have their source in a single experience, and that only the interrelation of these three signs enables us to understand the source of the formation of the symptoms. Disgust corresponds to the symptom of repression of the labial erogenous zone (spoilt by infantile sucking, as we shall see). The pressure of the erect member probably led to an analogous change in the corresponding female organ, the clitoris, and the stimulation of that second erogenous zone has been fixated by displacement on to the simultaneous sensation of pressure on the thorax. The fear of men in what may be a sexually excited state follows the mechanism of a phobia, to secure itself against a revival of the repressed perception.

In order to demonstrate the possibility of this deduction, I asked the patient as delicately as I could whether she knew anything about physical signs of excitement in the male body. The answer for now was: yes, and for then: she didn't think so. From the very outset I took the greatest care not to introduce this patient to any new knowledge from the realm of the sexual life, not for reasons of scruple, but in order to put my hypotheses to a severe test in this case. Accordingly, I only called a thing by its proper name when her own clear references showed that direct translation was hardly daring. Her prompt and honest reply also regularly showed that she knew already, but her memory was unable to solve the mystery of *how* she knew it. She had forgotten where all that knowledge came from.[16]

If I am correct in imagining the scene of the kiss in the shop as I have done, I am able to explain the disgust.[17] The sensation of disgust seems originally to have been a reaction to the smell (and later the sight) of excrement. But the genitals, and particularly the male member, can recall the excremental functions, because apart from the sexual function the male member also serves the function of evacuating urine. Indeed, this purpose is the older, and, during the pre-sexual phase, the only one that is known. In this way disgust enters the emotional expressions of sexual life. It is the *inter urinas et faeces nascimur* [we are born between faeces and urine] of the Church Father [St Augustine], which attaches itself to sexual life and cannot be parted from it, however many attempts at idealization one may undertake. But I wish to stress that my viewpoint is that I do not consider the problem solved by the discovery of this associative path. The fact that this association can be provoked does not explain how it was provoked. It is not provoked in this way under normal conditions. Knowledge of the paths does not render superfluous the knowledge of the forces that travel those paths.[18]

In addition, I did not find it easy to draw my patient's attention to her contact with Herr K. She claimed she had finished with him. The uppermost layer of all that occurred to her during our sessions, all that was readily conscious to her, and all that she remembered as conscious from the previous day, always referred to her father. It was quite correct that she could not forgive her father his continuation of relations with Herr K. and particularly with Frau K. But her interpretation of that contact was quite different from the way her father would have chosen to see it. As far as she was concerned there was no doubt that it was an ordinary love affair that bound her father to the beautiful young woman. Nothing capable of reinforcing that opinion had escaped her relentlessly keen perception about this matter, *no gap was to be found in her memories there*. The acquaintance with Herr and Frau K. had begun even before her father's serious illness; but it only became close when the young woman effectively nursed him during his illness, while Dora's mother stayed away from the sick man's bed. During the first summer holiday after the cure, certain things happened that should have opened everyone's eyes to the true nature of that 'friendship'. The two families had rented a floor in the hotel together, and one day Frau K. announced she could not keep the bedroom that she had been sharing up until that point with one of her children, and a few days later Dora's father gave up his bedroom, and they both moved into new rooms, the end rooms, which were separated only by the corridor, while the rooms which they had abandoned had not provided similar guarantees against possible disturbance. When she later reproached her father on the subject of Frau K., he said that he could not understand her hostility, and that the children in fact had every reason to be grateful to Frau K. Her Mama, to whom she then turned for an explanation of this obscure speech, told her that her Papa had at the time been so unhappy that he had wanted to commit suicide in the forest, but Frau K., who had sensed that this was happening, had come after him and had, with her pleading, persuaded him to stay alive for the sake of his family. Of course Dora didn't believe it, they had probably been seen together in the forest and her Papa had come up with this tale of a suicide in order to justify their rendezvous.[19] Then, when they returned to B., Papa had gone to see Frau K. at a particular time every day while her husband was in the shop. Everyone had talked about it and asked her about it in a significant way. Herr K. himself had often complained bitterly to her Mama, but spared her the object of his complaints by making only veiled allusions, which she appeared to interpret as sensitivity on his part. During their walks together, Papa and Frau K. regularly arranged matters so that he was alone with Frau K. There was no doubt that she took money from him, because she paid for things that she could not have afforded with her own money or her husband's. Her Papa also began to give Frau K. large gifts; in order to conceal them, he had at the same time become particularly generous to her mother and to Dora herself. The young woman, who had until then been sickly, and who had herself had to spend months in a sanatorium because she was unable to walk, had been healthy since that time, and full of life.

Even after leaving B., this contact, which they had maintained for several years, continued: from time to time Dora's father would declare that he could not bear the raw climate, that he had to think about himself, and he would start coughing and groaning until all of a sudden he would set off for B., from where he would write the most cheerful of letters. All these illnesses were merely excuses for seeing his girlfriend again. Then one day he announced that they were moving to Vienna, and she began to suspect a connection. They had actually only been in Vienna for three weeks when she heard that the Ks had moved to Vienna as well. They were here now, in fact, and she often encountered her Papa in the street with Frau K. She met Herr K. often as well; he always stared after her, and on one occasion when he met her walking on her own, he had followed her for a long way, in order to ascertain where she was going, and check that she wasn't on her way to a rendezvous herself.

According to Dora, Papa was insincere; there was a false trait to his character; he thought only of his own satisfaction and had the talent of organizing things in the way that best suited him. I often heard such criticisms, particularly during those days when her father felt that his condition had deteriorated again, and set off for several weeks in B., whereupon the keen-eyed Dora soon guessed that Frau K. had set off for the same destination to visit her relations.

I could not dispute this trait in Dora's father in general, and it was easy to see in what particular respects Dora was right to reproach him. In embittered mood, she found herself thinking that she had been handed over to Herr K. as a prize for his toleration of the relationship between Dora's father and his wife, and behind her affection for her father one could hear her fury at being used in such a way. On other occasions she knew that she had been guilty herself of exaggeration in coming out with such speeches. Of course the two men had never made a formal pact in which she had been used as an object of exchange; her father in particular would have recoiled in horror from such impertinence. But he was one of those men who can take the sting out of a conflict by falsifying his judgement of one of the two opposing arguments. Had his attention been drawn to the possibility that a growing girl might be put in danger by constant and unsupervised contact with a man who was not receiving satisfaction from his wife, her father would certainly have replied that he could rely on his daughter, that a man such as Herr K. could never be a danger to her, and that his friend himself was incapable of such intentions. Or: Dora was still a child, and Herr K. treated her as a child. But the truth was that each man avoided drawing from the behaviour of the other the conclusion unfavourable to his own desires. One year, Herr K. had been able to send Dora flowers on all the days when he had been in town, he had used every opportunity to give her expensive gifts, and spent all his free time in her company, although her parents did not recognize such behaviour as having the character of a declaration of love.

When a correctly founded and unobjectionable sequence of thoughts emerges during psychoanalytic treatment, there is a moment of embarrassment for the doctor, which the patient exploits in order to ask: 'Surely that's all true and accurate? What do you want to change, now that I've told it to you?' But one soon realizes that such thoughts, impervious to analysis, can be used to conceal others that seek to evade criticism and consciousness. A series of accusations levelled against other people makes one suspect a series of self-accusations with the same content. One need only turn each individual reproach back on the person of the speaker. There is something undeniably automatic about this way of defending oneself against self-reproach by directing the same reproach against someone else. It has its model in the ripostes that children give, when they answer without hesitation, 'You're the liar' if they are accused of lying. In striving for counter-insult, the adult would look for a genuine weak spot in his opponent, rather than relying on the repetition of the identical insult. In cases of paranoia, the projection of the accusation on to another, without any alteration of the content, and thus with no reference to reality, becomes manifest as a delusional process.

Without exception, Dora's reproaches against her father were also thoroughly reinforced, 'backed up' by the same content, as we shall show with reference to individual cases: she was correct in believing that her father did not want to understand Herr K.'s behaviour towards his daughter, lest his relationship with Frau K. be disturbed. But she had done exactly the same thing. She had turned herself into one of the guilty parties in that relationship and dismissed any clues that arose concerning its true nature. Her clarity about this had dated only from the adventure by the lake, and the strict demands she had made upon her father. Throughout all those previous years, in every possible respect she had encouraged her father's contact with Frau K. She never went to Frau K.'s if she suspected her father might be there. She knew the children would have been sent out, and arranged her route in such a way that she met the children and went walking with them. There had been one person in the house who wanted to open her eyes early on to her father's relations with Frau K., and to encourage her to take sides against her. It had been her last governess, an elderly, very well-read spinster who was free with her opinions.[20] Teacher and pupil had got on very well together for a while, until Dora had suddenly taken against her and insisted on her dismissal. As long as the governess had influence, she used it to stir Dora and her mother up against Frau K. She told Dora's Mama that it was irreconcilable with her dignity to tolerate such intimacy on her husband's part with a strange woman; she also brought to Dora's attention everything that was strange about that contact. But her efforts were in vain, Dora remained affectionately attached to Frau K. and would not hear of any reason to find her father's contact with her repellent. On the other hand, she was very clear about the motives driving her governess. Blind on one side, Dora was clear-sighted enough on the other. She noticed that her governess was in love with Papa. When Papa was present, she was quite a different person, and she could be amusing and helpful. When the family was staying in the factory town and Frau K. was not on the horizon, the governess had stirred things up against Mama, who was the next rival along. Dora held none of this against her. She was only angered when she noticed that the governess was quite indifferent to her, and that the love she had shown her was actually meant for her Papa. During Papa's absence from the factory town the spinster had had no time for her, would not go for walks with her, took no interest in her homework. Hardly had Papa returned from B. than she showed herself willing to undertake any service or assistance. Then Dora dropped her.

The poor girl had, with undesirable clarity, illuminated an aspect of her own behaviour. Just as the governess had sometimes behaved to Dora, so Dora had behaved towards the children of Herr K. She had acted as their mother, she had taught them, gone out with them, given them a complete substitute for the small amount of interest that their own mother showed them. There had often been talk of divorce between Herr and Frau K.; this did not take place because Herr K., who was an affectionate father, did not want to lose either of the two children. The common interest in the children had, from the start, brought Herr K. and Dora together. For Dora, busying herself with the children had clearly been a pretext designed to conceal something else from herself and others.

Her behaviour towards the children, as it was explained by the governess's behaviour towards her, yielded the same result as her tacit toleration of her father's relations with Frau K., namely that she had been in love with Herr K. for all those years. When I voiced this deduction, Dora disagreed. She immediately said that other people, such as a cousin who had visited B. for a while, had said to her, 'You're wild about that man'; but she herself claimed not to be able to remember such feelings. Later, when the wealth of material coming to light made denial more difficult, she admitted that she might have loved Herr K., but since the scene by the lake that was all over.[21] Be that as it may, it was clear that the reproach of having made herself deaf to unavoidable duties and having arranged things so that her own passionate love was left undisturbed, the very accusation that she levelled against her father rebounded upon herself.[22]

The other reproach against her father, that he turned his illnesses into means and pretexts, in turn conceals a whole part of her own secret history. One day she complained of a supposedly new symptom, acute stomach pains, and when I asked, 'Who are you copying with those?' I hit the nail on the head. The previous day she had paid a visit to her cousins, her late aunt's daughters. The younger of these had become engaged, the elder had in response fallen ill with stomach pains and had to be taken to the hospital in Semmering. She thought it was only envy on the part of the elder daughter, who always fell ill when she wanted to get something, and now she wanted to leave the house so that she would not have to witness her sister's happiness.[23] Her own stomach pains, on the other hand, made it clear that she identified with the cousin she had declared to be a fake, either because she also envied the happier party her love or because she saw her own fate reflected in that of the older sister, who had had an unhappy love affair shortly before.[24] But she had also learned how useful illnesses could be through her observations of Frau K. Herr K. spent part of the year travelling; every time he came back he found his wife indisposed, when, as Dora knew, she had been completely healthy the previous day. Dora understood that the husband's presence had the effect of making his wife ill, and that she found being ill a welcome way of escaping her hated marital duties. A remark concerning her own alternation of illness and health during the early girlhood years in B., suddenly introduced at this juncture, made me suspect that her own conditions should be considered in terms of a similar dependence to those of Frau K. In the technique of psychoanalysis, in fact, it is taken as a rule that an internal, but still hidden connection is announced through contiguity, the temporal proximity of ideas, just as the letters *a* and *b* written side by side indicate the formation of the syllable *ab*. Dora had often manifested attacks of coughing and loss of voice; might the presence or absence of her loved one have had an influence on this coming and going of her symptoms? If this was so, a coincidence that would reveal as much was bound to turn up. I asked what the average length of these attacks had been. About three to six weeks. And how long had Herr K.'s absences been? She had to admit, also between three and six weeks. So by being ill she was demonstrating her love for K., just as his wife demonstrated her repulsion. But conversely it might have been assumed that she would have been ill when he was absent and healthy after his return. And indeed that did appear to be the case, at least throughout the first period of these attacks: later on a need arose to cover over the coincidence between the attack of the illness and the absence of the secretly beloved man, so that the secret would not be betrayed by its constancy. Then, all that remained as a mark of its original meaning was the duration of the attack.

From my time in Charcot's clinic I remembered seeing and hearing that among people with hysterical mutism writing vicariously stood in for speech. They wrote more fluently, more quickly and better than other people did, or than they themselves had previously done. The same had been true of Dora. In the first days of her aphonia, 'writing had always flowed easily'. In fact this peculiarity did not, as the manifestation of a physiological substitute function, require any psychological explanation; but it was remarkable that such an explanation was so easy to come by. Herr K. wrote to her a great deal on his travels and sent her postcards; on some occasions she alone was told the date of his return, and his wife was surprised by his arrival. Incidentally, it is hardly less obvious that one should correspond with the absent one, to whom one cannot speak, than that one should seek to make oneself understood in writing if one's voice has failed. So Dora's aphonia allowed the following symbolic interpretation: when the loved one was far away, she did without speech; it had lost its value because she could not speak to *him*.

Writing, on the other hand, assumed significance as the only way of making contact with the absent one.

So am I about to conclude that in all cases of periodic aphonia we should diagnose the existence of a temporarily absent loved one? Of course that is not my intention. The determination of the symptom is, in Dora's case, far too specific for us to think in terms of the same accidental aetiology occurring with any great frequency. So what is the value of aphonia in our case? Have we allowed ourselves to be deceived by a *jeu d'esprit*? I think not. Let us remember the question that is posed so often, of whether hysterical symptoms are psychical or somatic in origin, or, if we allow the former, whether they are all necessarily psychically determined. This question is, like so many others which we see researchers struggling repeatedly and unsuccessfully to answer, inadequately framed. The true state of affairs is not covered by the alternatives that it contains. As far as I can see, any hysterical symptom needs input from both sides. It cannot come about without a certain *somatic compliance*, which is achieved by a normal or pathological process in or relating to one of the bodily organs. It does not occur more than once – and it is characteristic of the hysterical symptom that it is capable of repeating itself – unless it has a psychical significance, a *meaning*. The meaning is not inherent within the hysterical symptom, it is conferred upon it; it is, so to speak, soldered to it, and it can be different in each case, according to the nature of the suppressed thought that is struggling for expression. However, a series of elements join forces in order that the connections between the unconscious thought and the somatic processes at its disposal be made less random in form, and approach a number of typical combinations. Where therapy is concerned, the definitions present in the accidental psychical material are more important; symptoms are resolved by an examination of their psychical significance. Once that which can be removed by psychoanalysis has been cleared away one is able to have all manner of probably accurate thoughts about the somatic, generally constitutional and organic foundations of the symptoms. As to the attacks of coughing and aphonia in Dora's case we will not restrict ourselves to psychoanalytic interpretation, but demonstrate the organic element behind it, from which the 'somatic compliance' for the expression of affection for a temporarily absent loved one emerged. And if, in this case, the link between symptomatic expression and unconscious thought-content strikes us as adroit and skilful, we will be happy to hear that it can achieve the same impression in every other case, in every other example.

Now I am prepared to hear it said that it is a very moderate gain if, thanks to psychoanalysis, we no longer seek the problem of hysteria in the 'particular instability of the nerve molecules' or in the possibility of hypnoid states, but in 'somatic compliance'.

In reply, however, I should like to stress that as a result of this process the problem is not only pushed back to some degree, it is also somewhat diminished. What is at issue is now no longer the problem as a whole, but one piece of it, containing the particular character of hysteria *as distinct from* other psychoneuroses. The psychical processes at work in all psychoneuroses remain for a long time identical, and only then does the 'somatic compliance' come into consideration, giving the unconscious psychical processes an escape route into the physical. Where this element is not available, the condition as a whole is no longer a hysterical symptom, but becomes something related to it, a phobia, for example, or a compulsive idea, in short a psychical symptom.

I shall now return to the accusation of the 'simulation' of illnesses that Dora levelled against her father. We soon noticed that this reproach corresponded not only to instances of self-reproach concerning earlier illnesses, but also to some concerning the present. At this point the doctor usually has the task of guessing and completing what the analysis only hints at. I had to draw the patient's attention to the fact that her current illness was just as motivated and tendentious as the illness she saw in Frau K. There was no doubt, I told her, that she had a purpose in mind which she hoped to achieve through her illness. But it could only be to turn her father away from Frau K. She could not achieve this with pleading and arguments; perhaps she hoped to accomplish it by frightening her father (see her suicide note) or arousing his sympathy (with her fainting attacks), and if none of that was of any use, then at least she could avenge herself on him. She knew how fond he was of her, and that tears came to his eyes if anyone asked him how his daughter was. I was quite convinced, I told her, that she would immediately become well if her father declared that he would sacrifice Frau K. for the sake of her health. I hoped he would not allow this to happen, because then she would have learned what power she held in her hands, and would certainly not have neglected to use the opportunities presented by sickness again on any future occasion. But if her father did not give in to her, I was quite sure that she would not relinquish her illness so readily.

I shall pass over the details which proved all these hypotheses completely correct, preferring instead to add some general observations about the role of *motives for illness* in hysteria. The motives for illness should be sharply distinguished from the possible ways of being ill, the material from which symptoms are created. The motives themselves play no part in the formation of symptoms, and neither are they present at the beginning of the illness; they only appear secondarily, but the illness is not fully constituted until they appear.[25] The motives for illness are dependably present in every case that constitutes a genuine illness and lasts for a long time. At first the symptom is an unwelcome guest of the psychical life, it has everything going against it, and that is also why it disappears so easily of its own accord, it would seem, under the influence of time. At first it has no useful application in the psychical economy, but it very often achieves such an application secondarily; some psychical current finds it convenient to use the symptom, and for that reason it has achieved a *secondary function*, effectively anchoring itself in the life of the mind. Anyone wishing to improve the health of the patient will, to his astonishment, encounter a great resistance, which teaches him that the patient is not completely serious about his intentions of relinquishing the illness.[26] Imagine a workman, a roof-builder, for example, who has been crippled and now begs his livelihood on the street corner. Along comes a miracle worker and promises him that he will make his crooked leg straight and fit to walk once more. One should not necessarily prepare oneself to see a particularly joyful expression appearing on his face. Of course he felt extremely unhappy when he suffered the injury, realizing that he would never be able to work again, and would have to starve or live on alms. But since then, the very thing that initially made him unemployable has also become his source of income; he lives off his crippled state. Take that away from him and one may render him completely helpless; he will have forgotten his craft in the meantime, lost his working habits, and become accustomed to idleness, and possibly taken to drink.

The motives for illness often begin to stir in childhood. The love-hungry little girl, unhappy at having to share her parents' affection with her brothers and sisters, realizes that all that tenderness comes flowing back when her parents are made anxious by her illness. The girl now knows a way of calling forth her parents' love, and will use this as soon as she has at her disposal the psychical material necessary to produce a morbid state. Once the child has become a woman and, in contradiction of the demands of childhood, has married an inattentive man who suppresses her will, unstintingly exploits her work and expends neither affection nor money upon her, illness becomes the only weapon with which she can assert herself in life. It gives her the rest she craves, it forces the man to make sacrifices of money and care that he would not have made to the healthy woman, and it requires him to treat her with care if she recovers, because otherwise a relapse would be waiting in the wings. Her illness is apparently objective and involuntary, as even her doctor will be obliged to testify, and it enables her to employ, without conscious self-reproach, this useful application of a means that she found effective during childhood.

And yet the illness is indeed intentionally produced! States of illness are generally directed at a certain person, so that they disappear when that person goes away. The crudest and most banal judgement about the illness of the hysteric, which one may hear from uneducated relatives and nurses, is in a sense correct. It is true that the paralysed and bedridden patient would leap to his feet if fire broke out in his room, that the spoilt woman would forget all her troubles if a child fell seriously ill or the house was threatened with disaster. All those who speak of sick people in these terms are right up to a point, but they are ignoring the psychological difference between the conscious and the unconscious, which the child may still be allowed, but which is no longer acceptable for the adult. For that reason, protestations that it is all to do with the will, and attempts to cheer up or abuse the patient, will be in vain. One must first try to convince her, along the roundabout way of analysis, of the existence of her intention to be ill.

It is in the struggle against motives for illness in hysteria that the weakness of all therapy, psychoanalytic therapy included, generally lies. This makes matters easier for destiny; it does not need to assail either the patient's constitution or her pathogenic material. It removes a motive for illness, and the patient is freed from the illness, temporarily, or perhaps even in the longer term. If we doctors only had a greater insight into our patient's hidden interests in life, how many fewer miracle cures, how many fewer spontaneously disappearing symptoms would we allow in our hysterical cases! In one case, a date has finally arrived, in another, concern for another person has become superfluous, a situation has been fundamentally altered by external events, and all of a sudden the patient's suffering, so stubborn until now, is removed, apparently spontaneously, but in fact because its strongest motive, one of its applications in life, has been withdrawn.

Motives supporting illness will probably be found in all fully developed cases. But there are cases with purely internal motives, such as self-punishment, regret and atonement. In cases such as these the therapeutic task will be easier to resolve than in those in which the illness is related to the achievement of an external goal. Dora's goal was obvious: to win over her father and turn him away from Frau K.

None of his actions seemed, incidentally, to have left her so embittered as his readiness to see the scene by the lake as a product of her imagination. She was beside herself when she reflected that she was supposed to have imagined it all. For a long time I was unable to guess the self-reproach that lay concealed behind the passionate rebuttal of this explanation. One was right to suspect that there was something hidden behind it, for a false accusation is a lasting insult. On the other hand, I reached the conclusion that

Dora's story must entirely correspond to the truth. After she had understood Herr K.'s intention, she had not allowed him to have his say, she had slapped his face and run off. Her behaviour at the time probably seemed just as incomprehensible to the man she left behind as it does to us, for he must have deduced long before from countless little signs that he could be sure of the girl's affection. In our discussion of the second dream we will find the solution both to this problem and, at the same time, to the self-reproach that we were searching for at the beginning.

When Dora's accusations against her father recurred with wearying monotony, and the cough refused to go away, I found myself thinking that the symptom might have a significance in relation to her father. Furthermore, the conditions that I am accustomed to imposing on the explanation of a symptom were far from fulfilled. According to a rule that I have seen confirmed time and again, but did not yet have the courage to postulate as being universal, a symptom signifies the representation – the realization – of a fantasy with a sexual content: that is, a sexual situation. I should rather say, at least *one* of the meanings of a symptom corresponds to the representation of a sexual fantasy, while for the other meanings, such restrictions concerning content do not exist. When we embark upon psychoanalytical work, we very quickly learn that a symptom has more than one meaning, and serves to represent several unconscious trains of thought. I should like to add that in my view a single unconscious train of thought or fantasy is hardly ever sufficient for the production of a symptom.

The opportunity to interpret nervous coughing in terms of a fantasized sexual situation arose very soon. When Dora stressed once again that Frau K. only loved Papa because he was 'ein *vermögender* Mann' [a wealthy man], I noticed from certain little details in her expression – which I shall pass over here as I shall most of the purely technical aspects of the work of analysis – that the sentence concealed its opposite: Father was 'ein *unvermögender* Mann' [an incapable, or impotent man]. This, then, could only have a sexual meaning: Father was '*unvermögend*', impotent, as a man. After she had confirmed this interpretation on the basis of her conscious knowledge, I showed her the contradiction she would fall into if, on the one hand, she maintained that the relationship with Frau K. was an ordinary love affair, and on the other, claimed that her father was impotent, and was thus incapable of exploiting such a relationship. Her answer showed that she did not need to acknowledge the contradiction. She was very well aware, she said, that there was more than one kind of sexual satisfaction. She was, however, unable to identify the source of that knowledge. When I went on to ask whether she meant the application of organs other than the genitals for sexual intercourse, she said yes, and I was able to continue: she was thinking of precisely those body parts which were in an aroused state in her own body (throat, oral cavity). She claimed to know nothing of these thoughts, but then, in order for the symptom to appear, she could not have had a full understanding of them. It was therefore impossible to avoid the deduction that her spasmodic coughing, which usually began with a tickle in the throat, represented a situation of sexual gratification *per os* [oral sexual gratification] between the two people whose amorous relationship was a source of constant preoccupation to her. It was of course very true that the cough had disappeared within a very short time after this elucidation, which was tacitly accepted; none the less we did not want to place too much value on this change, because it had appeared spontaneously so often before.

If this little piece of the analysis has aroused surprise and horror in the medical reader, quite apart from the incredulity that is his prerogative, I am prepared to test the justification of these two reactions at this point. Surprise is, I think, motivated by my audacity in talking to a young girl – or a woman of a sexual age – about such delicate and repellent matters. Horror probably relates to the possibility that a chaste young girl might know about such practices and that her imagination might revolve around them. On both of these points I should recommend reserve and level-headedness. In neither case is there cause for indignation. One can talk to girls and women about all kinds of sexual matters without doing them any harm, first if one adopts a particular way of doing this, and secondly if one can convince them that it is unavoidable. Under the same conditions, after all, a gynaecologist will demand all kinds of exposure. The best way of talking about these things is coolly and directly; at the same time it is the furthest removed from the salaciousness with which the same subjects are dealt with in 'society', and with which both girls and women are very familiar. I give both organs and processes their technical names, and inform the patient of them if they – the names – are unknown to them. '*J'appelle un chat un chat.*' [I call a spade a spade.] I have heard of medical and non-medical people who are scandalized by a form of therapy in which such discussions take place, and who seem to envy both me and the patient the thrill that they believe must occur. However, I am too familiar with the respectability of the gentlemen in question to get annoyed with them. I shall not rise to the temptation of satirizing them. I should only like to mention that I often have the satisfaction of hearing a patient, for whom frankness in sexual matters has not at first been easy, later exclaiming, 'No, your cure is far more respectable than Herr X's conversation!'

One must be convinced of the unavoidability of touching upon sexual themes before undertaking a treatment of hysteria, or else one must be prepared to be convinced by experiences. Then one will say to oneself: *pour faire une omelette il faut casser des oeufs*. [You can't make an omelette without breaking eggs.] The patients themselves are easily persuaded; there are only too many opportunities in the course of the treatment. One does not need to reproach oneself for discussing facts from normal or abnormal sexual life with them. If one is relatively careful, one is simply translating into consciousness what they already know in the unconscious, and the whole effect of the cure is based on the insight that the emotional effects of an unconscious idea are more violent and, because invulnerable to inhibition, more dangerous than the effects of a conscious idea. One never risks corrupting an inexperienced girl; and where there is no knowledge of sexual processes in the unconscious, no hysterical symptom will come into being. Wherever one encounters hysteria one can no longer talk of 'pure thoughts' in the sense used by parents and teachers. Among ten-, twelve- and fourteen-year-old children, both boys and girls, I have convinced myself of the utter dependability of this proposition.

A second emotional reaction occurs, which, if I am correct, is directed not at myself but at the patient: this reaction finds the perverse character of the patient's fantasies horrifying. I should stress that such vehement condemnation is not appropriate in a doctor. I also find it, amongst other things, superfluous that a doctor writing about the confusions of the sexual drives should take every opportunity to express his personal revulsion at such unpleasant things. Here is a fact to which I hope, if we suppress our personal tastes, we shall become accustomed. As regards what we call the sexual perversions, transgressions of the sexual function in terms of area of the body and sexual object, we must be able to discuss them without indignation. The very vagueness of the boundaries of what might be called a normal sexual life in different races and at different periods of time should cool the protesters down. But we must not forget that the perversion most repellent to us, the sensual love of man for man, was not only tolerated by the Greeks, a people culturally far superior to ourselves, but even endowed with important social functions. Each one of us goes a bit too far, either here or there, in transgressing the boundaries that we have drawn up in our own sexual lives. The perversions are neither bestialities nor degeneracies in the dramatic sense of that word. They are the development of germs that are all contained within the undifferentiated sexual predisposition of the child, the suppression of which, or their application to higher, asexual goals – their *sublimation* – is destined to supply the forces behind a large number of our cultural achievements. So if someone has become coarse and manifestly perverse, it would be more accurate to say that he has *remained* so, that he represents a stage of an *arrested development*. Psychoneurotics are all people with inclinations that are strongly formed, but which in the course of their development have been repressed and become perverse. Their unconscious fantasies thus reveal exactly the same content as the authentically established actions of perverts, even if they have not read Krafft-Ebing's *Psychopathia sexualis*, which naïve people hold responsible to some degree for the origins of perverse tendencies. The psychoneuroses are, we might say, the *negative* of the perversions. In neurotics the sexual constitution, which also contains the expression of heredity, works alongside the accidental influences of life, which disturb the development of normal sexuality. Water that encounters an obstacle in one river-bed is driven back into older courses previously destined to be abandoned. The drive-forces for the formation of hysterical symptoms are fed not only by repressed normal sexuality but also by unconscious perverse impulses.[27]

The less repellent so-called sexual perversions are the most widespread among our population, as everyone knows apart from medical authors on the subject. Or rather the authors know it too; they just try to forget they do the moment they pick up their pens to write about them. So it can hardly be surprising if our hysteric, who is shortly to be nineteen years of age, and who has heard of the occurrence of one such form of sexual intercourse (the sucking of the member), should develop an unconscious fantasy of this kind and express it with the sensation of irritation in the throat and with coughing. Neither would it be surprising if she had arrived at such a fantasy without external information, something that I have observed with certainty in other patients. The somatic precondition for such an autonomous creation of a fantasy, which coincides with the actions of a pervert, was, in her case, the result of a remarkable fact. She very clearly remembered that in childhood she had been a '*Lutscherin*', or 'thumb-sucker'. Her father also remembered that he had weaned her off the habit when it continued into her fourth or fifth year. Dora herself had kept in her memory a distinct image from early childhood, in which she sat in a corner on the floor, sucking on her left thumb, while tugging with her right hand on the earlobe of her brother, who sat peacefully beside her. This is the kind of utter self-gratification through sucking that other – later anaesthetic and hysteric – patients have described to me. One of these patients has given me an account that casts a clear light on the origin of this strange habit. The young woman in question, who had never given up sucking, saw herself in a childhood memory, supposedly from the first half of her second year, drinking at her nurse's breast and at the same time pulling rhythmically on her nurse's earlobe. I do not believe that anyone would wish to dispute that the mucous membrane of the lips and the mouth may be declared to be a primary *erogenous zone*, since it has preserved part of that significance for kissing, which is considered normal. The early and generous activation of this erogenous zone, then, is the condition for the later somatic compliance from the mucous tract that begins with the lips. If then, at a time when the actual sexual object, the male member, is already known, situations arise which cause excitement of the still erogenous zone of the mouth to increase once again, it does not take a great deal of creative imagination to substitute for the original nipple and the fingers standing in for it, the actual sexual object, the penis, in a situation of satisfaction. Thus, the perverse fantasy, so shocking to us, of sucking the penis, has the most harmless of origins; it is the reworking of what we might term a 'prehistoric' impression of sucking at the breast of the mother or nurse, which has been revived later on by seeing children at the breast. In the majority of cases, the cow's udder has served a suitable intermediate notion between the nipple and the penis.

The interpretation of Dora's throat symptoms, which we have just discussed, also prompts another observation. The question arises: to what extent can this fantasized sexual situation coincide with the other explanation: that the coming and going of the symptoms of the illness mirrors the presence and absence of the beloved man? If we take the woman's behaviour into account, the idea expressed is the following: if I were his wife, I would love him quite differently, I would be sick (with longing, for example) if he went away, and healthy (with joy) when he came home again. My experiences in the solution of hysterical symptoms lead me to give the following reply: the various meanings of a symptom need not be compatible with one another, that is, they need not connect into a coherent whole. It is enough that the connection is produced by the theme that has given rise to all of these fantasies. Incidentally, in the case under consideration, compatibility of this kind is not excluded: one meaning is more attached to the cough, the other more to the aphonia and the development of conditions; deeper analysis would probably reveal a much greater psychical determination of the details of the illness. We have already seen that a symptom can regularly correspond to several meanings *at once*; let us now add that it can also express several meanings *in sequence*. The symptom can change one of its meanings or its principal meaning over the years, or else the leading role can pass from one meaning to another. It is like a conservative trait in the character of the neurosis that the symptom, once formed, may be maintained even after the unconscious thought that it expresses has lost its meaning. But this tendency to preserve the symptom can also be easily expressed in mechanical terms; the production of such a symptom is so difficult, the transfer of purely psychical to physical excitement, which I have called *conversion*, is dependent upon so many favourable conditions, the somatic compliance required for conversion is so difficult to attain, that the compulsion to discharge the excitement from the unconscious may mean that it contents itself with the already accessible discharge channel. It would appear much easier to produce associative relations between a new thought that needs discharging and the old one, which no longer needs it, than to create a new conversion. Along a path thus traced, excitement flows from the new source of excitement to the old, and the symptom, as the Gospel puts it, resembles an old skin that has been filled with new wine. If, after these discussions, the somatic portion of the hysterical symptom appears to be the one that is more constant, more difficult to replace, and the psychical to be the one that changes, the element more easily replaced, it would not be correct to deduce from this that there was a difference in rank between them. For psychical therapy, the psychical portion is always the more significant.

Dora's tireless repetition of the same thought about the relationship between her father and Frau K. presented the opportunity for another important discovery to be made in her analysis.

Such a train of thought may be called excessively strong, *reinforced* or *supervalent* in Wernicke's sense [Carl Wernicke in *Grundriss der Psychiatrie* (*Outline of Psychiatry*), 1900]. It proves to be pathological, despite the apparent correctness of its content, because of the peculiar fact that despite all conscious and deliberate efforts it cannot be broken down or removed. One finally comes to terms with a normal train of thought, however intense it may be. Dora felt, quite correctly, that her thoughts about her Papa called for a special assessment. 'I can't think about anything else,' she complained repeatedly. 'My brother tells me that we children have no right to criticize these actions of Papa's. We shouldn't worry about them, and should perhaps even be pleased that he has found a woman to attach himself to, since Mama has so little understanding of him. I can see that, and I would also like to think as my brother does, but I can't. I can't forgive him.'[28]

What is one to do in the face of such a supervalent thought, having listened both to its conscious explanation and the unsuccessful objections to it? One tells oneself *that this excessively strong series of ideas owes its reinforcement to the unconscious*. It cannot be resolved by intellectual work, either because its own roots extend into unconscious, repressed material or because it masks another unconscious thought. This latter is usually its exact opposite. Opposites are always closely linked, and often paired in such a way *that one thought becomes conscious in an excessively strong way, while its opposite number is repressed and becomes unconscious*. This relationship is the result of the process of repression. The repression, in fact, has often been carried out in such a way that the opposite of the thought to be repressed is excessively reinforced. I call this a *reaction* reinforcement, and the thought which is asserted with excessive strength in the consciousness, and which, like a prejudice, proves impossible to break down, the *reaction thought*. These two thoughts relate to one another more or less after the fashion of a pair of astatic needles. With a certain excess of intensity, the reaction thought keeps the unpleasant thought in the repression; but in the process it is itself 'muffled' and rendered immune to conscious intellectual work. The way to remove the excessive strength from the excessively strong thought, then, is to return the unconscious idea opposed to it into consciousness.

Neither should one rule out the possibility that in certain cases one may be presented not with one of two reasons for supervalence, but with a competition between the two. Other combinations may also arise, but these are easily incorporated into the process.

Let us attempt to do this with the example given to us by Dora, first of all with the first hypothesis: that the roots of her compulsive anxiety about her father's relationship with Frau K. are unknown to her because they lie in the unconscious. It is not hard to guess these roots from the situation, and from the symptoms. Dora's behaviour clearly went far beyond a daughter's sphere of interest, and she felt and acted more like a jealous wife, in a way that might have been understandable if her mother had been acting in the same way. In confronting her father with an alternative: 'Either her or me', in the scenes she made and the threat of suicide which she allowed her parents to glimpse, she was clearly putting herself in her mother's position. If we are correct in guessing that the fantasy of a sexual situation is at the root of her cough, then in that fantasy she took the place of Frau K. So she was identifying with both of the women her father had loved, now and in the past. The obvious conclusion to draw is that her inclination towards her father was stronger than she knew or would have wished to admit, that she was in love with her father.

I have learned to see such unconscious love affairs between father and daughter, mother and son – identifiable by their abnormal consequences – as a revivification of the seeds of certain impressions from infancy. Elsewhere[29] I have explained how early sexual attraction becomes apparent between parents and children, and shown that the Oedipus fable should probably be understood as the poetic treatment of what is typical about such relationships. This precocious inclination of the daughter towards the father, of the son towards the mother, a distinct trace of which is probably to be found in most people, must be seen as having been originally more intense in children constitutionally predisposed towards neurosis, precocious and hungry for love. After this, certain influences which cannot be discussed here come into play, fixating the rudimentary amorous excitement or intensifying it in such a way that from childhood, or only from puberty, it becomes something which might be compared to a sexual attraction and which, like a sexual attraction, monopolizes the libido.[30] The external circumstances in our patient's case certainly do not discourage such an assumption. She had always been temperamentally drawn to her father, and his many illnesses must have heightened her affection for him; in some of his illnesses she herself was entrusted with the minor tasks involved in nursing him; proud of her precocious intelligence, he had chosen her as a confidante even when she was a child. The arrival of Frau K. meant that it was not really her mother but Dora herself who was driven out of more than one job.

When I told Dora I assumed that her inclination towards her father had had the characteristics of passionate love, even early on, she gave her usual answer: 'I can't remember', but then she immediately told me something similar about her seven-year-old cousin (on her mother's side), in whom she often thought she saw something like a reflection of her own childhood. The little girl had once witnessed a heated argument between her parents, and had whispered in Dora's ear, when she had visited shortly afterwards: 'You can't imagine how I hate that (pointing at her mother) person! And when she dies I'm going to marry Papa.' I have become used to seeing such instances, which in some respects accord with what I am asserting, as a confirmation issuing from the unconscious. No other 'yes' can be heard from the unconscious; there is no such thing as an unconscious 'no'.[31]

This passionate love for her father had not manifested itself for years; rather, Dora had enjoyed excellent relations with the very woman who had replaced her in her father's life, and had even, as we know from her instances of self-reproach, favoured that woman's relationship with her father. So that love had recently been revived, and if that was the case, we had cause to wonder why it should have happened. Clearly it was a reaction symptom, its purpose being to suppress something else that was still powerful in the unconscious. As things stood, the first thing that occurred to me was that what had been repressed was Dora's love for Herr K. I had to accept that her passionate love was still there, but since the scene by the lake – for unknown reasons – a violent resistance to it had developed, and the girl had revived and intensified her old inclination towards her father, lest she should retain any conscious thought of the love of her first years of girlhood, which was now embarrassing to her. Then I also gained an insight into a conflict that had the potential to shatter the girl's psychical life. On the one hand, she was filled with regret at having repelled the man's proposal, she was filled with longing for him and the little signs of his affection; on the other hand, powerful motives, pride being one that could easily be guessed, did battle with those affectionate and lovelorn impulses. As a result she had managed to persuade herself that she had finished with Herr K. – that was her gain in this typical process of repression – and yet as a protection against her passion, which was constantly forcing its way into her consciousness, she had to appeal to and exaggerate her infantile inclination towards her father. But the fact that she had been almost incessantly dominated by bitter jealousy seemed capable of a further determination.[32]

The most intense denial that I received when I put this interpretation to Dora certainly did nothing to contradict my expectations. The 'no' that one hears from the patient when one first presents the repressed thought to their conscious perception merely confirms the repression and its intensity; it is a measure of its strength, so to speak. If we do not take this 'no' to be the expression of an objective judgement, of which the patient would not in fact be capable, but instead go beyond it and take the work further, we soon have our first proof that in such cases 'no' means the 'yes' one is hoping for. She admitted that she could not be as angry with Herr K. as he deserved her to be. She said that she had met Herr K. in the street one day when she was with her female cousin, who did not know him. Her cousin suddenly called out, 'Dora, what's wrong with you? You're as white as a ghost!' She had felt nothing of this change in herself, but I had to tell her that facial expressions and affective manifestations obey the unconscious rather than the consciousness, and give the unconscious away.[33] On another occasion, after several days of uniform cheerfulness, she came to see me in the most terrible mood, which she was unable to explain. She felt so dreadful today, she explained; it was her uncle's birthday and she could not bring herself to congratulate him; she didn't know why. As my interpretative art was not working that day, I let her go on speaking, and she suddenly remembered that it was Herr K.'s birthday today as well, which I did not neglect to use against her. Then it became relatively easy to explain why the lovely presents on her own birthday a few days previously had brought her no joy. She was missing the one present from Herr K. that would obviously have been the most precious of all.

Meanwhile, she maintained her denial of my assertion for a long time, until, towards the end of the analysis, the crucial proof of its correctness came to light.

I must now mention a further complication to which I would certainly give no space here if I were inventing, as a writer, such a mental state for a novella, rather than dissecting it as a doctor. The element to which I shall now refer can only dull and blur the beautiful conflict, worthy of poetic treatment, which we may assume in Dora; it would rightly fall victim to the censorship of the writer, who carries out a process of simplification and elimination when he deals with psychological matters. But in the reality that I am attempting to describe here, the rule is the complication of motives, the accumulation and composition of mental stimuli, in short: over-determination. The supervalent train of thought, dealing with her father's relationship with Frau K., concealed an impulse of jealousy whose object was Frau K. herself – an impulse, then, that could only be based on an inclination towards her own sex. It has long been known and often stressed that even normal boys and girls may, during puberty, show clear signs of the existence of same-sex inclinations. Infatuated friendship for a fellow schoolgirl, with sworn oaths, kisses, promises of eternal correspondence, and with all the sensitivity of jealousy, is the usual forerunner of the first more intense passionate love for a man. In favourable circumstances the homosexual current often wins out completely; where happiness in love for a man does not come about, in later years it is often reawakened by the libido and heightened to a particular intensity. If this can be observed without much difficulty in healthy people, following on from earlier observations concerning the stronger formation of the normal germs of perversion in neurotics, we may also expect to find a stronger homosexual predisposition in their constitution. This must be so, because I have never carried out psychoanalytic treatment of a man or a woman without bearing such a highly significant homosexual inclination in mind. Among hysterical women and girls, whose sexual libido as directed towards men has been energetically suppressed, one regularly finds that the libido directed towards women has undergone a vicarious kind of reinforcement, and one that can even be said to be partially conscious.

I shall not go into this important theme, which is particularly indispensable for an understanding of hysteria in men, because Dora's analysis came to an end before it could shed any light on these relations in her own case. But I might recall that governess with whom she at first lived in intellectual intimacy, before she noticed that the governess cherished her and treated her well not for her own sake but for her father's. Then she forced the governess to leave the house. She dwelt with striking frequency and special emphasis on the story of another falling-out that she herself considered mysterious. She had always got on well with her second cousin, the one who later became engaged, and had shared all kinds of secrets with her. Now, when her father returned to B. after the interrupted visit to the lake, and Dora naturally refused to go with him, this cousin was asked to travel with Dora's father and agreed to do so. From that point onwards, Dora felt cold towards her cousin, and was herself startled at how indifferent she had become towards her, although she admitted that she had nothing major to reproach her with. These susceptibilities led me to ask what her relationship with Frau K. had been like before the disagreement. I learned then that the young woman and the barely adult girl had lived for years in the greatest intimacy. When Dora was living with the Ks, she had shared a bedroom with the wife; the husband was moved elsewhere. She had been the wife's confidante and adviser throughout all the problems of her married life; there was nothing that they had not talked about. Medea was perfectly happy for Creusa to draw the two children to herself; she certainly did nothing to obstruct contact between the children's father and the girl. One interesting psychological problem is how Dora managed to love the man about whom her beloved friend had so many bad things to say. We may probably solve this with the insight that thoughts dwell particularly comfortably side by side in the unconscious, that even opposites can bear one another without conflict, and that this state is often perpetuated in the consciousness.

When Dora talked of Frau K., she praised the 'delightful whiteness of her body' in a tone more that of a girl in love than a defeated rival. More melancholic than bitter, on another occasion she told me she was convinced that the presents her Papa had brought back for her had been bought by Frau K.; she recognized her taste. On another occasion she stressed that she had clearly been given a present of some pieces of jewellery through the intercession of Frau K., because they were very similar to the ones that she had seen Frau K. wearing, for which she had, on that occasion, expressed a vociferous desire. Indeed, I must say in general that I never heard her utter a harsh or angry word about the woman, whom she must have seen, from the point of view of her supervalent thoughts, as the source of her unhappiness. Her behaviour seemed inconsistent, but that apparent inconsistency was the expression of a complicated current of emotion. For how had the friend she loved with such infatuation behaved towards her? After Dora had made her accusation against Herr K., and her father had demanded an explanation in writing, he first replied with protestations of respect, and offered to come to the factory town to clear up any misunderstandings. A few weeks later, when her father spoke to him in B., there was no longer any sign of respect. He disparaged the girl and played his trump card: a girl who read such books and took an interest in such things had no claim to a man's respect. So Frau K. had betrayed her and blackened her character; it was only with Frau K. that she had talked of Mantegazza and related subjects. It was the same as with the governess; Frau K., too, had loved her not for her own sake but for her father's. Frau K. had thoughtlessly sacrificed Dora so as not to have her own relationship with Dora's father disturbed. Perhaps this insult was more wounding to Dora, was more pathogenically effective, than the earlier wound that had been inflicted when her father had sacrificed her, and with which she wanted to mask the wound inflicted by Frau K. Did such a stubbornly maintained amnesia concerning the sources of her forbidden knowledge not point directly to the emotional value of the accusation, and thus to her betrayal by her friend?

I believe, then, that I am not mistaken in putting forward the hypothesis that the purpose of Dora's supervalent train of thought about her father's relationship to Frau K. was to suppress not only her formerly conscious love for Herr K., but also her profoundly unconscious love for Frau K. It was directly opposed to the latter current. She told herself incessantly that her Papa had sacrificed her to Frau K., and vociferously demonstrated that she would not grant Frau K. possession of her Papa, and in that way she concealed the opposite, that she could not grant her Papa the love of this woman, and that she had not forgiven this beloved woman the disappointment of her own betrayal. In her unconscious, the feminine impulse of jealousy was coupled with jealousy as it might have been felt by a man. These masculine or, we might say, *gynaecophilic* currents of emotion must be considered typical of the unconscious love-life of hysterical girls.

Notes

1. *The Interpretation of Dreams*, Chapter II [*Gesammelte Werke*, vol. II/III, p. 104ff.].

2. A colleague once passed his sister to me for psychoanalytic treatment after, he told me, she had been unsuccessfully undergoing treatment for years for hysteria (pains and ambulatory disorders). The brief information seemed to accord well with the diagnosis; in one of the first sessions I had the patient tell me her story herself. When this story, despite the curious details to which she referred, turned out to be perfectly clear and orderly, I told myself that the case could not be one of hysteria, and immediately undertook a careful physical examination. The result was the diagnosis of moderately advanced tabes [a wasting disease], which was then considerably improved with Hg injections (Ol. Cinereum, performed by Professor Lang).

3. Amnesias and false memories are complementary to one another. Where

large gaps appear in the memory, few errors of memory will be encountered. Conversely, the latter can completely conceal the presence of amnesias at first glance.

4. A rule gained by experience tells us that if an account is given hesitantly, one should learn from this manifestation of the narrator's judgement. In an account hovering between two versions, the first should be taken to be correct, and the second seen as a product of repression.

5. I do not hold the view that the sole aetiology of hysteria is hereditary, but, with reference to earlier publications ('L'hérédité et l'étiologie des névroses' ['The Heredity and Aetiology of Neuroses'], *Revue neurologique*, 1896, in vol. I of the complete edition [of the *Gesammelte Werke*]), in which I dispute the above sentence, I do not wish to give a sense that I underestimate heredity in the aetiology of hysteria, or that I consider it to be utterly dispensable. For our patient's case enough of a taint is present in what I have revealed about the father and his brother and sister; indeed, if one takes the view that illnesses like that of the mother are impossible without a hereditary disposition, one will be able to declare the heredity of this case to be a convergent one. For the hereditary or, more precisely, the constitutional predisposition of the girl, another element seems to me to be more significant. I have mentioned that her father had suffered a bout of syphilis before his marriage. Now a *strikingly large* percentage of the patients whom I have treated with psychoanalysis are descended from fathers who have suffered from tabes or paralysis. Because my therapeutic procedure is a new one, only *serious* cases come to me, those which have already been treated for years without any success. In accordance with the Erb-Fournier theory, tabes or paralysis in the father can be seen as references to a syphilitic infection in the past, which I too have directly identified in a number of cases with fathers such as these. In the last discussion of the descendants of syphilitics (XIIIth International Conference of Medicine in Paris, 2–9 August 1900, papers by Finger, Tarnowsky, Jullien and others) I find no mention of the fact that my experience as a neuropathologist forces me to acknowledge: that syphilis in the father is certainly worthy of consideration as an aetiology for the neuropathic constitution of the children.

6. For the probable cause of this first illness, see below.

7. Cf. on the same subject the analysis of the second dream.

8. This cure, and consequently my insight into the concatenations of the case, has, as I have already stated, remained fragmentary. For that reason I can provide no information on certain points, or only hints and suspicions. When this letter came to be discussed in one session, the girl asked, as

though astonished: 'How did they find the letter in the first place? After all, it was locked in my desk.' But as she knew that her parents had read this draft of a suicide note, I conclude that she had played it into their hands herself.

9. I believe that in this attack cramps and deliriums were also apparent. But, as the analysis did not get as far as this event either, I do not have access to any definite memory of it.

10. Here is an example of the latter. One of my Viennese colleagues, whose conviction of the lack of importance of sexual elements in hysteria has probably been strongly reinforced by such experiences, forced himself, in the case of a fourteen-year-old girl with dangerous hysterical vomiting, to ask the awkward question of whether she might not even have had a love affair. The child answered, 'No', probably with well-acted astonishment, and in her disrespectful way said to her mother, 'Imagine, the fool even asked me if I was in love.' She then entered my treatment and revealed herself – although not at our first discussion – as a masturbator of long standing with a strong fluor albus (which was closely related to the vomiting). She had finally given up the habit of her own accord. In her abstinence, though, she had been so severely tormented by the most violent sense of guilt that she saw all accidents that befell the family as divine punishment for her sins. She was also influenced by the story of her aunt, whose extramarital pregnancy (providing a second determination for her vomiting) her family thought they had successfully kept secret from her. She was considered to be 'entirely a child', but proved to be initiated in all the essentials of sexual relationships.

11. I have gone beyond this theory without abandoning it, that is, I now declare it not to be incorrect, but incomplete. I have abandoned only my emphasis on the so-called hypnoid state, which is thought to appear in the patient as a result of the trauma, and to serve as an explanation of any psychologically abnormal events that subsequently occurred. If one might be permitted in a collaborative work to undertake a retrospective distribution of property, I should like to state that the hypothesis of the 'hypnoid states', which some people see as the core of our work, is the sole initiative of Breuer. I consider it unnecessary and misleading to interrupt the continuity of the problem in which the psychical process consists in hysterical symptom formation by bestowing this name upon it.

12. Cf. my essay: 'Zur Ätiologie der Hysterie' [On the Aetiology of Hysteria'], *Wiener klinische Rundschau*, 1896, vol. 22–6 (Sammlung kl. Schriften zur Neurosenlehre, I. Folge, 1906. 3. Aufl. 1920. – Contained in vol. I of this complete edition [*Gesammelte Werke*]).

13. The appraisal of these circumstances will be made easier by an explanation later on.

14. Dora's disgust in response to this kiss certainly did not have accidental causes, since these would certainly have been remembered and mentioned. I happen to know Herr K.; he is the same person who accompanied the patient's father when he came to see me, a man who was still young and with appealing looks.

15. Such displacements are not being assumed for the purpose of this single explanation, for example, but arise as an indispensable requirement for a whole series of symptoms. Since writing this I have heard from a fiancée who had previously been very much in love, and who turned to me because of a sudden cooling towards her betrothed, which occurred at the same time as a profound depression. She told me of the same effect of horror as the result of an embrace (without a kiss). In this case the fear was traced back without further difficulty to the man's erection, perceived but removed from consciousness.

16. Cf. the second dream.

17. Here, as at all similar places, one should prepare oneself, not for a single, but for several reasons, for *over-determination*.

18. All these discussions contain much that is typical of hysteria and universally applicable to it. The theme of erection provokes some of the most interesting of hysterical symptoms. Female sensitivity to the outlines of the male genitals perceptible through the clothing often becomes, once repressed, the motive for fear of people and of human society. The broad connection between the sexual and the excremental, whose pathogenic significance can probably not be overstated, is the basis for a very considerable number of hysterical phobias.

19. This is connected to her own suicidal drama, which therefore expresses something like the longing for a similar love.

20. This governess, who read all the books about the sexual life etc., and talked to the girl about them, but candidly asked her to keep everything relating to them secret from her parents, since one could not know what their attitude might be – in this girl, for a while, I sought the source for all of Dora's secret knowledge, and perhaps I was not entirely wrong to do so.

21. Cf. the second dream.

22. Here the question arises: if Dora loved Herr K., how are we to explain her dismissal of him in the scene by the lake, or at least the brutal form of that dismissal, with its suggestion of bitterness? How could a girl in love see an insult in a declaration which – as we shall later hear – was far from brash or repellent?

23. An everyday occurrence between sisters.

24. The further conclusion I drew from the stomach pains will be discussed below.

25. [*Addition 1923*:] This is not entirely correct. We would not be justified in our suggestion that the motives for the illness are not present at the beginning of the illness and are only secondary phenomena. On the next page, in fact, motives for the illness are mentioned which exist before the outbreak of the illness and which contribute to it. Later on in the text I have given a better account of this subject by introducing the distinction between *primary and secondary gain from illness*. The motive for illness is the sole intention of such a gain. What is subsequently said in this section applies to the secondary gain from illness. But a primary gain from illness must be acknowledged for any neurotic illness. Becoming ill first of all spares the patient a psychical task, and presents itself as the most comfortable solution in the case of a psychical conflict (*flight into illness*), although in most cases such an escape proves to be unambiguously pointless. This portion of the primary gain from illness can be described as the *internal*, psychological part. In addition, external elements such as the example quoted of the situation of the woman oppressed by her husband, can provide motives for becoming ill and thus produce the *external* portion of the primary gain from illness.

26. A poet, albeit one who is also a doctor, Arthur Schnitzler gave most correct expression to this idea in his *Paracelsus*.

27. These sentences about sexual perversions were written several years before the excellent book by I. Bloch (*Beiträge zur Ätiologie der Psychopathia sexualis* [*Contributions to the Aetiology of Psychopathia Sexualis*], 1902 and 1903). Cf. also in that year (1905) *Drei Abhandlungen zur Sexualtheorie* [*Three Essays on Sexual Theory*] (5th edn, 1922).

28. This kind of supervalent thought is, along with profound depression, often the only symptom of a condition that is usually called 'melancholia', but it can be resolved by psychoanalysis like a case of hysteria.

29. In the *Interpretation of Dreams*, Chapter V, Section D (ß) [*Gesammelte Werke*, vol. II/III], and in the third of the *Three Essays on Sexual Theory*.

30. The crucial element in this is probably the premature appearance of real genital sensations, whether they be spontaneous or provoked by seduction and masturbation (see below).

31. [*Addition 1923*:] Another very curious and entirely dependable form of confirmation from the unconscious, with which I was unfamiliar at the time, is the patient's exclamation: 'That's not what I was thinking' or 'I hadn't thought of that'. This statement can be practically translated as: 'Yes, that was unconscious to me.'

32. Which we shall [shortly] encounter.

33. Cf: '*Ruhig kann* [correctly: *mag*] *ich Euch erscheinen,*
Ruhig gehen sehn.'

> [Quietly can I watch you coming, Quietly watch you go.]
> From Schiller, 'Ritter Toggenburg' ('Toggenburg the Knight').

II

The First Dream

Just as we had the prospect of shedding some light on a dark corner of Dora's childhood thanks to the material that had thrust its way into the analysis, Dora told me that one night recently she had once again had a dream which she had repeatedly dreamed in exactly the same way. A periodically recurring dream was always particularly apt, by virtue of that very characteristic, to arouse my curiosity; in the interest of the treatment, one could envisage weaving this dream into the analysis as a whole. I therefore decided to examine this dream with especial care.

First dream: '*A house is on fire,*'[1] Dora said, '*Father stands by my bed and wakes me up. I get dressed quickly. Mama wants to rescue her jewellery box, but Papa says: I don't want me and my two children to burn to death because of your jewellery box. We dash downstairs, and as soon as I'm outside I wake up.*'

As this is a recurring dream, I naturally ask when she dreamed it first. – She doesn't know. She does remember, though, that she had the dream in L. (the lakeside town where the scene with Herr K. took place) three nights in a row, and then she had dreamed it again here a few days ago.[2] – The connection, thus established, between the dream and the events in L. naturally raises my expectations about the solution of the dream. But first I should like to learn what prompted its last recurrence, so I ask Dora, who has already been trained in dream interpretation through some small examples which we have analysed before, to break down the dream and tell me what comes to mind.

She says: 'Something that can't have anything to do with it, because it's quite fresh, while I've had the dream before.'

It doesn't matter, just say it; it will be the most recent thing connected with the dream.

'Well, around this time Papa has been arguing with Mama because she locks the dining room at night. My brother's room has no door of its own, and can only be reached through the dining room. Papa doesn't want my brother to be locked in like that at night. He said that wouldn't do; something might happen at night and he would need to get out.'

Did that refer to the danger of fire?

'Yes.'

Please take note of your own expressions. We may need them. You said: That *something might happen* (at night), *and he would need to get out.*[3]

But now Dora has found the link between the recent and the earlier causes for the dream, because she goes on:

'When we arrived in L. that time, Papa and I, without beating about the bush he expressed his fear of a fire. We arrived during a violent thunderstorm and saw the little wooden house with no lightning conductor. So that fear was quite natural.'

I am now concerned to establish the connection between the events in L. and the similar-sounding dreams. So I ask: Did you have the dream during the first nights in L., or the last nights before you left, before or after the scene that we know about in the forest? (I know that the scene did not take place on the first day, and that she subsequently stayed in L. for a few days without mentioning what had happened.)

She first answered: 'I don't know.' After a while: 'Actually I think it was afterwards.'

So now I knew that the dream was a reaction to that experience. But why did it recur three times there? I go on: How long did you stay in L. after that scene?

'Another four days, and on the fifth I left with Papa.'

Now I'm certain that the dream was the immediate effect of the experience with Herr K. You dreamed it there first, and not before then. You only added the uncertainty of your memory in order to blur the connection.[4] But I still can't get the numbers to add up. If you stayed in L. for four nights, you may have repeated the dream four times. Was that perhaps the case?

She no longer denies my claim, but rather than answering my question she continues:[5] 'On the afternoon after our trip on the lake, from which we, Herr K. and I, returned at noon, I had lain down as usual on the sofa in the bedroom to have a quick sleep. I suddenly woke up and saw Herr K. standing in front of me . . .'

Just as you saw Papa standing by your bed in the dream?

'Yes. I asked him what he was doing. He replied that no one could stop him going into his bedroom whenever he felt like it; and anyway he wanted to get something. Having been made uneasy by this, I asked Frau K. if there was no key to the bedroom, and the next morning (on the second day) I locked myself in to make my toilet. Then, when I was about to lock myself in in the afternoon to lie down on the sofa again, the key was missing. I am convinced that Herr K. had removed it.'

So that is the theme of locking or not locking the door, which appears in the first dream associations, and which happened to play a role in the recent occasion for the dream.[6] Should the phrase: *I get dressed quickly* be placed in that context as well?

'On that occasion I decided not to stay at the Ks without Papa. The next morning I was worried that Herr K. might surprise me while I was at my toilet, and so *I* always *got dressed* very *quickly*. Papa was staying in the hotel, and Frau K. had gone out very early for an outing with Papa. But Herr K. didn't bother me again.'

I understand that on the afternoon of the second day you resolved to escape these vexations, and now, on the second, third and fourth night after the scene in the forest, you had time to repeat this intention in your sleep. You already knew you would not have the key the next – the third – morning to lock yourself in when you got dressed on the second afternoon, before the dream, and you were able to resolve to make your toilet as quickly as possible. But your dream recurred that night precisely because it corresponded to an *intention*. An intention exists until it has been carried out. You told yourself, so to speak: I have no peace, I can't sleep peacefully, until

I've left this house. Conversely, you say in the dream: *Once I'm outside I wake up*.

Here I shall interrupt the account of the analysis to measure parts of a dream interpretation against my general principles about the mechanism of dream-formation. In my book[7] I explained that every dream is a desire represented as fulfilled, and the representation is a disguise if the desire is a repressed one which belongs to the unconscious; apart from the dreams of children, only unconscious desires, or those that extend into the unconscious, have the power to form a dream. I think I should have been more certain of general agreement if I had been content to claim that every dream had a meaning that could be revealed by a certain piece of interpretative work. After complete interpretation the dream could be replaced by thoughts, which could be inserted at an easily identifiable point in the waking mental life. I could then have gone on to say that this meaning of the dream proves just as diverse as waking trains of thought. On one occasion it is a fulfilled desire, on another it is a realized fear, or a continued reflection, an intention (as in Dora's dream), a piece of intellectual production during sleep, and so on. This representation would certainly have been distinguished by its comprehensibility, and would have been supported by a good number of well-interpreted examples, such as the dream analysed here.

Instead I put forward a general assertion restricting the meaning of dreams to a single form of thought, the representation of desires, and provoked a general tendency to contradiction. But I must say that I do not believe I have either the right or the duty to simplify a psychological process in order to make things more agreeable for the reader, when that process presented the investigation with a complexity whose solution could generally be found only in other spheres. For that reason it will be particularly valuable for me to show that the apparent exceptions, such as Dora's dream here, which seems first of all to reveal an intention formed during the day and continued in sleep, none the less reinforce this contentious rule.

*

We still have a large part of the dream to interpret. I continue: What about the jewellery box that Mama wants to save?

'Mama is very fond of jewellery, and got a lot of it from Papa.'

And what about you?

'I used to love jewellery too: since my illness I've stopped wearing it. – Four years ago (a year before the dream) Mama and Papa had a big row about a piece of jewellery. Mama wanted to wear something particular, drop pearls, in her ears. But Papa doesn't like that kind of thing, so instead of the drop pearls he brought her a bracelet. She was furious, and told him that if he'd spent so much money on a present that she didn't like then he should give it to someone else.'

And you thought you'd have been happy to have it yourself?

'I don't know,[8] I really don't know how Mama ended up in this dream; she wasn't even in L. at the time.'[9]

I'll explain it to you later. Can't you think of anything else about the jewellery box? So far you've only talked about jewellery and said nothing about a box.

'Yes, Herr K. had given me a valuable jewellery box as a present some time before.'

So there was the gift you received in return. You may not know that 'jewellery box' is a popular expression used to refer to something you recently alluded to when you talked about the handbag,[10] that is to say, the female genitals.

'I knew *you'd* say that.'[11]

That means, *you* knew it. – The meaning of the dream now becomes even clearer. You say to yourself: the man is pursuing me, he wants to get into my room, he's threatening my 'jewellery box' and if something awful happens it will be Papa's fault. For that reason you brought into the dream a situation that expresses the opposite, a danger from which Papa is saving you. In this region of the dream, everything is turned into its opposite; you will soon hear why. The mystery, however, lies with your mother. How did she come to be involved? She is, as you know, your former competitor for Papa's favour. In the incident with the bracelet you would gladly have accepted what your Mama rejected. Now let us replace 'accept' with 'give', 'reject' with 'refuse'. It now means that you would be prepared to give Papa what Mama refused him, and what we're dealing with has something to do with jewellery.[12] Now remember the jewellery box that Herr K. gave you. There you have the beginning of a parallel sequence of thoughts in which, as in the situation in which he stood by your bed, Herr K. replaces Papa. He gave you a jewellery box, in order that you should give him your 'jewellery box'; that's why I was just talking of a 'reciprocal gift'. In this sequence of thoughts your Mama will be replaced by Frau K., who was present at the time. So you're ready to give Herr K. what his wife refuses him. Here you have the thought that must be so strenuously repressed, and which requires the transformation of all elements into their opposite. As I have already told you before we discussed this dream, the dream once again confirms that you are awakening your old love of Papa in order to protect yourself against your love of K. But what do all these efforts prove? Not only that you are afraid of Herr K., but that you are more afraid of yourself, and of your temptation to yield to him. In that way you're confirming the intensity of your love for him.[13]

Of course she would not go along with this piece of interpretation.

However, a continuation of the dream interpretation had also presented itself to me, which seemed equally indispensable to the anamnesis of the case and the theory of dreams. I promised to tell Dora about it at the next session.

I could not, in fact, forget the reference that seemed to arise out of the ambiguous words noted above (*that we had to get out, that there might be a mishap during the night*). I put this down to the fact that the elucidation of the dream seemed incomplete to me without the fulfilment of a certain requirement that I do not wish to set up as a universal principle, but which I none the less wished to see observed. A regular dream stands, so to speak, on two feet, one of which is the actual and essential cause, while the other touches on an important event in childhood. The dream establishes a connection between the two, the childhood experience and the experience in the present day, it seeks to remould the present according to the model of the most distant past. The desire that creates the dream always comes from childhood, it repeatedly seeks to reawaken childhood to reality, to correct the present in terms of childhood. In the dream content, I thought I could already clearly discern the pieces that could be assembled into a reference to an event in childhood.

I began my discussion of this with a little experiment, which was, as usual, successful. A large match-holder happened to be standing on the table. I asked Dora to look around and see if she could see anything in particular on the table that was not usually there. She could not see anything. Then I asked her if she knew why children were forbidden to play with matches.

'Yes, because of the risk of fire. My uncle's children love playing with matches.'

Not just because of that. They are warned: 'Don't play with fire', and there's a particular belief associated with that.

She knew nothing of this.

Well: the fear is that they will then wet the bed. That is probably based on the opposition of *water* and *fire*. The idea is more or less that they will dream of fire and then try to put it out with water. I don't know exactly. But I can see that the opposition of water and fire is doing excellent service in your dream. Mama wants to save the jewellery box so that it doesn't *burn*, in the dream thought it's important that the 'jewellery box' shouldn't get *wet*. But fire isn't only used as the opposite of water, it also directly represents love, being in love, being burned. From fire, then, one track leads via this symbolic meaning to thoughts of love, while the other leads off via its opposite, water – after another connection to love, which also makes things *wet*, has branched off – in another direction. Where to now? Think of your expressions: that *there might be a mishap* at night, that you'd have to *get out*. Doesn't that signify a physical need, and if you transfer that 'mishap' to childhood, could it be anything other than the bed getting wet? But what does one do to protect children against bedwetting? Isn't it the case that you wake them from their sleep during the night, *just as your Papa does with you in the dream*? That, then, would be the real event from which you derive the right to replace Herr K., who wakes you from your sleep, with Papa. I must therefore conclude that you suffered from bedwetting for longer than children usually do. Papa says: *I don't want* [. . .] *my two children* . . . to perish. Your brother has otherwise nothing to do with the current situation at the Ks', and he had not gone to L., either. What do your memories tell you about that?

'I don't know about myself,' she answered, 'but my brother wet the bed until he was six or seven, and sometimes it even happened during the day.'

I was about to draw her attention to how much easier it was to remember such a thing about one's brother than about oneself, when she continued with a memory that had come back to her: 'Yes, it did happen to me for a while, but not until I was seven or eight. It must have been bad, because I know they called the doctor in. It was just before the nervous asthma.'

What did the doctor say?

'He said it was a weakness of the nerves; it would pass, he said, and prescribed a tonic.'[14]

The interpretation of the dream now struck me as complete.[15] She added a supplement to the dream the following day. She had forgotten to mention that after waking up she had always smelled smoke. The smoke accorded well with the fire, and also referred to the fact that the dream had a particular relationship to me, because if she claimed that one thing did not conceal another, I would often say, 'There's no smoke without fire.' But to that exclusively personal interpretation she objected that both Herr K. and Papa were passionate smokers, as, indeed, was I. She herself smoked by the lake, and Herr K. had rolled himself a cigarette before making his unfortunate declaration. She thought she was sure she could remember that the smell of smoke had appeared not only in the last occurrence of the dream, but on the three occasions when she had had the dream in L. As she refused to provide any further information, I had to work out how I was to incorporate this supplement within the fabric of the dream thoughts. One possible clue was that the sensation of smoke had presented itself in the form of a supplement, which meant that it had had to overcome a particular effort of repression. Consequently, it was probably among the most obscurely represented and most repressed ideas; the temptation to appear willing to Herr K. If that was so, it could hardly mean anything but the longing for a kiss, which, from a smoker, would inevitably taste of smoke; but there had been a kiss between them about two years previously, and it would certainly have been repeated more than once if the girl had yielded to Herr K.'s advances. In this way, ideas of temptation seemed to have referred back to the earlier scene, and to have reawoken the memory of that kiss. At that time Dora, the thumb-sucker, had protected herself against its enticement with disgust. If I finally bring together all these clues, which suggest a transference to myself, since I am also a smoker, I come to the view that it probably occurred to her during a session between us that she desired a kiss from me. That, for her, was the cause to repeat the warning dream and resolve to abandon the cure. Everything accords very well if this is so, but because of the characteristics of the 'transference' it cannot be proven.

I might now hesitate about whether I should first tackle the result of this dream as it relates to this particular case history, or whether I should deal with the objection against dream theory that it raises. I shall choose the former of these.

It is worth going in some detail into the meaning of bedwetting in the prehistory of neurotics. For the sake of comprehensibility I shall restrict myself to stressing that Dora's case of bedwetting was not an ordinary case. The disorder had not simply continued beyond the time that is considered normal, but by her own definite account had first gone away and then returned relatively late, after the age of six. Such bedwetting has, to my knowledge, no more probable cause than masturbation, the role of which is still grossly under-estimated in the aetiology of bedwetting. In my experience children are well aware of this connection, and all psychical consequences thus follow on from it as though it were something they had never forgotten. Now, at the time when the dream was related, we found ourselves pursuing a line of research that led directly to just such an admission of childhood masturbation. A little while previously Dora had asked why it was she who had fallen ill, and, before I could reply, had placed the responsibility upon her father. She based her explanation not on unconscious thoughts but on conscious know-ledge. To my astonishment, the girl knew the nature of her father's illness. She had eavesdropped on a conversation after her father's return from surgery, in which the illness was called by its name. In even earlier years, at the time of his detached retina, an optician who had been called in must have referred to its venereal aetiology, because the curious and concerned girl had heard an old aunt saying to her mother, 'He was sick before the marriage', adding something that she didn't understand, and which she later interpreted as referring to indecent things.

So her father had fallen ill because of his licentious ways, and Dora assumed that he had passed on the illness in hereditary fashion. I was careful not say that I, as I mentioned above (p. 51, note 5), am also of the view that the descendants of syphilitics are particularly prone to serious neuropsychoses. The continuation of this train of thought, in which she levelled accusations against her father, passed through unconscious material. For a few days she identified with her mother, in little symptoms and peculiar habits, and this gave her the opportunity to reach new heights in intolerable behaviour, and then led me to suspect that she was considering a stay in Franzensbad, which she had visited in the company of her mother – I can't remember the year. Her mother had suffered from pains in the lower abdomen, and a discharge (catarrh) that called for a cure in Franzensbad. It was her opinion – probably justified, once again – that the source of this illness was Papa, who had therefore passed on his venereal infection to Dora's mother. It was quite understandable for her, like many non-specialists in general, to lump together gonorrhoea and syphilis, hereditary diseases and those passed on through intercourse. Her insistence on their identification almost made me ask whether she suffered from a venereal disease herself, and now I learned that she suffered from a catarrh (fluor albus) and could not remember when it had started.

Now I understood that the train of thought that vociferously levelled accusations against her father concealed, as usual, a self-reproach, and I met her half-way by telling her that, in my eyes, fluor in young women usually suggested masturbation, and that all the other causes posited for such a condition are relatively unimportant compared to that one.[16] So she was on the way to answering her own question about why she had fallen ill, by admitting masturbation, probably in childhood. She categorically denied being able to remember any such thing. But a few days later she mentioned something that I must take to be a further approach towards confession. On that day, unlike any day before or after, she was wearing a little purse around her neck, in the style that was modern at the time, and played with it as she lay there, opening it up, inserting a finger, closing it again, and so on. I watched her for a while and then explained to her what a *symptomatic action* was.[17] Symptomatic actions are what I call those activities that a person performs automatically, unconsciously, without noticing, as though playing, which the person would dismiss as meaningless and which, if asked, he would describe as unimportant and random. More careful observation then shows that such actions, of which the consciousness knows nothing, or wishes to know nothing, express unconscious thoughts and impulses, which are both valuable and instructive as tolerated expressions of the unconscious. There are two kinds of conscious relation towards symptomatic actions. If an inoffensive motivation can be found for them, one becomes aware of them; if such a pretext is absent from consciousness, one will generally be quite unaware that one is doing them. In Dora's case the motivation was easy: 'Why shouldn't I wear a little bag like this, when it happens to be in fashion?' To such a justification the possibility of an unconscious origin of the action in question does not arise. On the other hand, no compelling proof can be demonstrated for such an origin and the meaning that one assigns to the action. One must content oneself with observing that such a meaning fits very well into the context of the situation in question, into the agenda of the unconscious.

On another occasion I shall present a collection of such symptomatic actions as one can observe among healthy and nervous people. The interpretations are sometimes very easy. Dora's bifoliate bag is nothing other than a representation of the genitals, and her playing with it, opening it and inserting her finger, is an unabashed but unmistakable mimed communication of what she would like to do, the act of masturbation. Recently, a similar case presented itself to me, one which was very cheering. In the middle of a session an elderly lady, supposedly wishing to moisten her throat with a sweet, takes out a small bone box, tries to open it and hands it to me to convince me how hard it is to open. I voice my suspicion that the box must signify something in particular, pointing out that this is the first time I've seen it, despite the fact that its owner has been visiting me for over a year. To which the lady says eagerly: 'I always carry this box with me, I take it with me wherever I go!' She only calms down after I point out to her with a laugh how well her words apply to another meaning. The box – *Dose*, πύξις – is, like the little bag, like the jewellery box, once again a representative of the Venus shell, the female genitals!

There is much symbolism of this kind in life that we normally pass by without noticing. When I gave myself the task of bringing to light what people hide, not through the compulsion of hypnosis, but through what they say and show, I thought the task more difficult than it actually is. Anyone with eyes to see and ears to hear will be convinced that mortals cannot hide a secret. If one's lips are silent, one will be voluble with one's finger-tips; betrayal seeps through every pore. And for that reason the task of bringing the most hidden parts of the soul to consciousness is very easy to accomplish.

Dora's symptomatic action with the little bag was not the immediate predecessor of the dream. She introduced the session that brought us the relation of the dream with another symptomatic action. When I walked into the room where she was waiting, she rapidly concealed a letter she was reading. Of course I asked her who the letter was from, and at first she refused to admit it. Then something emerged that was utterly irrelevant and unrelated to our cure. It was a letter from her grandmother, asking her to write more often. I think she just wanted to play 'secrets' with me, and hint that the doctor was now going to wrest her secret from her. I now explain her aversion to any new doctor with reference to her anxiety that he might get to the bottom of her illness through physical examination (catarrh), or questioning (the communication about bedwetting), and guess her masturbation. She always spoke very dismissively of doctors, whom she had evidently overestimated in the past.

Accusations against her father for having made her ill, with the self-accusation behind them – fluor albus – playing with the little bag – bedwetting after the sixth year – secrets that she doesn't want the doctor to wrest from her: I consider the clues about childhood masturbation to have been definitively proven. In this case I had begun to guess about the masturbation when she had told me about her cousin's stomach cramps (see p. 29) and had then identified with her by complaining for several days about the same painful sensations. It is well known how often stomach cramps occur among those who masturbate. A personal communication from W. Fliess states that precisely such gastralgias can be interrupted by a cocaine injection to the 'gastric point' that he found in the nose, and by cauterization of that point. Dora was consciously confirming two things to me: that she herself had often suffered from stomach cramps, and that she had had good reasons for thinking her cousin was a masturbator. It is very common among patients to recognize in others a connection that they could not, because of their emotional resistance, recognize in themselves. And she no longer denied it, although she did not yet remember it. The temporal definition of the bedwetting 'just before the nervous asthma' I also consider clinically valid. Hysterical symptoms hardly ever arise as long as children are masturbating, but only during abstinence.[18] They express a substitute for masturbatory gratification for which a yearning remains in the unconscious while other, more normal gratification has not yet begun and while masturbation remains a possibility. The latter condition determines the possibility of hysteria being cured through marriage and normal sexual intercourse. If gratification in marriage is removed once again, through coitus interruptus, psychical aversion and so on, the libido seeks out its old river bed and expresses itself once more in hysterical symptoms.

I should like to be able to say with certainty when and through what particular influence Dora's masturbation was suppressed, but the fact that the analysis was terminated prematurely requires me to present incomplete material. We have heard that the bedwetting lasted almost up to the first case of dyspnoea. Now the only explanation that she was able to suggest for that first condition was that her Papa had then travelled away for the first time since his recovery. I could not help seeing that preserved piece of memory as indicating a connection with the aetiology of the dyspnoea. Now, because of symptomatic actions and other clues, I had good reason to assume that the child, whose bedroom was near her parents' room, had listened to a nocturnal visit of the father to his wife, and had heard the panting of the breathless man during coitus. In such cases children sense the sexual in disturbing sounds. The movements demonstrating sexual excitement are already present as innate mechanisms. I demonstrated years ago that the dyspnoea and rapid heartbeat of hysteria and anxiety neurosis are only isolated fragments of the act of coitus, and in many cases, such as Dora's, I was able to trace the symptom of dyspnoea, or nervous asthma, back to the same cause, that of listening to adults having sexual intercourse. The influence of co-excitement can cause a drastic change in the child's sexuality, replacing the inclination to masturbation with an inclination to anxiety. A while later, when her father had been absent and the child, in love with him, remembered him with longing, she then repeated the impression as an attack of asthma. From the cause of this illness preserved in the memory, we may still guess the anxious train of thought that accompanied the attack. The first time she had such an attack was after over-exerting herself on an outing to the mountains, when she had probably been really short of breath. Along with this came the idea that her father was forbidden to climb mountains, that he was not allowed to over-exert himself because he suffered from breathlessness; then there was the memory of how much he had exerted himself at night in Mama's room, and the worry that he might have injured himself, the worry that she might have over-exerted herself in her masturbation, which also led to sexual orgasm with some dyspnoea; and then the intensified return of that dyspnoea as a symptom. I was still able to draw some of this material from the analysis, and had to supply the rest myself. We have been able to see, with reference to masturbation, that the material relating to a theme is only assembled fragmentarily at various times and in various contexts.[19]

Now a series of extremely important questions arises concerning the aetiology of hysteria: whether Dora's case might be seen as typical of the aetiology, whether it represents the only type of cause, and so on. But I am certainly correct in making the answer to these questions wait for the communication of a larger series of similarly analysed cases. I would have to begin by turning the question on its head. Instead of saying simply yes or no, in response to the question of whether or not the aetiology of this illness lies in childhood masturbation, I would first of all discuss the conception of aetiology in psychoneuroses. The point of view from which I replied would be significantly remote from the point of view from which the question was put. It is enough for us to convince ourselves that childhood masturbation is demonstrably present in this case, that it is not a random factor, and that it cannot be irrelevant to the form of the symptoms.[20] We may more readily understand Dora's symptoms if we consider the meaning of the fluor albus to which she admitted. The word 'catarrh', which she learned to apply to the infection when her mother had to go to Franzensbad for a similar reason, is in turn a 'switch' that opened up access, via the symptom of coughing, to a whole series of thoughts about her Papa's responsibility for his own illness. This cough, which certainly had its origins in an insignificant and real catarrh, was, furthermore, an imitation of her father, who also suffered from a lung condition, and was capable of expressing her sympathy and concern for him. But in a way it also announced to the world something that she might not yet have been aware of: 'I am Papa's daughter. I have catarrh just as he does. He made me ill just as he made Mama ill. It is from him that I have the bad passions that are punished with illness.'[21]

We may now attempt to bring together all the various determinations that we have found for the attacks of coughing and hoarseness. At the very bottom of this stratification is a real, organically caused coughing irritation, the grain of sand around which the mollusc forms the pearl. This irritation may be fixated because it affects a region of the body that has to a large degree preserved the significance of an erogenous zone in the girl. It is also suited to expressing the excited libido. It is fixated by what is probably the first psychical coating – sympathetic imitation of the sick father –

and subsequently by self-reproach because of 'catarrh'. The same group of symptoms also proved capable of representing relations with Herr K., regretting his absence and expressing the desire to be a better wife to him. Once a part of the libido has turned back towards the father, the symptom acquires what may be its final meaning: identification with Frau K. I would like to guarantee that this series is by no means complete. Unfortunately this unfinished analysis cannot pursue the change of meaning over chronological time, or reveal the sequence and co-existence of different meanings. One might make such demands upon a complete analysis.

At this point I must not neglect to examine further connections between genital catarrh and Dora's hysterical symptoms. At a time when we were still a long way away from a psychical explanation of hysteria, I heard other, experienced colleagues assert that among hysterical patients with fluor a deterioration in the catarrh generally means an intensification of the hysterical illness, particularly in terms of appetite loss and vomiting. No one knew very much about this connection, but I believe that they were inclined towards the view of the gynaecologists, who, as we know, assume genital infections to have a very great direct and disturbing effect on the nervous functions, although proof of this is generally lacking. As regards the state of our knowledge today, such a direct and organic influence cannot be ruled out, but its psychical form is more easily identifiable. Women take a special pride in the state of their genitals; if these succumb to illnesses which seem likely to prompt distaste or even disgust, women's self-esteem is injured and humiliated to a quite incredible extent. Abnormal secretions of the vaginal mucous membrane are considered disgusting.

Let us recall that Dora had a vivid feeling of disgust after Herr K.'s kiss, and that we found reason to complete her narration of the kissing scene with reference to the fact that she felt the pressure of the erect member against her body during that embrace. Now we learn further that the same governess whom she had rejected because of her disloyalty had told her from the experience of her own life that all men were flighty and unreliable. For Dora this meant that all men were like Papa. She believed her father to be suffering from a venereal disease, and her concept of venereal disease was of course formed from her own personal experience. Suffering from venereal disease, then, meant being afflicted with a disgusting discharge – might this not be a further motivation for the disgust that she felt at the moment of the embrace? That disgust, transposed to the man's touch, would in that case be disgust projected on to the primitive mechanism mentioned above (see p. 26), which finally referred to her own fluor.

I suppose that these may be unconscious thoughts, stretched out over prefigured organic relations like garlands of flowers draped over metal wire, so that in another case one might be able to find different paths of thought leading between the same starting and finishing points. But knowledge of those chains of thought, which have been individually effective, is of indispensable value in terms of resolving symptoms. If we are obliged to fall back on suppositions and deductions in Dora's case, this is only because the analysis was prematurely terminated. Without exception, the material that I have used to fill the gaps is based on other cases in which the analysis was completed.

The dream whose analysis provided us with the above conclusions corresponds, as we found, to an intention of Dora's, which she takes with her into sleep. For that reason the dream is repeated every night until the intention is fulfilled, and it reappears years later when the occasion arises to form an analogous intention. The intention may be consciously expressed more or less in the following terms: from this house, in which, as I have seen, my virginity is threatened, I set off with Papa, and in the morning at my toilet I seek to take precautions not to be disturbed. These ideas find their clear expression in the dream; they belong to a current which has attained consciousness and which dominates the waking state. Behind them we may guess a more obscure train of thought which corresponds to the opposite current, and which has for that reason succumbed to repression. It culminates in Dora's temptation to give herself to the man in thanks for the love and affection he has shown her for the past few years, and perhaps evokes the memory of the only kiss that she has had from him. But according to the theory developed in my *Interpretation of Dreams*, such elements are not sufficient to form a dream. A dream is not an intention represented as accomplished, but a desire represented as fulfilled, and possibly a desire from childhood. We are duty-bound to examine whether this proposition is not contradicted by our dream.

The dream, in fact, contains infantile material that is not at first glance explicably connected with the intention to flee Herr K.'s house and the temptation emanating from him. Why does the memory arise of bedwetting as a child, and of the trouble that her father had taken then to accustom the child to cleanliness? Because, one might reply, only with the help of this train of thought is it possible to suppress the intense thoughts of temptation and allow the intention of defeating them to triumph. The child decides to flee *with* her father; in reality she is fleeing *to* her father, for fear of the man who is propositioning her; she reawakens an infantile inclination towards her father, an inclination that is supposed to protect her against her recent inclination towards a stranger. Her father is himself to some extent guilty of the present danger, having abandoned her to a stranger in the interest of his own love affair. How much nicer it was, though, when the same father loved no one more than her, and made every effort to save her from the dangers that threatened her then. The infantile and now unconscious desire to place her father in the position of the stranger is the power that forms the dream. If there has been a situation resembling this one in all respects except for the person involved, this becomes the main situation of the dream content. Such a situation exists: her father had, like Herr K. the day prior to the dream, once stood by her bed and woken her with a kiss or something similar, as perhaps Herr K. intended to do. So the intention to flee the house is not in itself enough to facilitate a dream, but is made capable of doing so by the fact that it is joined by another intention, based on infantile desires. The desire to substitute her father for Herr K. provides the driving force for the dream. I would remind the reader of the interpretation, imposed upon me by the intensified train of thought referring to her father's relationship with Frau K., that an infantile attachment to her father had been awoken to keep her repressed love for Herr K. in the repressed state; this abrupt change in the patient's mental life is reflected in the dream.

As regards relations between waking thoughts that continue in sleep – the day's residues – and the unconscious dream-forming desires, I have in the *Interpretation of Dreams*, Chapter VII, Section C, set down some observations that I shall quote here in full, because I have nothing to add to them, and because the analysis of this dream of Dora's proves once again that this is an accurate representation of things.

'I am prepared to admit that there is a whole class of dreams whose *stimulus* consists primarily or even exclusively in the residues of daily life, and I think that my own wish finally to be *Professor extraordinarius* (extraordinary professor)[22] would have allowed me to sleep in peace on that night had not my concern for my friend's health the previous day still been active. But that concern had not yet formed a dream; the *driving-force* needed by the dream had to be supplied by a desire; it was up to that concern to create such a desire as a driving-force for the dream. To put it metaphorically: it is entirely possible that a diurnal thought should act as the *entrepreneur* for the dream; but the entrepreneur, who, as they say, has the idea and the drive to put it into action, can do nothing without capital; he requires a *capitalist* with the necessary outlay, and that capitalist, who provides the psychical outlay for the dream, is always and inevitably, whatever the diurnal thought may be, *a desire from the unconscious*.'

No one familiar with the delicacy of the structure of such formations as dreams will be surprised to discover that the desire for the father to assume the place of the tempting man calls to memory not random material from childhood, but material most intimately related to the repression of that temptation. For if Dora feels incapable of yielding to her love for that man, if she represses that love rather than giving in to it, that decision is not more intimately connected with any element than with her precocious sexual pleasures and their consequences, bedwetting, catarrh and disgust. Such antecedents can, according to the sum of constitutional conditions, explain two attitudes towards demands made by the erotic life in adulthood: either unresisting abandon to sexuality, bordering on perversion, or, a reaction involving the rejection of sexuality, accompanied by neurotic illness. Our patient's constitution and level of intellectual and moral education had led to the latter outcome.

In particular, I should also like to point out that the analysis of this dream has led us to information concerning pathogenically effective experiences which were not otherwise accessible to memory, let alone to reproduction. The memory of childhood bedwetting had, as it turned out, already been repressed. Dora had never mentioned the details of Herr K.'s pursuit of her, as it had not occurred to her to do so.

A few additional remarks[23] concerning the synthesis of this dream. The dream-work begins on the afternoon of the second day after the scene in the forest, when Dora notices that she can no longer lock the door to her room. Then she says to herself: I'm in serious danger here, and forms the intention not to stay alone in the house, but to leave with her Papa. This intention becomes available for dream-work because it is able to continue into the unconscious. Corresponding to this intention within the unconscious is the fact that it conjures up the infantile love of the father as a protection against the present temptation. The reversal that consequently occurs within her is fixated and leads her to the point of view represented by her supervalent train of thought (jealousy of Frau K. over her father, as though she were in love with him). There is a struggle within her between the temptation to yield to the man who is courting her, and complex resistance to that temptation. The latter is assembled from motives of respectability and good sense, hostile impulses resulting from the governess's revelation (jealousy, wounded pride, see below) and an element of neurosis, the pre-existing sexual repugnance deriving from her childhood history. Dora's love for her father, awakened to protect her against temptation, derives from that childhood history.

The dream transforms the intention, deep within the unconscious, to flee to the father, into a situation that represents the desire for her father to save her from danger as being already fulfilled. For this to be achieved, an obstructive thought must be removed, that it is her father who has put her in that danger. We will encounter the hostile impulse (inclination towards revenge) against her father, which is here suppressed, as one of the motors of the second dream.

According to the conditions of dream-formation, the fantasized situation is selected in such a way that it repeats an infantile situation. It is a most particular triumph if it manages to transform a recent situation, such as that which occasioned the dream, into an infantile situation. This can occur in this case because of a coincidence in the material. Herr K. stood by her bed and woke her, just as her father often did in the years of her childhood. The complete reversal that Dora effected can be accurately symbolized by substituting her father for Herr K. in that situation.

But in those days her father woke her so that she would not wet the bed.

This idea of 'wet' becomes defining for the rest of the dream content, although in that content it is represented only by a remote reference and by its opposite.

The opposite of 'wet', 'water', can easily be 'fire', 'burning'. The coincidental fact that her father voiced a fear of the fire on their arrival at the town [L.] contributes to the danger from which her father saves her: the danger of fire. The chosen situation of the dream image is based on this coincidence and the opposition to 'wet': there is a fire, her father stands by her bed to wake her. Her father's chance remark would not achieve this significance in the dream content if it did not accord so excellently with the victorious emotional current that wishes to see the father as helper and saviour. He sensed the danger immediately upon their arrival, and he was right! (In fact it was he who put the girl in that danger.)

Within the dream thoughts, easily traceable connections give the idea of 'wet' the role of an intersection point for several different circles of representation. 'Wet' belongs not only to bedwetting, but also to the circle of thoughts of sexual temptation, which are suppressed behind this dream content. She knows that there is also a wetness in sexual intercourse, that the man gives the woman something liquid in *the form of drops* in the act of intercourse. She knows that the danger lies there, that she is given the task of protecting the genitals from being made wet.

At the same time, with 'wet' and 'drop', the other circle of associations closes, that of the disgusting catarrh, which in her more mature years has the same shaming significance as bedwetting had in her childhood. Here 'wet' is equated with 'contaminated'. The genitals, which should be kept clean, are contaminated by catarrh, both in her Mama's case and her own (p. 70). She appears to believe that her Mama's addiction to cleanliness is a reaction to this contamination.

The two circles are superimposed here: Mama has had both from Papa, the sexual 'wet' and the contaminating fluor. Dora's jealousy of her Mama is inseparable from the circle of thoughts concerning the infantile love of her father, which is conjured up here as a means of protection. This material is not yet capable of representation. But if a memory can be found which stands in a similar relation to both circles of 'wet', but which manages not to be offensive, that memory will be able to assume the function of representation in the dream content.

One example of this is to be found in the detail of the 'drops' that Mama wanted as a piece of jewellery. Apparently the link between this reminiscence and the two circles of the sexual 'wet' and of contamination is an external and superficial one, conveyed through words, because 'drop' is used as a 'switch', an ambiguous word, and 'jewellery' is used more or less as 'clean', a rather forced opposition to 'contaminated'. In fact very firm underlying associations can be demonstrated. The memory emerges from the material of Dora's jealousy of her Mama, which had infantile roots but continued long after childhood. Through these two verbal associations all significance attached to the ideas of sexual intercourse between the parents, the fluor infection and Mama's irritating habit of cleaning is transferred to a single reminiscence of 'jewellery drops'.

But a further displacement must occur for the purposes of the dream content. What finds its way into the dream is not the 'drops', which are close to the original 'wet', but the more remote 'jewellery'. So, if this element is incorporated into the previous fixated dream situation, it could have meant the following: 'Mama still wants to save her jewellery.' In the new alteration, 'jewellery box', the influence of elements from the underlying circle of temptation on the part of Herr K., assumes belated validity. Herr K. did not give her jewellery, but he did give her a 'little box' for it, the substitute for all the favours and affection for which she should now be grateful. And the resulting composite, 'jewellery box', has another particular representational value. Is 'jewellery box' not a commonplace image for the immaculate, intact female genitals? And, on the other hand, an innocuous word, ideally suited both to suggest the sexual thoughts behind the dream and to conceal them?

Thus we find, at two points in the dream: 'Mama's jewellery box', and this element replaces the mention of infantile jealousy, the drops, and thus the sexual 'wet', at once contamination by fluor and the now current thoughts of temptation, which urge towards a reciprocal love and depict in anticipation the sexual situation, both longed-for and threatening. The element of the 'jewellery box' is, more than any other, the product of condensation and displacement, and a compromise between opposing currents. Its multiple origin – from both an infantile and a contemporary source – is indicated by its twofold appearance in the dream content.

The dream is the reaction to a fresh and stimulating experience, which necessarily awakens the memory of the only analogous experience from earlier years. That is the scene with the kiss in the shop, during which Dora felt disgust. But the same scene can be reached from elsewhere, from the circle of thoughts around catarrh (see pp. 70–71) and from the circle of the current temptation. So it makes a contribution of its own to the dream content, which must adapt to the preformed situation. Something is on fire . . . the kiss probably tasted of smoke, so Dora smells smoke in the dream content, which in this case continues after she has awoken.

Unfortunately, I inadvertently left a gap in the analysis of this dream. The speech is put into the mouth of the father: 'I didn't want my two children to perish' etc. (we may probably add, on the basis of the dream thought: through the consequences of masturbation). Such a speech in a dream is generally assembled from pieces of real speech, whether heard or uttered. I should have inquired into the true origin of this speech. The result of that would have made the construction of the dream more complicated, but it would also certainly have rendered it more transparent.

Should we assume that this dream had exactly the same content in L. as it did when repeated during the cure? That would not seem necessarily to be the case. Experience shows that people often claim to have had the same dream while the individual phenomena of the recurring dream differ in numerous details and other modifications. Thus one of my patients tells me she has had her favourite recurring dream once again, and in the same way: she is swimming in the blue sea, parting the waves with pleasure, and so on. Closer examination shows that against a common background sometimes one detail and sometimes another is applied; on one occasion, indeed, she was swimming in the sea when it was frozen, surrounded by icebergs. Other dreams, which she herself does not try to present as being identical, prove to be intimately connected with this recurring dream. For example, she sees at the same time, from a photograph, the highlands and lowlands of Heligoland in real dimensions, a ship on the sea bearing two friends from her youth, and so on.

It is certain that Dora's dream, which occurred during the cure – perhaps without changing its manifest content – had acquired a new and current significance. Its dream thoughts included a connection with my treatment, and corresponded to a renewal of her intention at the time to escape from a danger. If her memory was not in error, when she claimed to have smelled the smoke after waking up in L., we must acknowledge that she very skilfully incorporated my utterance: 'There's no smoke without fire' into the fully formed dream, where the words appear to be used to over-determine the last element. Incontestably, it was the result of chance that the final cause, her mother's locking of the dining room, which meant that Dora's brother was locked in his bedroom, produced a connection with Herr K.'s pestering of her in L. It was here, when she could not lock her bedroom, that her resolution reached maturity. Perhaps her brother did not appear in her dreams at that time, with the result that the words 'my two children' entered the dream content only after the final cause of the dream.

Notes

1. There was never a real fire at our house, she said in answer to my question.
2. The content allows us to conclude that the dream was *first* dreamed in L.
3. I emphasize these words because they make me suspicious. They sound ambiguous to me. Does one not use the same words for certain physical needs? But ambiguous words are like switches or points at a railway junction, changing the course of associations. If the switch is changed from the way it appears in the dream content, in all likelihood one ends up on the track on which the thoughts behind the dream sought, and still hidden, are moving.
4. Concerning what was initially said about doubts when remembering, see above pp. 12–13.
5. In fact we must wait for new remembered material before my question can be answered.
6. I assume, although without telling Dora, that she picked up this element because of its symbolic significance. '*Rooms*' (*Zimmer*) in dreams often seek to represent women (*Frauenzimmer*), and it can of course not be a matter of indifference whether a woman is 'open' or 'closed'. The 'key' that opens in this case is well known.
7. *The Interpretation of Dreams*, 1900.
8. The usual phrase with which she acknowledged something repressed.
9. This observation, which testifies to a complete misunderstanding of the rules of dream interpretation with which she was otherwise familiar, as well as the hesitancy and sparse exploitation of her ideas about jewellery boxes, proved to me that this was material that had been most emphatically repressed.
10. About this little bag see below.
11. A very common way of rejecting an item of knowledge arising from the repressed.
12. For the drops we will later also be able to find an interpretation required by the context.
13. To this I add: Incidentally, I must conclude from the recurrence of the dream over recent days that you consider the same situation to have recurred, and that you have decided to stay away from the cure, to which only your father brings you. – Subsequent events showed how correct my guess had been. Here my interpretation touches upon the theme of

'transference', extremely significant both from the practical and theoretical points of view, to which I will have little opportunity to refer further in this essay.

14. This doctor was the only person in whom she showed any trust, because the experience made her aware that he had not discovered her secret. With anyone else whom she could not yet assess she felt anxiety, now motivated by the possibility that he might guess her secret.

15. The core of the dream, translated, would be more or less as follows: The temptation is so strong. Dear Papa, protect me once again as you did in my childhood days, so that my bed doesn't get wet!

16. [*Addition 1923*:] An extreme view that I would no longer hold today.

17. Cf. my essay *Zur Psychopathologie des Alltagslebens* [*Psychopathology of Everyday Life*], 1901, Chapter IX.

18. The same thing is true in principle of adults, but here, too, relative abstinence, a restriction of masturbation, is enough for a high level of libido-hysteria and masturbation to appear together.

19. In a similar way, proof of infantile masturbation is also produced in other cases. The material for this is generally similar in nature: indications of fluor albus, bedwetting, ceremonial related to the hands (compulsive washing) and so on. One can always tell with certainty by the set of symptoms connected with the case whether or not the habit has been discovered by a carer, or whether a campaign of dissuasion or a sudden volte-face has put an end to the sexual activity. In Dora's case masturbation had remained undiscovered, and had come to an end all of a sudden (secrecy, fear of doctors – substitution of dyspnoea). It is true that patients regularly dispute the capacity of these clues to supply proof, even when the memory of catarrh or their mother's warning ('it'll make you stupid; it's poisonous') has remained in conscious memory. But some time later the memory of this piece of the child's sexual life appears with certainty in all cases – as for instance in a patient with obsessive ideas deriving directly from infantile masturbation. Here the traits of self-prohibition and self-punishment – if they have done one thing, they mustn't do another, they mustn't be disturbed, they insert pauses between one performance (with the hands) and the next, hand-washing, and so on – prove to be pieces of deterrence on the part of their carers, preserved unaltered. The warning: 'Now, that's poisonous!' was the only thing that had been preserved in the memory. On this subject, compare my *Drei Abhandlungen zur Sexualtheorie* [*Three Essays on Sexual Theory*], 1905, 5th German edition, 1922 [the second essay].

20. The learning of the habit of masturbation must somehow be connected to her brother, for in this context she told me with the emphasis that reveals a 'screen memory' that her brother had regularly passed on all his infections to her. He endured them easily, she with difficulty. In the dream, her brother is also protected against 'perishing'; he himself has suffered from bedwetting, but stopped before his sister did. In a sense it was also a 'screen memory' when she announced that she was able to keep pace with her brother up until her first illness, and from then on she had lagged behind him in her school work. As though she had been a boy until that point, and only then become girlish. She was really a wild thing, but from her 'asthma' onwards she became quiet and well-behaved. This illness formed [in her] the borderline between two phases of sexual life, the first of which was male in character, the second female.

21. The word ['catarrh'] played the same role in the fourteen-year-old girl whose case history I have crammed into a few lines on p. 52, note 10. I had placed the child with an intelligent lady, who performed the services of a carer for me, in a pension. The lady told me that her little patient could not bear her presence at bedtime, and that in bed she developed a strikingly bad cough of which there was no sign throughout the day. When she was asked about these symptoms, all the little girl could think was that her grandmother coughed the same way, and she was said to have catarrh. It then became clear that she too had catarrh, and that she did not want to be observed when washing in the evening. The catarrh which had been pushed *from top to bottom* by means of this word even showed an unusual level of intensity.

22. This refers to the analysis of the dream taken as a model at this point [Chapter V, Section D], II/III.

23. [The remainder of this chapter was printed as a footnote in editions earlier than 1924.]

III

The Second Dream

A few weeks after the first dream came the second, and the analysis was terminated after its elucidation was complete. It cannot be rendered as completely transparent as the first, but it brought the desired confirmation of a hypothesis that had become necessary concerning the patient's state of mind, filled a gap in the memory and provided a deep insight into the origin of another of Dora's symptoms.

Dora related her dream: '*I am going for a walk in a town I don't know, I see streets and squares that are strange to me.*[1] *Then I enter a house where I live, go to my room and find a letter from my Mama lying there. She writes: As I am away from home without my parents' knowledge, she was not going to write to tell me that Papa was ill. Now he has died, and if you want*[2] *you can come. Now I make for the station and ask about a hundred times: Where is the station? I keep getting the answer: five minutes away. Then I see a dense forest ahead of me, walk into it and there ask a man I meet. He tells me: Another two and a half hours.*[3] *He offers to come with me. I decline and go on my own. I see the station ahead of me and can't reach it. At the same time there's that habitual feeling of anxiety that you have when you can't get any further in the dream. Then I'm at home, I must have travelled in the meantime, but I can't remember anything about it. – I walk into the porter's lodge and ask about our apartment. The maid opens the door for me and answers: Mama and the others are already at the cemetery.*'[4]

The interpretation of this dream was not without its difficulties. Because of the particular circumstances in which we broke up, which related to its content, not everything was explained, and this in turn has something to do with the fact that I have not been able to remember the whole sequence of revelations with equal exactitude. First of all I shall mention the subject that we were analysing when this dream occurred. For some time Dora herself had been asking questions about the connection between her actions and what one took to be the motives for them. One of these questions was: 'Why did I remain silent for the first few days after the scene by the lake?' The second: 'Why did I then suddenly tell my parents about it?' I thought we still needed an explanation of why she had felt so gravely insulted by Herr K.'s advance, particularly as I was beginning to understand that his courtship of Dora had not been a frivolous attempt at seduction on Herr K.'s part either. I interpreted the fact that she had informed her parents about the event as an action already influenced by pathological revenge. A normal girl would, I should have thought, have come to terms with such events on her own.

So I shall set out the material that presented itself to the analysis of this dream in the rather haphazard order in which it comes to mind.

She is wandering alone in a strange town, and sees streets and squares. She assures me that it was certainly not B., my first guess, but a town where she had never been. Naturally I continued: You might have seen paintings or photographs from which you have taken these dream-images. It was after this observation that she mentioned a monument in a square, and immediately after that revealed that she knew the source of the idea. She had been given an album of views of a German spa town for Christmas, and had taken it out again the previous day to show the relatives with whom she was staying. It was in a box of pictures that she could not immediately find, and she had asked her Mama: *Where is the box*?[5] One of the pictures showed a square with a monument. But the present had been given to her by a young engineer whom she had once fleetingly known in the factory town. The young man had taken a job in Germany in order to achieve his independence more quickly, and used every opportunity he had to make her remember him, and it was easy to guess that if his position improved he planned to propose to Dora. But that would take time, and he would have to wait.

The idea of wandering around in a strange town was overdetermined. It led back to one of the diurnal causes of the dream. During the holidays a young cousin had come on a visit, and she was to show him the city of Vienna. This external cause was clearly one of extreme indifference. But the cousin reminded her of a brief first stay in Dresden. On that occasion she had wandered around as a stranger, and of course had not neglected to visit the famous gallery. Another cousin, who was with them and knew Dresden, wanted to act as guide in the gallery. *But she turned him away and went on her own*, stopping by paintings that she liked. Before the Sistine Madonna she stopped for *two hours*, in silently dreaming admiration. She had no clear answer to the question of what she had liked so much about the painting. In the end she said: the Madonna.

It is certain that these ideas really are part of the dream-forming material. They incorporate components which we find unaltered in the dream content (she turned him away and went on her own). I make a note that 'pictures' correspond to an intersection in the fabric of the dream thoughts (the pictures in the album – the paintings in Dresden). And I might single out the theme of the *Madonna*, the virgin mother, for further examination. But above all I see that in this first part of the dream she is identifying with a young man. He is wandering around in a strange place, trying to find a goal, but he is held back, he needs patience, he must wait. If she was thinking about the engineer, then that goal would have been the possession of a wife, Dora herself. Instead it was a station, although according to the connection that exists between the question posed in the dream and the one posed in reality, we can substitute a box for this. A box and a woman go better together.

She asks about a hundred times . . . That leads to another, less insignificant cause for the dream. The previous evening, after the party, her father had asked her to bring him the brandy; he could not get to sleep without drinking brandy. She had asked her mother for the key to the larder, but her mother was in the middle of a conversation and did not answer, until Dora erupted with the impatient exaggeration: Now I've asked you *a hundred times* where the key is. In fact, of course, she had only repeated the question about *five times*.[6]

Where is the key? strikes me as the masculine counterpart to the question: Where is the box? (see the first dream, p. 60). So these are both questions – about the genitals.

At the same family gathering, someone had raised a toast to Papa and expressed the hope that he would long remain in the best of health, etc. At that, her father's tired features had twitched in a very strange way, and she had understood the thoughts he had to suppress. The poor, sick man! Who could tell how much life he still had ahead of him?

This brings us to the *content of the letter* in the dream. Her father had died, she had left home of her own volition. When we came to the letter in the dream, I immediately reminded her of the suicide note that she had written to her parents, or had at least left out where her parents could find it. That letter was designed to frighten her father so that he would leave Frau K., or at least to allow Dora to avenge herself on him if he could not be persuaded to do that. We have reached the subject of her death and the death of her father (*cemetery*, later in the dream). Are we mistaken in assuming that the situation which forms the façade of the dream corresponds to a fantasy of revenge against her father? Her thoughts of pity the previous day would have tallied well with that. But according to the fantasy, she went away from home to a strange place, and out of concern for her, out of longing for her, her father's heart had broken. That meant that she would have had her revenge. She understood very well what her father was lacking, if he was unable to get to sleep without cognac.[7]

Let us keep *vengefulness* as a new element for a later synthesis of the dream thoughts.

But the content of the letter must have allowed further determination. Hence the addition: *If you want?*

Then it occurred to her that after the word 'want' there was a question mark, and this reminded her that the words were a quotation from the letter from Frau K., containing the invitation to L. (by the lake). In this letter, after the words: 'if you want to come?' there had been a question mark that looked very odd in the middle of the sentence.

So that takes us back to the scene by the lake and the mysteries connected with it. I asked her to relate that scene to me in detail again. At first she did not introduce much that was new. Herr K. had begun quite seriously; but she would not let him finish. Once she had understood what was happening, she slapped his face and dashed away. I wanted to know what words he had used; she could only remember his explanation: 'You know, I get nothing from my wife.'[8] Then, lest she bump into him again, she set off walking around the lake towards L., and *asked a man she met how far away she was*. Hearing his answer: 'Two and a half hours', she abandoned that plan and went back to find the boat which would soon be setting off. Herr K. was there, too, and he approached her, asking her to forgive him and to tell no one of what had happened. She did not reply. – Yes, the *forest* in the dream was quite similar to the forest on the shores of the lake, where the scene she had just described again had taken place. She had seen exactly the same dense forest in a painting in the exhibition at the Secession the previous day. In the background of the painting there were *nymphs*.[9]

Now one of my suspicions became a certainty. '*Bahnhof*' ['station'][10] and '*Friedhof*' ['cemetery'], in place of female genitals, was striking enough, but had directed my sharpened attention towards the similarly formed '*Vorhof*' ['vestibule'], an anatomical term for a particular region of the female genitals. But that could be an error conjured by the mind. Now, when the 'nymphs' were added, seen against the background of the 'dense forest', no doubts were permitted any longer. This was symbolic sexual geography! 'Nymphae', as a doctor will know and the layman will not – and not even every doctor will – is the name given to the small labia in the background of the 'dense forest' of pubic hair. But anyone using such technical names as '*Vorhof*' and '*Nymphen*' must have taken their knowledge from books, and not popular books but anatomical textbooks or a dictionary, the usual refuge of young people consumed with sexual curiosity. If this interpretation were correct, behind the first dream there lay a defloration fantasy, in which a man tried to force his way into a woman's genitalia.[11]

I shared my conclusions with her. The impression must have been compelling, because a forgotten fragment of the dream immediately followed: *That she was walking peacefully*[12] *back and forth in her room, reading a big book that lay on her desk*. Here the emphasis is on the two details: peaceful and with a big book. I asked: Was it in dictionary format? She said it was. But children never look up forbidden material in a dictionary *peacefully*. They tremble and quake, and look anxiously around to see if anyone is coming. Parents are very much in the way where such reading is concerned. But the wish-fulfilling power of the dream had fundamentally improved the uncomfortable situation. Dora's father was dead and the others had already gone to the cemetery. So she could go on reading as she pleased. Did that not mean that one of her reasons for revenge had also been her rejection of the constraints imposed by her parents? If her father was dead, she could read or love as she wished. At first she claimed not to remember ever having looked things up in a dictionary, but then she admitted that she did have such a memory, although it was innocuous in content. When her favourite aunt had been so seriously ill, and it was already decided that she should travel to Vienna, her parents received a *letter* from another uncle, saying that they could not travel to Vienna, since a child, a cousin of Dora's, had fallen dangerously ill with appendicitis. Of what she had read, she still remembered the description of the characteristic pain located in the abdomen.

Now I reminded her that she had supposedly had appendicitis shortly after her aunt's death. I had previously not dared to include this illness among her hysterical accomplishments. She told me that for the first few days she had had a high temperature and felt in her abdomen the same pain that she had read about in the dictionary. She had had cold compresses, but had been unable to bear them; on the second day, amidst violent pains, her period had begun, and was very irregular following her illness. At that time she had suffered constantly from constipation.

It would not have been correct to see this condition as purely hysterical. Although hysterical fever does doubtless occur, it seems arbitrary to relate the fever of this questionable illness to hysteria rather than to an organic cause, which was in fact active at the time. I was about to abandon that trail, when she herself helped me, bringing the final supplement to the dream: *She sees herself particularly clearly going up the stairs*.

Of course I demanded a particular determination for that. She objected, probably not in all seriousness, that she had to go upstairs to get to her apartment on that floor. I was easily able to dismiss this by remarking that if she could travel from the strange town to Vienna in her dream, and skip the railway journey, she could also manage to leave out the steps of the stairs in her dream. She then went on with her story: after her appendicitis she had found walking difficult, and her right foot had dragged. That had remained the case for a very long time, and for that reason she had avoided stairs whenever she could. Even now her foot sometimes dragged. The doctors she consulted on her father's orders had been very surprised by this quite unusual leftover from a case of appendicitis, particularly since the pain in her body had not recurred, and did not accompany the dragging foot in any way.[13]

So that was a genuine hysterical symptom. Even if the fever had also been organically caused – one of those cases of influenza without a particular location, for example – it was securely established that the neurosis had appropriated a chance factor in order to use it for one of its manifestations. So Dora had created for herself an illness that she had read about in the dictionary, and had punished herself for reading about it; she then had to tell herself that the punishment could not apply to the reading of an innocent article, but had come about as the result of a displacement, when this act of reading had been followed by another, less innocent one, now concealed in the memory behind the innocent act of reading that had occurred around the same time.[14] Perhaps we could discover what subjects she had been reading about.

What, then, was the significance of the condition that wished to imitate perityphlitis? The leftover from the infection, the dragging of a leg, which did not really accord with a case of perityphlitis, might accord better with the secret, sexual – let us say – meaning of the illness, and might in turn, if explained, shed some light on the meaning that we were looking for. I tried to find a way into this mystery. Times had appeared in the dream: time is far from irrelevant in all biological events. So I asked when that appendicitis had occurred, whether it had been before or after the scene by the lake. The prompt answer, removing all difficulties at a stroke, was: nine months afterwards. This date is characteristic. So the supposed appendicitis could have realized the fantasy of a *childbirth* with the modest means at the patient's disposal: pains and a period.[15] Of course she knew the significance of the date and could not dismiss the likelihood that she had read about pregnancy and birth in the dictionary. But what about the dragging foot? I would have to guess. That's how you walk when you've put a foot wrong. So she really would have 'put a foot wrong' [*einen Fehltritt gemacht*] if she was giving birth nine months after the scene by the lake. But I had to make one additional demand. I am convinced that one can develop such symptoms only if one has an *infantile* model for them. The memories that one has of later impressions do not, as I must maintain on the basis of my own previous experiences, have the power to be realized as symptoms. I barely dared hope that she would deliver the desired material from childhood, because in reality I cannot yet assert the above proposition, in which I should very much like to believe, as a universal principle. But here the confirmation came *immediately*. Yes, she had once put the same foot wrong as a child, she had slipped in B. when going down the *stairs*: her foot – it was even the same one that had later dragged – swelled up and had to be bandaged, and she took to her bed for several weeks. It was a short time before she developed her nervous asthma, in her eighth year.

Now it was time to turn to account our knowledge of this fantasy: If you give birth nine months after the scene by the lake, and then walk around until the present day with the consequences of 'putting a foot wrong', that proves that in your unconscious you regret the outcome of the scene. So you correct it in your unconscious thought. The precondition for your fantasy of childbirth is that something took place on that occasion,[16] that you had experienced everything on that occasion that you later had to read in your dictionary. You see that your love of Herr K. did not end with that scene, that, as I have claimed, it has continued until the present, albeit unconsciously. – She did not contradict that, either.[17]

This work towards the elucidation of the second dream occupied two sessions. When, after the conclusion of the second session, I expressed my satisfaction with what we had achieved, she replied dismissively: 'So what's really come out?' thus preparing me for the approach of further revelations.

She began the third session with the words: 'You do know, doctor, that this is the last time I'll be coming here?'

I couldn't have known, as you haven't said anything to me about it.

'Yes, I've decided to stick it out until the New Year[18] but I'm not going to wait any longer than that for the cure.'

You know you are free to leave at any time. But let us work today. When did you reach this decision?

'Fourteen days ago, I think.'

That sounds like a servant-girl, or a governess: fourteen days' notice.

'A governess who resigned had been at K.'s once when I visited them in L. by the lake.'

Really? You've never mentioned that to me. Please tell me about it.

'Well, there was a young girl in the house acting as governess to the children, who behaved in a very curious way towards Herr K. She didn't greet him, she didn't reply to him, she didn't hand him anything at table if he asked for something; in short, she treated him like so much air. Incidentally, he wasn't much more polite to her. One or two days before the scene by the lake the girl took me to one side; she had something to tell me. She told me then that on one occasion, when his wife had been away for several weeks, he had approached her, had insistently wooed her and asked her to be nice to him; he got nothing from his wife, etc.'

Those are the same words that he used in his advances to you, when you slapped his face.

'That's right. She yielded to him, but after a short time he stopped paying her any attention, and since then she had hated him.'

And that governess had handed in her notice?

'No, she wanted to hand it in. She told me that immediately she had felt abandoned she had related what had happened to her parents, who are respectable people and live somewhere in Germany. Her parents demanded that she leave the house immediately, and then wrote to tell her that if she didn't they would have nothing more to do with her, and she couldn't come home again.'

And why didn't she leave?

'She said she would wait a short time and see if things changed with Herr K. She couldn't bear living like that. If she saw no changes she would hand in her notice and leave.'

And what became of the girl?

'I only know that she left.'

And she didn't leave the affair with a child?

'No.'

Here, then, in the middle of the analysis, as is generally the rule, a piece of factual material had come to light that helped to solve problems thrown up earlier. I was able to tell Dora: now I know the reason behind the slap with which you responded to his advances. It wasn't hurt at his impertinence to you, but jealous revenge. When the girl told you her story, you used your skill to sweep aside everything that didn't suit your emotions. The moment Herr K. used the words: I get nothing from my wife, which he also used to the girl, fresh impulses were awoken in you, and the scales tipped over. You said to yourself: so he dares to treat me like a governess, a servant? That injury to self-esteem was associated with jealousy and also with sensible motives: in the end it was all too much.[19] As proof of how profoundly you were influenced by the girl's story, I present you with your repeated identification with her in the dream and in your behaviour. You tell your parents something that we haven't previously understood, just as the girl wrote to her parents. You dismiss me like a governess with fourteen days' notice. The letter in the dream, which enables you to come home, is a pendant to the letter from the girl's parents, who had forbidden her to do the same.

'Why didn't I tell my parents straight away?'

How much time did you allow to pass?

'The scene took place on the last day of June; on 14 July I told my mother.'

So, fourteen days again, the characteristic period for a servant to give her notice! I can now answer your question. You understood the poor girl very well. She didn't want to go because she still had hopes, because she expected that Herr K. would return his affections to her. So that must have been your motive, too. You waited for that date to see if he would repeat his advances, and from that you would have concluded that he was serious, and that he didn't mean to play with you as he had with the governess.

'He sent a postcard a few days after he left.'[20]

Yes, but when nothing more came, you gave your revenge free rein. Maybe you even thought at the back of your mind that you might persuade him, by means of your accusations, to travel to the place where you were staying.

'. . . As he at first proposed doing,' she interjected.

Then your longing for him would have been satisfied – here she nodded her confirmation, which I hadn't expected – and he could have given you the satisfaction you demanded.

'What satisfaction?'

I'm actually starting to sense that you took matters with Herr K. much more seriously than you previously wished to reveal. Wasn't there often talk of divorce between the Ks?

'Of course, at first they didn't want to because of the children, and now she wants to but he no longer does.'

Might you not have thought that he wanted to divorce his wife to marry you? And that he no longer wanted to because he had no one to replace you with? Two years ago, of course, you were very young, but you yourself have even told me that your Mama was engaged at seventeen and then waited a further two years for her husband. The story of the mother's love usually becomes a model for the daughter. So you wanted to wait for him, too, and assumed that he was just waiting until you were mature enough to become his wife.[21] I imagine you had quite a serious plan for your life. You didn't even have the right to claim that such an intention was ruled out where Herr K. was concerned, and you have told me enough about him that directly indicates such an intention.[22] His behaviour in L. doesn't contradict that, either. You didn't let him finish, and you don't know what he was going to tell you. At the same time the plan would not have been so impossible to carry out. Your Papa's relationship with Frau K., which you had probably only supported for so long for this reason, offered you the certainty that his wife might agree to a divorce, and you can get your Papa to do what you want. Indeed, if the temptation in L. had had another outcome, that would have been the sole possible solution for all parties. I also think that was why you so regretted the other outcome, and corrected it in the fantasy which took the form of appendicitis. So it must have been a severe disappointment for you when, instead of renewed advances, your accusation provoked a denial and insults from Herr K. You concede that nothing makes you so furious as when people think you imagined the scene by the lake. I now know what you didn't want to remember, that Herr K.'s declaration was serious and Herr K. would not give up until he married you.

She had been listening, without contradicting as she usually did. She seemed moved, said goodbye as sweetly as anything, with warmest wishes for the New Year and – never came back. Her father, who visited me a few more times, assured me that she could come back if she wished to; one could tell, he said, that she was longing for the treatment to continue. But he was probably never entirely sincere. He had been supporting the cure, as long as he was able to hope that I would 'dissuade' Dora from believing that there was anything but friendship between himself and Frau K. His interest faded away when he realized that this success was not part of my intention. I knew she would not come back. It was undoubtedly an act of revenge on her part, just when my expectations of a happy conclusion to the cure were at their highest point, to interrupt the analysis and dash those hopes in such an unexpected way. Her tendency to harm herself was also accounted for in this process. Anyone who, like myself, awakens the most wicked demons that dwell untamed in the human breast in order to do battle with them must be prepared to suffer some damage in the course of that struggle. Could I have kept the girl in treatment if I had found a part for myself to play, if I had exaggerated the importance of her presence for myself, and shown her a keen interest, which, in spite of the attenuation caused by my position as a doctor, would have resembled a substitute for the tenderness she longed for? I don't know. Since a part of the factors that we encounter as resistance in any case remains unknown to us, I have always avoided acting out roles, and contented myself with a more modest psychological art. In spite of all my theoretical interest and all my attempts to help as a doctor, I tell myself that boundaries are necessarily set on the psychical influence that one may legitimately exert, and in consequence of this I also respect the patient's will and insight.

Neither do I know whether Herr K. would have achieved more if he had been told that that slap in the face did not mean a definitive 'no' on Dora's part, but corresponded to her recently awakened jealousy, while the strongest impulses of her psychical life sided with him. If he had ignored that first 'no' and continued his advances with convincing passion, his love might have conquered all internal problems in order to win the girl's affection. But I believe that she might equally have been impelled to satisfy her vengeance upon him all the more violently. It is never possible to calculate the direction in which the decision will tend to go in a conflict between motives, whether towards the abolition or the intensification of repression. The inability to satisfy the *real* demands of love is one of the most significant character traits of neurosis; neurotics are dominated by the opposition between reality and fantasy. What they long for most intensely in their fantasies they flee from when they encounter it in reality, and they yield most readily to fantasies when there is no longer any need to fear their realization. The barrier erected by repression can, however, fall to the onslaught of violent excitements with real causes; neurosis can still be overcome by reality. But generally speaking we have no way of knowing in which patient and through which event that cure might be possible.[23]

Notes

1. To this is later added the important supplement: *In one of the squares I see a monument*.
2. With the addition: *By this word there was a question mark: want?*
3. On a second occasion she repeats: *2 hours*.
4. Two additions in the next hour: *I see myself particularly clearly going up the stairs*, and: *After her answer I go to my room, although not the slightest bit sad, and read a big book on my desk*.
5. In the dream she asks: *Where is the station?* From this convergence I drew a conclusion that I shall develop below.
6. In the dream content the number five is present in the statement of time: *five minutes*. In my book on the interpretation of dreams I have shown with reference to several examples how numbers occurring in the dream thoughts are treated by the dream; one often finds them torn from their contexts and inserted into new ones.
7. Without a doubt sexual satisfaction is the best sleeping draught, just as sleeplessness is generally the consequence of the absence of satisfaction. Her father could not sleep because he lacked intercourse with the woman he loved. Cf. what follows below: I get nothing from my wife.
8. These words will lead to the solution of our mystery.
9. Here for the third time: painting [*Bild*] (cityscapes, gallery in Dresden), but in a much more significant connection. What is seen in the painting turns it into a female [*Weibsbild*] (forest, nymphs).
10. The 'station' incidentally facilitates '*Verkehr*' ['traffic', or 'intercourse']. The psychical coating of some instances of fear of railways.
11. The defloration fantasy is the second component feature of this situation. The emphasis on the difficulty of going forward, and the anxiety felt in the dream, refer to the readily emphasized virginity that we find suggested elsewhere by the 'Sistine Madonna'. These sexual thoughts produce an unconscious background for the desires, which are perhaps kept secret, that deal with the suitor waiting in Germany. We have encountered the first component of this dream situation in the revenge fantasy. The two are not entirely identical, but only partially so. We will encounter the traces of an even more significant third train of thought below.
12. On another occasion, rather than using the word 'peacefully', she said 'not the slightest bit sad' (note 4 above). I can adduce this dream as a new proof for the correctness of an assertion contained in the *Interpretation of Dreams*, Chapter VII, Section A, II/III that the first forgotten and

subsequently remembered fragments of the dream are always the most important for the understanding of the dream. There I draw the conclusion that the forgetting of dreams also demands to be explained with reference to internal psychical resistance. [The first sentence of this footnote was added in 1924.]

13. We may assume a somatic connection between painfulness identified between the 'ovaries' in the abdomen, and locomotor disturbance of the leg on the same side. In Dora's case this has a particularly specialized interpretation, that is, it is subject to psychical overlayering and utilization. Cf. the analogous observation in the analysis of the coughing symptoms and the connection between catarrh and lack of appetite.

14. A very typical example of symptoms arising out of causes that apparently have nothing to do with sexual matters.

15. I have already suggested that most hysterical symptoms, once they have reached their full formation, represent a fantasized situation of sexual life – a scene of sexual intercourse, a pregnancy, childbirth, etc.

16. The defloration fantasy, then, is applied to Herr K., and it becomes clear why the same region of the dream content includes material from the scene by the lake. (Rejection, two and a half hours, the forest, invitation to L.)

17. Some later additions to these interpretations: The 'Madonna' is clearly Dora herself, first because of the 'admirer' who sent her the pictures, then because she won Herr K.'s love above all through her maternal treatment of his children, and finally because as a virgin she had had a child, a direct reference to the fantasy of childbirth. The Madonna, incidentally, is a common oppositional idea when a girl is under pressure of sexual accusations, as is the case with Dora. I first suspected this connection as a doctor in the psychiatric clinic, when I was treating a case of hallucinatory confusion that had followed a very swift course, and which turned out to be a reaction to an accusation by the bridegroom.

Had the analysis continued, it would probably have become possible to demonstrate maternal longing for a child as an obscure but powerful motive for her behaviour. The many questions that she had recently thrown up seem to be belated offspring of the questions of sexual curiosity that she had sought to satisfy from the dictionary. We may assume that she had read about pregnancy, childbirth, virginity and similar themes. In reproducing the dream, she had forgotten one of the questions that could be incorporated within the context of the second dream situation. It could only be the question: Does Herr X live here? or: Where does Herr X live? There must be a reason why she forgot this apparently innocent question after introducing it into the dream. I find the reason in the surname itself, which also has a meaning referring to an object, and can thus be said to be an '*ambiguous*' word. Unfortunately I cannot communicate this name to show how skilfully it has been used to refer to 'ambiguous' and 'indecent' matters. This interpretation is supported in another region of the dream, where the material is drawn from the memories of the death of Dora's aunt, in the sentence, 'They have already gone to the cemetery', which also contains a reference to the aunt's *name*. These indecent words probably indicate to a second, *oral* source, as the words in question would not have been found in a dictionary. I should not be surprised to hear that Frau K. herself, the traducer, was the source. Dora would then have been nobly sparing her, while pursuing everyone else with an almost sly revenge; behind the multitude of displacements arising in this way we might suspect a simple element, her deep-rooted homosexual love for Frau K.

18. It was 31 December.

19. It was perhaps not irrelevant that she could also have heard the same complaint about his wife, the meaning of which she probably understood, from her father, as I heard it from him.

20. This refers to the engineer, concealed behind the 'I' in the first dream situation.

21. Waiting until one has reached one's goal: that is found in the content of the first dream situation. In this fantasy of waiting for the bride, I see part of the third component of this dream. I have alluded to that component above.

22. Particularly a speech with which he had accompanied the Christmas present of a writing-case during the last year of their stay together in B.

23. Some additional remarks on the structure of this dream, which cannot be so thoroughly understood that we might attempt a synthesis of it. Dora's fantasy of revenge against her father stands out like a prominent façade: She has left home of her own volition. Her father has fallen ill, then died . . . Now she goes home, the others are all already at the cemetery. She goes to her room, not at all sad, and peacefully reads the dictionary. This includes two references to the other act of revenge that she actually carries out by allowing her parents to find her farewell letter: the letter (Mama's letter in the dream) and the mention of the funeral of the aunt who had been a model to her. This fantasy conceals ideas of revenge against Herr K., for which she has found an outlet in her behaviour towards me. The maid – the invitation – the forest – the two and a half hours come from the material of events in L. The memory of the governess and her correspondence with Dora's parents, along with the element of her letter of farewell, joins the letter in the dream content which allows her to come home. The refusal to allow herself to be accompanied, the decision to go on her own, can probably be translated as follows: Because you have treated me as a maid, I am going to leave you behind, go my own way alone and stay unmarried. Elsewhere, covered over by these ideas of revenge, material from affectionate fantasies of unconsciously continued love for Herr K. shines through: I would have waited for you until I had become your wife – the defloration – childbirth. Finally, it is part of the fourth, most deeply hidden circle of thoughts, that of Dora's love for Frau K., that the defloration fantasy is represented from the man's point of view (identification with the admirer, who is now abroad) and that at two points the clearest references to ambiguous words (does Herr X live here) and the non-oral source of her sexual knowledge (the dictionary). Cruel and sadistic impulses find fulfilment in this dream.

IV

Afterword

It is true that I introduced this account as the fragment of an analysis; but the reader will probably have found that it is far more incomplete than its title might lead him to expect. I shall now attempt to explain the reasons for these far from arbitrary omissions.

Some results of the analysis have been left out partly because by the time the analysis was interrupted they had not been identified with sufficient certainty, and partly because they failed to continue through to a general result. In other instances, when it seemed appropriate to me, I have referred to the probable course that individual solutions would have taken. In these passages I have entirely passed over the technique – far from obvious – that is the only way of extracting the raw material from the ideas that occur to the patient. The disadvantage of this is that the reader is unable to confirm the correctness of my working method on the basis of my account. But I found it quite impracticable to deal simultaneously with the technique of an analysis and with the internal structure of a case of hysteria. It would have been an almost impossible task for me, and it would certainly have made a disagreeable experience for the reader. The technique needs to be represented quite separately, and to be explained with reference to examples taken from a wide variety of cases, whereby it would not be necessary to give the results of each individual case. I have not attempted to explain the psychological hypotheses revealed in my descriptions of psychical phenomena. A fleeting explanation would achieve nothing; a thorough explanation would be a task in itself. I can only assure the reader that without being wedded to a particular psychological system, I set about studying phenomena revealed by the observation of psychoneurotics, and that I then adjusted my opinions until they seemed suited to give a full account of all the patient's symptoms. I am not proud to have avoided speculation; but the material for these hypotheses has been gained through the most extensive and exhaustive observation. In particular, the resoluteness of my point of view concerning the unconscious has provoked dissent, since I work with unconscious ideas, trains of thought and impulses as though, as objects of psychological study, they were just as good and as certain as conscious phenomena; but I am sure that anyone setting out to examine the same field using the same method will be unable to avoid reaching the same point of view, in spite of all attempts by philosophers to persuade him otherwise.

Those among my colleagues who have considered my theory of hysteria to be purely psychological, and who have therefore declared it incapable of solving a pathological problem, will probably conclude from this account that in levelling their accusation, they are unfairly transferring a characteristic of the technique to the theory. It is only the therapeutic technique that is purely psychological; the theory does not neglect to refer to the organic basis of neurosis, although it does not seek that basis in pathological and anatomical change, substituting for chemical changes – which cannot currently be grasped – the provisional nature of the organic function. No one will be able to deny that the sexual function, in which I see the cause of hysteria and of psychoneuroses in general, has an organic element. No theory of sexual life will, I suppose, be able to avoid admitting the exciting action of particular sexual materials. Of all the syndromes that clinical practice teaches us about, the intoxications and the kinds of abstinence produced by the chronic use of certain toxins are closest to genuine psychoneuroses.

Neither have I written in this account about what we can say at present on the subject of 'somatic compliance', about the infantile seeds of perversion, about the erogenous zones and the predisposition to bisexuality. I have only emphasized those points at which the analysis comes into contact with these organic foundations of the symptoms. More could not be done on the basis of an individual case, and for the same reasons I also had to avoid a fleeting discussion of those elements. This will provide ample material for other works, based on a large number of analyses.

Nevertheless, in publishing this account, incomplete though it is, I had two aims: first to provide a supplement to my book about the interpretation of dreams, explaining how this otherwise useless art can be applied to the revelation of that which is hidden and repressed within the life of the human soul; in the analysis of the two dreams reported here, the technique of dream interpretation, similar to the technique of psychoanalysis, must be taken into account. Secondly, I wished to awaken interest in a series of connections at present completely unknown to science, because they are only discovered in the application of this particular process. No one has had a proper idea of the complications of the psychical processes at work in hysteria, the juxtaposition of the most diverse impulses, the reciprocal connection of opposites, instances of repression and displacement, and so on. Pierre's Janet's emphasis on the *idée fixe*, which metamorphoses into the symptom, amounts to nothing but a pitiful schematization. In addition, it will not be possible to avoid the suspicion that excitements attached to ideas which are not capable of becoming conscious act upon one another in a different way, run a different course and manifest themselves differently from those which we refer to as 'normal', and the ideas attached to which do reach consciouness. Once we have grasped this, nothing stands in the way of our understanding of a therapy which stresses neurotic symptoms by transforming the former kind of ideas into normal ideas.

I was also concerned to show that sexuality does not intervene only once in the working of those processes that are characteristic of hysteria, as a *deus ex machina*, but that it provides the driving force for each individual symptom and each individual manifestation of a symptom. The manifestations of the illness are, to put it bluntly, the *patient's sexual activity*. No individual case will ever be capable of proving such a general principle, but I can only repeat it over and over again, because I never encounter anything else: sexuality is the key to the problem of psychoneuroses and neuroses in general. No one who scorns this idea will ever be in a position to solve this problem. I am still waiting for the research that might contradict or restrict this principle. But all that I have heard said against it so far has been in the form of expressions of personal displeasure or scepticism, which we need only counter with Charcot's phrase: '*Ça n'empêche pas d'exister*' [That doesn't mean it doesn't exist].

Neither is this case of whose history and treatment I have published a fragment here well suited to cast a proper light on the value of psychoanalytic therapy. Not only the brevity of the treatment, barely three months, but also another factor inherent within the case, prevented the cure from concluding with an improvement admitted both by the patient and by her relatives, which would be attainable otherwise, and would have corresponded more or less closely to a complete cure. Gratifying successes of this kind are achieved where symptoms are maintained only by internal conflict between impulses related to sexuality. In such cases one sees the condition of the patient improving to the extent that one has contributed to the solution of their mental difficulties by translating pathogenic into normal material. The cure proceeds differently when symptoms have been placed at the service of external motives concerning the patient's life, as had been the case with Dora over the previous two years. It is surprising, and it could easily be misleading, to learn that the state of the patient has not noticeably altered as a result even of highly advanced work. In fact, things are not as serious as they might appear; the symptoms may not disappear as a result of the work, but may do so a short while afterwards, once relations with the doctor have been severed. The delay of the cure or improvement is really only down to the personality of the doctor.

Let us add something further to our understanding of this state of affairs. We may say that as a general rule the new formation of symptoms is suspended during a psychoanalytical cure. The productivity of the neurosis is, however, by no means extinguished, but activated in the creation of thought formations of a particular kind, generally unconscious, to which we can give the name '*transferences*'.

What are transferences? They are new editions, facsimiles of the impulses and fantasies that are to be awakened and rendered conscious as the analysis progresses, whose characteristic trait is the substitution of the person of the doctor for a person previously known to the patient. To put it another way: a whole series of earlier psychical experiences is brought to life not as something in the past, but as a current relationship with the doctor. There are transferences which differ from their model only in this substitution. To remain with the same metaphor, these are simply reprints, unmodified new editions. Others are made with greater skill, they have undergone an attenuation of their content, a *sublimation*, as I put it, and are even capable of reaching consciousness by basing themselves on some skilfully evaluated, real particularity in the person or the circumstances of the doctor. Those are revised and corrected editions, no longer mere reprints.

If one goes into the theory of analytical technique, one comes to the understanding that the transference is something that it necessarily requires. In practical terms, at least, one becomes convinced that one cannot by any means avoid it, and that this final creation of the illness is something to be struggled against, like all the others. Now this piece of work is by far the most difficult. The interpretation of dreams, the extraction of the unconscious thoughts and memories from the ideas that occur to the patient, and similar arts of translation, are easily learned; the patient always supplies the text himself. But the transference one must effectively guess on one's own, from little signs, taking care not to be guilty of arbitrariness. The transference is inescapable, however, because it is used in the production of all the obstacles that render the material of the cure inaccessible to treatment, and because the patient only becomes convinced of the correctness of the reconstructed connections after the transference has been resolved.

One will be inclined to consider it a serious disadvantage of the analytic process – troublesome enough already – that it increases the doctor's work by creating a new kind of pathological psychical product. One might, in fact, be tempted to conclude that the existence of transferences actually harms the patient in the course of the analytical cure. In both instances one would be mistaken. The doctor's work is not increased by the transference; it may be a matter of indifference to him whether he has to overcome the impulses of patient as regards himself or another. But the cure also requires the patient to accomplish something new that he would not otherwise have been able to do. If the healing of neuroses takes place in institutions where psychoanalytic treatment is excluded, if, as we might say, hysteria is not healed by the method but by the doctor, if the result tends to be a kind of blind dependency and lasting attachment between the patient and the doctor who has freed him from his symptoms by means of hypnotic suggestion, the scientific explanation for all this lies in a 'transference', which the patient generally effects towards the person of the doctor. The psychoanalytic cure does not create the transference, it only reveals it, as it does other phenomena hidden in the mental life. The difference is expressed in the fact that the patient spontaneously calls upon only affectionate and friendly transferences leading towards his cure; where this cannot take place, he breaks off the treatment as quickly as possible, uninfluenced by the doctor, whom he does not find 'sympathetic'. In psychoanalysis, on the other hand, since the play of motives is different, all impulses, even hostile ones, are awoken, and made available to the analysis by being made conscious. The transference, destined to be the greatest obstacle to psychoanalysis, becomes its most powerful aid if one succeeds in guessing it correctly on each occasion and translating it to the patient.[1]

I had to mention the transference, because that factor alone enables me to explain the peculiarities of Dora's analysis. Its quality, which makes it appear suitable for a first, introductory publication, its particular transparency, is most intimately involved with its great shortcoming, which led to its premature interruption. I did not succeed in mastering the transference in time; the readiness with which Dora put part of the pathogenic material at my disposal meant that I neglected to pay attention to the first signs of the transference, which she prepared with another part of the same material, a part that remained unknown to me. At first it clearly appeared that I was replacing her father in her imagination, which will be readily understood given the difference in our ages. In addition, she always consciously compared me to him, anxiously seeking to reassure herself about whether I was also being quite honest with her, since her father 'always opted for secrecy and a roundabout way'. Then, when she had her first dream, in which she warned herself to abandon the cure as she had abandoned Herr K.'s house, I should have been on my guard, and told her: 'Now you have made a transference from Herr K. to me. Have you noticed anything to make you suspect bad intentions on my part, similar to those of Herr K., either directly or in some sublimated form, or has something struck you about me, or have you discovered something about me that compels your affection, as happened with Herr K.?' Then I would have drawn her attention to some detail from our relationship, in my person or my situation, concealing something analogous but a great deal more important about Herr K., and as a result of the solution of this transference the analysis would have gained access to new material, probably based on real memories. But I ignored that first warning, telling myself that we had plenty of time, since no other signs of transference were apparent, and since the material for the analysis was not yet exhausted. So the transference took me by surprise, and because of whatever unknown factor it was that made me remind her of Herr K., she avenged herself on me, as she wanted to avenge herself on Herr K., and left me, just as she believed herself deceived and abandoned by him. In that way she was *acting out* a significant part of her memories instead of reproducing them in the cure. What that unknown factor was of course I cannot know: I suspect it may have related to money, or it might have been jealousy of another patient who had stayed in contact with my family after her cure. Where a transference can be prematurely incorporated into the analysis, it develops more slowly and obscurely, but it is better equipped against sudden and invincible resistance.

In Dora's second dream the transference is represented by several clear references. When she told me the dream, I did not know, and learned only two days later, that we only had *two hours* of work ahead of us, the same amount of time that she had spent in front of the Sistine Madonna, the same amount of time, after she had corrected herself (two rather than two and a half hours), as the walk that she had not taken back around the lake. The striving and waiting in the dream, both of which referred to the young man in Germany, and to the length of time she would have to wait before Herr K. could marry her, had been manifest in the transference a few days previously. The cure, she said, was taking too long for her, she wouldn't have the patience to wait that long, although, during the first few weeks, she had been sensible enough not to object when I told her that it would be a year before she had effected a complete recovery. The refusal to be accompanied in the dream, along with her insistence on going alone, which also came from the visit to the Dresden gallery: I was only to learn of these on the day appointed by Dora. The meaning was probably this: 'Since all men are so appalling, I would prefer not to marry. This is my revenge.'[2]

In those cases where impulses of cruelty and motives for revenge, which have already been used in life to maintain the symptoms, transfer themselves to the doctor in the course of the cure, before he has had time to free himself of them by returning to their sources, it can hardly come as a surprise if the patient's condition does not demonstrate the influence of his therapeutic efforts. For how better could the patient avenge herself than by demonstrating with her own person the doctor's impotence and incapacity? None the less, I am inclined not to underestimate the therapeutic value even of a fragmentary treatment such as Dora's.

Only a year and three months after the end of the treatment and the writing of this account of it, I received news of my patient's condition and thus of the outcome of the cure. On a date that was not quite indifferent, the 1st of April – we know that times were never insignificant for her – she appeared at my house to conclude the story and once again ask for help; but a glance at her face was enough to tell me that she was not serious in this respect. She had been in 'a confused state', as she put it, for four or five weeks after leaving the treatment. Then a great improvement began, the attacks became rarer, her mood lifted. In May of the past year, one of the K. children had died, the one who had always been sickly. She took this bereavement as an occasion to pay the Ks a visit of condolence, and was received by them as though nothing had happened over the past three years. On this occasion she was reconciled with them, took her revenge on them and brought the matter to a conclusion that was satisfying to her. To the wife she said: I know you have a relationship with Papa; and she did not deny it. She forced the husband to admit to the scene by the lake, and then took this vindicating information to her father. She did not resume contact with the family after that.

After that she was quite well until mid-October, when she lost her voice once again, not regaining it until six weeks later. Surprised by this information, I asked her whether there was any cause for this, and heard that the attack followed a violent shock. She had seen someone being hit by a car. She finally admitted that the victim of the accident had been none other than Herr K. She met him in the street one day; he approached her on a busy street, stopped in front of her as though confused and, in his distraction, was knocked over by a car.[3] She was sure, incidentally, that he had survived without any serious injuries. She said she still had a faint emotional reaction if she heard talk of her Papa's relationship with Frau K., in which she no longer involved herself. She lived for her studies, and did not think of marriage.

She sought my help for a facial neuralgia on the right-hand side, which had persisted day and night. For how long? 'For exactly fourteen days.'[4] – I had to smile, as I was able to show her that she had read a news item about me in the newspaper exactly fourteen days before, and she confirmed this (1902).

So the supposed neuralgia was a self-punishment, regret for the slap in the face that she had given Herr K., and a revenge-transference that she had passed from him to me. I do not know what kind of help she wanted to ask me for, but I promised to forgive her for losing me the satisfaction of freeing her much more thoroughly from her illness.

Years have passed since she visited me. Since then Dora has married, to the very same young man, if the signs do not deceive me, whom she mentioned at the beginning of the analysis of the second dream. Since the first dream indicated her detachment from the man she loved and a return towards her father, the flight from life into illness, this second dream signified that she was breaking away from her father and that life would win her back.

(1905)

Notes

1. [*Addition 1923*:] What is said here about transference is continued in the technical essay about 'transference love' (in vol. X [of the *Gesammelte Werke*]).

2. The further removed I am in time from the termination of this analysis, the more likely it seems to me that my technical error was the following: I failed to guess in time, and to inform the patient, that her homosexual (gynaecophilic) feelings of love for Frau K. were the strongest of the unconscious currents in her mental life. I should have guessed that no one other than Frau K. could have been the chief source of her knowledge of sexual matters, the same person who had condemned her for her interest in such questions. It was striking, after all, that she knew all manner of improper things and claimed never to know how she knew them. I should have followed up on that mystery, I should have sought the reason for that strange repression. The reckless desire for revenge expressed in this dream was ideally suited to mask the opposite current, magnanimity, with which she forgave her beloved friend's betrayal and concealed from everyone the fact that it was Frau K. who introduced her to knowledge that was later used to cast suspicion upon her. Before I came to acknowledge the significance of the homosexual current among psychoneurotics, I often found myself getting stuck in my treatment of cases, or else became completely confused.

3. An interesting contribution to the indirect suicide attempt discussed in my *Psychopathology of Everyday Life*.

4. See the significance of this date and its relationship to the theme of revenge in the analysis of the second dream.

Three Essays on Sexual Theory

Preface to the Second Edition

The author, who is under no illusions about the lacunae and obscurities of this little paper, has none the less resisted the temptation to incorporate in it the results of his research over the past five years, and thus to destroy its unified documentary character. He is therefore reproducing the original wording with minor changes, and contenting himself with the addition of a few footnotes, which are distinguished from older notes by being preceded by the sign*.[1] In addition, it is his devout wish that this book may rapidly age, while that which was once new in it finds general acceptance, and its inadequacies are replaced by something more correct.

Vienna, December 1909

Notes

1. [This sign was dropped from all subsequent editions.]

Preface to the Third Edition

After observing the reception and effect of this book over a decade, I should like to provide this third edition with a few preliminary remarks directed against misunderstandings and claims that cannot be fulfilled. Let us stress above all, then, that the account given in these pages proceeds directly from everyday medical experience, which should be deepened and rendered scientifically significant by the results of psychoanalytic investigation. The three 'essays on sexual theory' can contain only what psychoanalysis obliges us to accept or allows us to confirm. For that reason it is out of the question that they could ever be extended into a 'sexual theory', and understandable that they do not adopt a position on some important problems of the sexual life. But it should not be believed for that reason that these aspects of the larger subject have remained a closed book to the author, or that he has neglected them as trivial.

But the dependence of this paper on the psychoanalytic experiences that led to its writing is apparent not only in the selection, but also in the arrangement of the material. A certain sequence of agencies is maintained at all times, accidental elements are highlighted while dispositional elements are left in the background, and ontogenetic development is taken into account over and against phylogenetic development. For accidental factors play the principal part in analysis, it is almost entirely taken up with them; the dispositional aspect only appears behind them as something awoken by experience, but whose assessment leads far beyond the field of competence of psychoanalysis.

A connection of a similar kind governs the relationship between ontogenesis and phylogenesis. Ontogenesis can be seen as a repetition of phylogenesis, in so far as the latter has not been altered by a more recent experience. The phylogenetic predisposition makes itself apparent behind the ontogenetic process. Fundamentally, however, the disposition is the imprint of an earlier experience of the same kind, to which the individual's more recent experience is added as the sum of accidental elements.

Alongside the constant feature of dependence on psychoanalytic research I must emphasize that this work has remained deliberately independent of biological research. I have carefully avoided incorporating into the study scientific expectations from general sexual biology or particular animal species that the technique of psychoanalysis has enabled us to make of the human sexual function. My goal, however, was to examine the extent to which the biology of human sexual life can be guessed by the means of psychological inquiry; I was able to refer to connections and agreements produced in the course of this investigation, but I had to take care not to be misled whenever the psychological method led on some important points to views and results that deviated considerably from those which were merely biologically supported.

In this third edition, I have added numerous parentheses, but avoided making them identifiable, as in the previous edition, with particular signs. – Progress in scientific work in our field has slowed down at present, but certain additions to this paper were indispensable, if it was to remain in contact with more recent psychoanalytic literature.

Vienna, October 1914

Preface to the Fourth Edition

Once the floods of war have receded, we can establish with satisfaction that interest in psychoanalytical research has remained undamaged throughout the world. But not all parts of psychoanalytical theory have experienced the same fate. The purely psychological postulations and findings of psychoanalysis concerning the unconscious, repression, the conflict that leads to illness, the gain from illness, the mechanisms of symptom formation, amongst other things, are enjoying growing recognition and winning respect even among those opposed in principle to psychoanalysis. The part of the theory that borders on biology, the basis of which is provided in this little paper, still provokes undiminished contradiction, and has even led people who had for a time been closely preoccupied with psychoanalysis to reject it and move on to new concepts which once again reduce the role of the sexual element in both normal and pathological mental lives.

None the less I cannot support the hypothesis that this aspect of psychoanalytic theory could be much further away from the reality that we are attempting to guess than the rest. My memory, and repeated examination of the material, tell me that it has proceeded from equally careful and unbiased observation, and it is not difficult to explain this discrepancy in its reception by the public. First of all, only those investigators with sufficient patience and technical skill to carry the analysis back to the first years of childhood can confirm the beginnings of human sexual life as described in these pages. This is often impossible, as medical procedure demands that the illness should, at least in appearance, be treated more rapidly. But apart from doctors who practise psychoanalysis, no one has any access to this field, or any possibility of forming a judgement uninfluenced by their own aversions and prejudices. If people were able to learn from direct observation of children, these three essays could have gone unwritten.

But we must also remember that some of the content of this paper – the emphasis on the significance of the sexual life for all human achievements and the attempt made here to extend the concept of sexuality – has always generated the strongest motives for resistance to psychoanalysis. In the need for resounding slogans some have gone so far as to speak of the 'pan-sexualism' of psychoanalysis, and to level the absurd accusation that it explains 'everything' with reference to sexuality. One could be amazed at this, if we were ourselves capable of forgetting the effect of affective elements that confuse us and render us forgetful. For the philosopher Arthur Schopenhauer also showed people, a considerable time ago, the extent to which their actions and endeavours were defined by sexual strivings – in the familiar sense of the word – and a world of readers should surely be incapable of striking so gripping a reminder so completely from their minds! But as regards the 'extension' of the concept of sexuality that is made necessary by the analysis of children and so-called perverts, everyone who looks down contemptuously upon psychoanalysis should remember how closely the extended sexuality of psychoanalysis coincides with the Eros of the divine Plato. (See: Nachmansohn, 'Freuds Libidotheorie verglichen mit der Eroslehre Platos' ['Freud's Theory of the Libido Compared with Plato's Theory of Eros'], *Internationale Zeitschrift für Psychoanalyse*, III, 1915.)

Vienna, May 1920

I

The Sexual Deviations[1]

When biologists discuss the sexual needs of men and animals, they assume the existence of a 'sexual drive', following the analogy of the drive to seek food – hunger. The vernacular lacks a term corresponding to the word 'hunger'; for this purpose, science uses the word 'libido'.[2]

Popular opinion has quite particular notions of the nature and properties of this sexual drive. It is supposed to be absent from childhood, and to set in with the maturing process of puberty, when it finds expression in the irresistible attraction that one sex exerts upon the other, and its goal is supposed to be sexual union or at least the actions that lie on the route to that union.

But we have every reason to see this account as a very unfaithful depiction of reality; if we take a closer look at it, it proves to be abundant in errors, imprecision and hasty judgements.

Let us introduce two terms: if we call the person exuding the sexual attraction the *sexual object*, and the action towards which the drive urges the *sexual goal*, scientifically examined experience reveals numerous deviations in relation to both sexual object and sexual goal, whose relationship towards the accepted norm calls for detailed examination.

1) Deviations Regarding the Sexual Object

The popular theory of the sexual drive is most beautifully expressed by the poetic fable of the division of the human being into two halves – man and woman – which seek to reunite in love. So it seems to come as a great surprise to hear that there are men whose sexual object is not women but men, and women whose sexual object is not men but women. Such people are called 'countersexual' or, more exactly, inverts, and the fact is that of *inversion*. The number of such people is very considerable, although it is difficult to arrive at precise figures.[3]

A) Inversion

(Behaviour of Inverts)

The people in question behave in different ways in different contexts.
a) They may be *absolutely* inverted, which is to say that their sexual object can only be of the same sex, while the opposite sex is never the object of their sexual longing, but leaves them cold or even provokes sexual repulsion in them. As men they are then, by virtue of this repulsion, incapable of performing the normal sex act, or else they lack all pleasure in its performance.
b) They may be *amphigenically inverted* (psychosexually hermaphroditic), that is, their sexual object can belong equally well to the same as to the other sex; so their inversion lacks the character of exclusivity.
c) They may be *occasionally* inverted, that is, under certain external conditions, chief among which are a lack of access to the normal sexual object and imitation, they can take a person of the same sex as their sexual object, and feel satisfaction in the sexual act with that person.

Inverts also demonstrate different attitudes in their assessment of the special nature of their sexual instinct. Some take inversion perfectly for granted, just as a normal person will take the direction of his libido to be quite natural, and keenly stress their equality with normal people. But others reject the fact of their inversion and perceive it as a morbid compulsion.[4]

Other variations apply to relations over time. The characteristic nature of an individual's inversion either dates from as far back as his memory goes, or has only made itself apparent at a particular time before or after puberty.[5] The characteristic is either maintained throughout the whole of life, or subsides for periods of time, or represents an episode on the path towards normal development; indeed it is sometimes manifested only late in life, after a long period of normal sexual activity. A periodic vacillation between the normal and the inverted sexual object has also been observed. Of particular interest are those cases in which the libido changes its direction to move towards the inversion, after a painful experience with the normal sexual object.

These different series of variations generally exist independently of one another. Where the most extreme form is concerned, for example, we might generally assume that the inversion has existed since very early on, and that the person feels himself to be at one with its peculiarity.

Many authors would refuse to assemble the cases enumerated here into a unit, preferring to stress the differences between these groups rather than what they have in common, and this has to do with their preferred judgement of inversion. But while there may be considerable justification for separating out certain cases, there is no mistaking the fact that all intermediate stages are to be found in abundance, so that series might be said to form of their own accord.

(Concept of Inversion)

The first concept of inversion consisted in the notion that it was an innate sign of nervous degeneracy, and was in harmony with the fact that medical observers first encountered it among patients suffering from, or appearing to suffer from, nervous disorders. This characteristic contains two features that should be judged independently of each other: innateness and degeneracy.

(Degeneracy)

The term 'degeneracy' is vulnerable to all those objections that can be raised against the unselective use of the word in general. None the less it has become customary to impute to degeneracy any expression of an illness that is not precisely traumatic or infectious in origin. According to Magnan's categorization of degenerates, even the most excellent general formation of neural functioning need not exclude the concept of degeneracy. In such circumstances we might wonder what use and what new content the diagnosis of 'degeneracy' might possess, if any. It seems to make more sense not to speak of degeneracy:

1) where several serious deviations from the norm do not coincide;

2) where the capacity for achievement and existence do not in general appear to be seriously damaged.[6]

That inverts are not degenerates in this justified sense emerges from several facts:

1) inversion is encountered amongst people who show no other serious deviations from the norm;

2) the same is true of people whose capacities are not impeded, and who are distinguished by particularly high levels of intellectual development and ethical culture;[7]

3) if we ignore those patients whom we have encountered in our own medical experience and attempt to encompass a further range of views, in two directions we run into facts which prohibit us from viewing inversion as a sign of degeneracy:

a) we must stress that inversion was a common phenomenon, almost an institution, entrusted with important functions, among ancient peoples at the peak of their culture;

b) we find it to be uncommonly widespread among many savage and primitive peoples, despite the fact that we usually restrict the concept of degeneracy to high civilization (I. Bloch); even among the civilized peoples of Europe, climate and race have the most powerful influence on the distribution and assessment of inversion.[8]

(Innateness)

Understandably, the innate source of inversion has only been suggested for the first and most extreme class of inverts, based on their assurance that they had never in their lives shown any other direction in their sexual drives. The very existence of the other two classes, particularly the third, is difficult to reconcile with the view of a congenital character. Hence the tendency among those who hold this view to separate the group of absolute inverts off from all others, leading to the abandonment of a universally valid understanding of inversion. This would mean that inversion had an innate characteristic in one series of cases; in others it could have come about in a different way.

The antithesis to this view is that inversion is an *acquired* characteristic of the sexual drive. It is based on the idea that:

1) among many inverts (some of them absolute), an influential sexual impression early in life can be demonstrated, having the lasting consequence of an inclination towards homosexuality;

2) in many other cases it is possible to reveal the external encouraging and inhibiting influences of life that have led, sooner or later, to the fixation of the inversion (exclusive intercourse with the same sex, comradeship in war, detention in prisons, dangers of heterosexual intercourse, celibacy, sexual weakness, etc.);

3) that the inversion can be abolished by hypnotic suggestion, which would be astonishing if the characteristic were innate.

From this point of view, it is possible to dispute the certainty of the occurrence of innate inversion in general. One might object (with Havelock Ellis) that a more precise examination of the cases claimed for innate inversion would probably also tend to reveal an experience in early childhood which defined the direction of the libido, one which has not been stored in the person's conscious memory, but which could be remembered by recourse to the appropriate influence. According to these authors, inversion could only be characterized as a frequently occurring variation of the sexual drive, which can be determined by a considerable number of external circumstances in an individual's life.

But the certainty apparently achieved in this way is defeated by the contrary observation that many people demonstrably undergo the same sexual influences (even in early adolescence: seduction, mutual masturbation) without being inverted in the process or remaining so in the long term. One is therefore obliged to assume that the innate-acquired opposition is either incomplete or does not fully account for the conditions involved in inversion.

(Explanation of Inversion)

Neither the assumption that inversion is innate, nor that it is acquired, explains its essence. In the former case one must state what is innate about it if one is not to adopt the crudest explanation, that there is an innate link between a person's drive and a particular sexual object. In the other case the question arises of whether the diverse accidental influences alone adequately explain the acquisition of the inversions, and need no compliance from the individual to meet them. According to our earlier expositions, the denial of this latter element is not permissible.

(Invocation of Bisexuality)

Popular opinion is contradicted by the reflections of Frank Lydstone, Kiernan and Chevalier, in their endeavour to explain the possibility of sexual inversion. According to this view, a person is held to be either a man or a woman. But science is aware of cases in which the sexual characteristics appear blurred, and sexual definition consequently becomes more difficult, first of all in the anatomical field. The genitals of such people combine male and female characteristics (hermaphroditism). In rare cases, the two sexual apparatuses are formed side by side (true hermaphroditism); in the most usual cases one finds atrophy on both sides.[9]

What is significant about these abnormalities, however, is that they unexpectedly make it easier to understand the normal formation. A certain degree of anatomical hermaphroditism is actually part of the norm; all normally formed male or female individuals possess traces of the apparatus of the opposite sex, and these continue to exist either without a function as rudimentary organs, or have been reconstructed to assume other functions.

The understanding yielded by these long-known anatomical facts is that of an originally bisexual disposition, which changes in the course of its development into monosexuality, with small residues of the atrophied sex.

It seemed reasonable to transfer this understanding of inversion to the psychical sphere and see it in its deviant versions as the manifestation of a psychical hermaphroditism. For the resolution of this question, all that was required was a regular coincidence between inversion and the mental and somatic signs of hermaphroditism.

But this immediate expectation proves to be incorrect. We must not conceive such close relations between the assumed psychical and demonstrable anatomical hermaphroditism. What we find among inverts is frequently a reduction in the sexual drive in general (Havelock Ellis) and slight anatomical atrophy of the organs. Frequently, but by no means regularly or even predominantly. Thus we must concede that inversion and somatic hermaphroditism are entirely independent of one another.

In addition, great stress has been placed on the so-called secondary and tertiary sexual characteristics, and their accumulated occurrence among inverts (H. Ellis). This is also true in many respects, but we should not forget that the secondary and tertiary sexual characteristics in general appear very frequently in the opposite sex, and thus produce suggestions of hermaphroditism without the sexual object being altered in the sense of an inversion.

Psychical hermaphroditism would gain substance if the inversion of the sexual object were at least accompanied by a parallel change in the other mental qualities, drives and character traits into those characteristic of the other sex. However, such a character inversion can only be expected with any regularity among inverted women, while in men inversion may be reconciled with the most complete mental masculinity. If we are determined to establish the idea of mental hermaphroditism, we must add that in various respects its manifestations reveal only a very small degree of reciprocal causality. The same is also true of somatic hermaphroditism: according to Halban,[10] the atrophy of individual organs and secondary sexual characteristics appear fairly independently of one another.

The crudest form of the theory of bisexuality has been put forward by a spokesman for male inverts: a female brain in a male body. But we do not know what the characteristics of a 'female brain' might be. The substitution of the anatomical for the psychical problem is as futile as it is unjustified. Krafft-Ebing's attempt at an explanation seems to be more precisely put than that of Ulrichs, but is no different in its essentials: Krafft-Ebing says that the bisexual predisposition produces individual brain-centres that are just as male and female as the somatic sexual organs. These centres develop only during puberty, and mostly under the influence of glands that are independent of them within the sexual predisposition. We may, however, say the same of these male and female 'centres' as we do of the male and female brain. In addition, we do not even know whether we can assume that there are distinct points in the brain ('centres') as we can, for example, for language.[11]

These discussions leave us with two thoughts: that a bisexual predisposition also has some bearing on inversion, although we do not know what that predisposition consists of beyond anatomical formation, and that these are disorders which affect the development of the sexual drive.

(Sexual Object of Inverts)

The theory of psychical hermaphroditism assumes that the invert's sexual object is the opposite of a normal person's. According to this theory the male invert, like a woman, succumbs to the enchantment emanated by the male qualities of body and mind. He himself feels like a woman and seeks a man.

But however true this may be for large numbers of inverts, it is still a long way from revealing a general character of inversion. Beyond a doubt, a high proportion of male inverts have preserved the psychical character of masculinity, have relatively few secondary characteristics of the opposite sex, and actually seek female psychical traits in their sexual object. If this were not the case, we would be unable to understand why the male prostitutes available to the invert – today as in antiquity – copy women in all externals of clothing and posture; were this not the case, this imitation would surely insult the ideal of inverts. Among the ancient Greeks, among whom inverts included the most masculine of men, it is clear that it was not the masculine character of the boy but his physical similarity to women, along with his feminine mental qualities, such as shyness, reticence, a need to learn and to be helped, that fired the love of men. As soon as the boy became a man he ceased to be a sexual object for men, and in all likelihood became a lover of boys himself. So in this case, as in many others, the sexual object is not the same sex but the combination of both characteristics, the compromise, one might say, between one impulse that craves a man and another that craves a woman, with the body's permanent condition of maleness (the genitals) the reflection, so to speak, of the subject's own bisexual nature.[12]

Less ambiguous are conditions among women, whereby active inverts most usually bear male somatic and mental characteristics and demand femininity in their sexual object, although even here a greater variety might appear on closer examination.

(Sexual Goal of Inverts)

The important fact to bear in mind is that in inversion the sexual goal should by no means be considered uniform. Among men, intercourse *per anum* [anal intercourse] does not correspond to inversion; equally often, masturbation is the exclusive goal, and restrictions of the sexual goal – down to the mere outpouring of emotions – are even more frequent here than in heterosexual love. Among women, too, the sexual goals of inverts are highly diverse; among them, contact with the oral mucous membrane seems to be preferred.

(Conclusion)

We are not in a position to give a satisfactory explanation of the origin of inversion on the basis of this material, but we may observe that in the course of this investigation we have reached an insight that might be more significant to us than the solution of the task mentioned above. We are aware that we have considered the connection between sexual drive and sexual object to be deeper than it is. The experience of those cases which are considered abnormal tells us that a powerful bond exists between sexual drive and sexual object, and that we are in danger of overlooking it because of the uniformity of the normal arrangement, in which the drive itself appears to bring an innate object along with it. For this reason we tend to loosen the connection between drive and object in our minds. The sexual drive is probably at first independent of its object, and in all likelihood its origins do not lie in its object's attractions.

B) Sexually Immature People and Animals as Sexual Objects

While those people whose sexual objects do not belong to the normally appropriate sex, those whom we shall call inverts, may strike the observer as a collection of otherwise fully adequate individuals, the cases in which people who have not reached sexual maturity (children) are chosen as sexual objects immediately appear as individual aberrations. Only in exceptional cases are children the sole sexual objects; they usually attain this role if a cowardly individual, who has developed impotence, chooses them as a surrogate, or if an impulsive (urgent) drive can at that moment find no more suitable object. None the less, it casts a light on the nature of the sexual drive that it permits so much variation and such debasement of its object, something that hunger, which is far more energetic in its retention of its object, would only permit in extreme cases. A similar observation applies to sexual intercourse with animals, which is far from rare amongst rural people, in which sexual attraction goes beyond the boundaries of species.

For aesthetic reasons we would very much like to attribute these and other serious deviations of the sexual drive to the mentally ill, but we cannot do so. Experience teaches us that among the latter the observable disorders of the sexual drive are no different from those seen among healthy people, among entire races and social classes. Thus the sexual abuse of children occurs with extraordinary frequency among teachers and carers simply because they are presented with the best opportunity to abuse. The mentally ill only show the aberration in question in an intensified form or, very significantly, elevated to an exclusive role and replacing normal sexual satisfaction.

This very peculiar relationship between sexual variations and the range between health and mental disorder provides food for thought. I am inclined to the view that what needs to be explained is the fact that the impulses of sexual life are among those least effectively controlled by the higher activities of the mind. A person who is mentally abnormal in another context, in a social or ethical respect, will in my experience be regular in his sexual life. But there are many who are abnormal in their sexual life but who correspond in all other respects to the average, and who have personally played their part in the development of human civilization, the weak point of which is still sexuality.

The most general result of these discussions, however, would seem to be the insight that in a large number of conditions and among a surprisingly large number of individuals the nature and value of the sexual object are of secondary importance. The essential and constant feature of the sexual drive is clearly something else.[13]

2) *Deviations Regarding the Sexual Goal*

The normal sexual goal is generally supposed to be the union of the genitals in the act described as coitus, which leads to the release of sexual excitement (a satisfaction analogous to the sating of hunger). But even in the most normal sexual procedure we can see the first signs of something which, when fully developed, will lead to the aberrations described as *perversions*. Indeed, certain intermediate relationships towards the sexual object (along the path towards coitus), such as touching and looking at the object, are acknowledged as temporary sexual goals. On the one hand these activities are themselves connected with pleasure, while on the other they intensify the excitement that should lead to the achievement of the final sexual goal. One of these contacts in particular, the mutual contact of the mucous membrane of the lips, has also achieved high sexual value as a kiss among many peoples (including the most highly civilized), although the parts of the body in question are not part of the sexual apparatus, but in fact form the entrance to the alimentary canal. Here, then, we have elements which link perversions to normal sexual life, and which are applicable to their organization. The perversions are either a) anatomical *transgressions* of those areas of the body destined for sexual union or b) a *lingering* over the intermediate relations to the sexual object, which would normally be rapidly passed through on the way towards the final sexual goal.

A) Anatomical Transgressions

(Over-valuation of the Sexual Object)

The psychical esteem in which the sexual object is held as an ideal goal for the sexual drive is limited to the genitals only in the rarest cases, instead extending to the body as a whole, and tends to involve all the sensations emanating from the sexual object. The same over-valuation spreads into the psychical field, where it appears as a blinding of logic (weakness of judgement) concerning the sexual object's mental accomplishments and perfections, as well as a credulous submissiveness to the latter's judgements. The credulity of love thus becomes an important, if not the primary, source of authority.[14]

It is this sexual over-valuation that sits so ill with the restriction of the sexual goal to the union of the actual genitals, and contributes to the turning of other body parts into sexual goals.[15]

The significance of the element of sexual over-valuation can be most easily studied in men, whose love-life is the only one to have become amenable to examination, while that of women is still shrouded in impenetrable obscurity as a result both of cultural atrophy and of women's secrecy and insincerity.[16]

(Sexual Use of the Mucous Membrane of the Lips and Mouth)

The use of the mouth as a sexual organ is considered to be a perversion when the lips (or tongue) of one person are brought into contact with the genitals of the other, but not if the mucous membranes of the lips of both parties touch one another. The latter exception establishes contact with normality. Anyone who abhors the other practices, which have been customary since the earliest times of humanity, will yield to a distinct *feeling of disgust*, which protects him against the acceptance of such a sexual goal. The limit of this disgust, however, is often purely conventional; someone who ardently kisses the lips of a beautiful girl might not be able to use her toothbrush without a feeling of disgust, although there is no reason to assume that his own oral cavity, which does not disgust him, is any cleaner than the girl's. Our attention is drawn here to the element of disgust, which gets in the way of the libidinal over-valuation of the sexual object, but which can in turn be overcome by the libido. One would be inclined to see disgust as one of the powers which have imposed boundaries upon the sexual goal. As a rule, these stop short of the genitals themselves. But there is no doubt that the genitals of the opposite sex can in themselves be an object of disgust, and that this attitude is one of the characteristics of all hysterics (particularly among females). The strength of the sexual drive enjoys actively overcoming this disgust. (See below.)

(Sexual Use of the Anal Orifice)

Where the utilization of the anus is concerned, it is easier to see that it is disgust that stamps this sexual goal as a perversion than in the case mentioned above. But I do not wish it to be considered as bias on my part if I observe that the explanation for this disgust, the fact that this body part fulfils the purpose of excretion and comes into contact with something inherently disgusting – excrement – does not have much more validity than the explanation given by hysterical girls for their disgust in the face of male genitals: they serve to evacuate urine.

The sexual role of the anal mucous membrane is by no means restricted to intercourse between men, and there is nothing about it to make it characteristic of inverted feeling. On the contrary, it appears that pederasty among men owes its role to analogy with the act with a woman, while mutual masturbation is the most usual sexual goal in intercourse between inverts.

(Significance of Other Body Parts)

There is in principle nothing new about the sexual encroachment upon other parts of the body, in all its variations, and it adds nothing to our knowledge of the sexual drive, which is merely announcing its intention to go in every possible direction to take power of the sexual object. Sexual over-valuation aside, however, in anatomical transgressions a second element alien to popular knowledge becomes apparent. Certain parts of the body, such as the mucous membrane of the mouth and the anus, which repeatedly appear in these practices, effectively lay claim to be considered and treated as genitals in their own right. We will hear how this claim is justified by the development of the sexual drive, and how it is fulfilled in the symptomatology of certain illnesses.

(Inappropriate Replacement of the Sexual Object – Fetishism)

A quite particular impression is created by those cases in which the normal sexual object is replaced by another which is connected to it, but which is utterly unsuited to the accomplishment of the normal sexual goal. From the point of view of categorization we should perhaps have mentioned this extremely interesting group of deviations related to the sexual drive among the deviations related to the sexual object, but we have put off doing so until we have encountered the element of *sexual over-valuation* on which these phenomena depend, and which is connected with an abandonment of the sexual goal.

The substitute for the sexual object is a body part (foot, hair) which is generally unsuited to sexual purposes, or an inanimate object demonstrably connected to the sexual person, or best of all with that person's sexuality (items of clothing, white linen). It is not without some justification that this substitution is compared with the fetish in which primitive man sees his god embodied.

The transition to those cases of fetishism in which a normal or perverse sexual goal is abandoned occurs in cases where a fetishistic condition is required of the sexual object if the sexual goal is to be accomplished (a particular hair-colour, clothing, even physical imperfections). No other variation of the sexual drive verging on the pathological is of such great interest to us as this one, because of the strangeness of the phenomena to which it gives rise. A certain reduction in striving for the normal sexual goal seems to be the precondition for all such cases (executive weakness of the sexual apparatus).[17] The link to normality is conveyed by the psychologically necessary over-valuation of the sexual object, which inevitably encroaches upon everything connected with it by association. Hence a certain degree of such fetishism is a regular part of normal loving, particularly during those stages when one is in love, in which the normal sexual goal appears unattainable or its fulfilment cancelled.

Schaff' mir ein Halstuch von ihrer Brust,
Ein Strumpfband meiner Liebeslust!

[Bring me a kerchief from her breast, A garter of my love's delight!]
(Faust)

The pathological case only occurs when the striving for the fetish becomes fixated beyond such conditions and takes the place of the normal goal, or if the fetish breaks free of the particular person and itself becomes the sole sexual object. These are the general conditions for the transition from mere variations in the sexual drive to pathological aberrations.

In the choice of the fetish, as Alfred Binet first claimed – and this has subsequently been proven with ample evidence – what is revealed is the continuing influence of a sexual impression generally received in early childhood, and which we may place next to the proverbial retentiveness of first love in a normal person ('*on revient toujours à ses premiers amours*' ['we always return to our first loves']). Such a deduction is particularly clear in cases in which the sexual object is merely fetishistically conditioned. We shall encounter the importance of early sexual impressions elsewhere.[18]

In other cases it is a symbolic connection of ideas, of which the person affected is not generally conscious, that has led to the replacement of the object by the fetish. The routes of these connections are not always demonstrable with any great certainty (the foot is an ancient sexual symbol, even in myth,[19] and fur probably owes its fetishistic role to its association with the hair covering the mons veneris); but such symbolism does not always appear to be independent of childhood sexual experiences.[20]

B) Fixations of Temporary Sexual Goals

(Appearance of New Intentions)

All those external and internal conditions which obstruct or defer the accomplishment of the normal sexual goal (impotence, the high cost of the sexual object, dangers of the sexual act) understandably support the inclination to linger over the preparatory acts and turn them into new sexual goals which can replace the normal goals. On closer examination it always proves that those new intentions which appear most alien are already hinted at in normal sexual processes.

(Touching and Looking)

A certain degree of touching is, at least for human beings, indispensable for the achievement of the normal sexual goal. It is also a matter of general knowledge that the touch of the sexual object's skin constitutes on the one hand a great source of pleasure and on the other a great influx of arousal. Consequently, lingering over the touch, if the sexual act then continues further, can hardly be counted among the perversions.

Much the same is true of seeing, which is ultimately derived from touching. The optical impression remains the path along which libidinous arousal is most frequently awoken, and on whose viability – if this teleological way of looking at things may be permitted – breeding selection depends, in that it allows the sexual object to develop into something beautiful. The uncovering of the body, which is advancing along with civilization, keeps alive the sexual curiosity which seeks to complete the sexual object by revealing its hidden parts, but which can be diverted ('sublimated') into art if its interest can be distracted from the genitals to the form of the body as a whole.[21] Lingering over this intermediate sexual goal of sexually emphasized looking appears among most normal people, indeed it gives them the opportunity to elevate a certain proportion of their libido to higher artistic goals. The love of looking becomes a perversion, on the other hand, a) if it is restricted exclusively to the genitals, b) if it is linked to the overcoming of disgust (voyeurs: those who watch the functions of excretion, or c) if it represses the normal sexual goal rather than preparing for it. The latter is true to a most pronounced degree among exhibitionists who, if I may draw this conclusion on the basis of several analyses, show their genitals in order to see the genitals of the other party in return.[22]

In the perversion whose efforts are concerned with looking and being looked at, a very curious characteristic emerges, which will preoccupy us even more intensely in the next deviation. The sexual goal is present in two formations, the active and the passive.

The power which stands in the way of the love of looking, and which may be cancelled by it, is *shame* (as disgust was before).

(Sadism and Masochism)

The inclination to cause pain to the sexual object, and its counterpart, this most frequent and significant of all perversions, has been identified by Krafft-Ebing, in its two formations, the active and the passive, as *sadism* and *masochism*. Other authors prefer the narrower term *algolagnia*, which stresses the pleasure in pain and cruelty, while the names chosen by Krafft-Ebing stress the pleasure to be had from all kinds of humiliation and subjection.

Where active algolagnia, sadism, is concerned, its roots in the normal person can be easily demonstrated. Most men's sexuality reveals a certain quantity of *aggression*, of the inclination to overpower, whose biological significance lies perhaps in the need to overcome the resistance of the sexual object in a way other than the acts involved in *courtship*. In that case, sadism might be thought to correspond to an aggressive component of the sexual drive which has now become autonomous and exaggerated by virtue of being shifted into the leading position.

The concept of sadism varies in linguistic usage from a merely active, and violent, attitude towards the sexual object, to the exclusive derivation of satisfaction from the object's subjection and mistreatment. Strictly speaking, only the latter, extreme case may properly be deemed a perversion.

Similarly, the term masochism encompasses all passive attitudes towards sexual life and the sexual object, the most extreme form of which derives its satisfaction from the suffering of physical or mental pain inflicted by the sexual object. As a perversion, masochism seems further removed from the normal sexual goal than its positive counterpart; we may doubt whether it is ever a primary phenomenon, or whether it does not universally emerge as a transformation of sadism.[23] It is often apparent that masochism is nothing but an extension of sadism turned upon the subject's own person, which thereby comes to occupy the position of the sexual object. Clinical analysis of extreme cases of masochistic perversion suggests the combination of many elements working together to exaggerate and fixate the original passive sexual attitude (castration complex, sense of guilt).

The pain thus overcome joins the disgust and shame that had acted as resistances to the libido.

Sadism and masochism assume a particular place among the perversions, since their underlying opposition of activity and passivity is among the universal characteristics of sexual life.

The cultural history of mankind teaches us beyond any doubt that cruelty and the sexual urge belong most profoundly together, but in making this connection clear we have not gone beyond an emphasis on the aggressive element of the libido. According to some commentators, the combination of this aggression with the sexual drive is actually a leftover from cannibalistic pleasures, associated with the apparatus involved in overpowering, which serves to satisfy the other, ontogenetically older, major need.[24] It has also been asserted that every pain contains within itself the possibility of a feeling of pleasure. We shall merely observe that this perversion has not been satisfactorily explained, and that it may be the case that several different mental efforts combine within it to create a single effect.[25]

The most striking quality of this perversion, however, lies in the fact that its active and passive forms are regularly encountered in one and the same person. Anyone who takes pleasure in causing others pain in a sexual relationship is also capable of enjoying as pleasure the pain that can arise from his own sexual relations. A sadist is always at the same time a masochist, although the active or the passive side of the perversion may be more strongly developed in him, and either one can represent his predominant sexual activity.[26]

Thus we can see that certain inclinations towards perversion regularly appear as *pairs of opposites*; in relation to material which will be introduced below, this may claim a high level of theoretical significance. It is also illuminating that the existence of the pair of opposites, sadism and masochism, cannot simply be deduced by the presence of aggression. On the other hand, one might be tempted to connect such simultaneously existing opposites with the opposites of male and female united in bisexuality, for which active and passive can often be used in psychoanalysis.[27]

3) *General Observations Concerning all Perversions*

(Variation and Illness)

Doctors who have first studied the perversions in highly pronounced examples and under particular conditions have naturally been inclined to attribute to them the characteristics of illness or degeneracy, just as they have with inversion. In the latter case it is easier to reject this view. Everyday experience has shown that most of these transgressions, at least the less serious among them, form a component that is rarely absent from the sexual life of healthy people, and are also held by them to resemble other intimacies. Conditions permitting, even a normal person can replace the normal sexual goal with such a perversion for some considerable time, or allow the two to coincide. In every healthy person a supplement that might be called perverse is present in the normal sexual goal, and this universality is sufficient in itself to suggest the pointlessness of using the term 'perversion' in an accusatory sense. It is precisely in the area of sexual life that we encounter particular and currently insoluble difficulties if we wish to draw a sharp distinction between mere variation within the physiological range and pathological symptoms.

In some of these perversions the quality of the new sexual goal is such that it requires particular appreciation. Certain perversions are, in terms of their content, so far removed from normality that we cannot help but declare them 'pathological', particularly those in which the sexual drive performs astonishing feats (licking excrement, abusing corpses) in overcoming resistances (shame, disgust, fear, pain). But even in cases such as these we should not allow ourselves to expect with any certainty that the perpetrators will inevitably turn out to be people with different serious abnormalities, or people who are mentally ill. Here, too, we cannot escape the fact that individuals who behave normally in other respects reveal themselves in the area of sexual life alone, under the domination of the most unbridled of all the drives, to be ill. Manifest abnormality in other relations of life, on the other hand, always tends to show a background of abnormal sexual behaviour.

In the majority of cases we can find a pathological character in the perversion, not in the content of the new sexual goal, but in its relation to the normal. It is where the perversion does not appear *alongside* the normal (sexual goal and object), where favourable conditions encourage the perversion and unfavourable circumstances obstruct the normal, but has repressed and replaced the normal under all circumstances; it is in the *exclusiveness* and *fixation* of the perversion that we are most generally justified in diagnosing it as a pathological symptom.

(Mental Participation in the Perversions)

It is perhaps in the case of the most repellent perversions that we must acknowledge the most generous psychical participation in the transformation of the sexual drive. Here a mental task is being performed which, despite its grim consequences, we are obliged to see as an idealization of the drive. It may be that the omnipotence of love is nowhere more strongly apparent than in these deviations. Everywhere in sexuality, the highest and the lowest are most profoundly attached to one another ('from heaven through the world to hell' [*Faust*]).

(Two Results)

In the course of our study of perversions we have come to understand that the sexual drive has to struggle against certain mental forces which act as resistances, shame and disgust appearing most clearly among them. We may suppose that these forces are involved in keeping the drive within what may be seen as normal bounds, and if they have developed in the individual before the sexual drive has reached its full strength, it was probably they that suggested the direction of its development.[28]

We have also observed that some of the perversions investigated can only be understood where a number of motives coincide. If they permit analysis – or dissection – they must be composite in nature. We may take this as a sign that the sexual drive itself is perhaps not something simple, but is rather assembled out of components that come apart again in the perversions. If this is so, clinical observation has brought our attention to *fusions* that have lost their manifestation in uniform normal behaviour.[29]

4) The Sexual Drive in Neurotics

(Psychoanalysis)

One important contribution to our knowledge of the sexual drive in people who are at least close to normality is derived from a source that is only accessible in one particular way. There is only one means of forming thorough and reliable conclusions abut the sexual life of so-called psychoneurotics (hysteria, compulsive neurosis, wrongly called neurasthenia, certainly also dementia praecox, paranoia), and that is by subjecting them to psychoanalytical investigation, using the healing process employed by J. Breuer and myself in 1893, which we then called 'cathartic'.

I should first explain, or rather repeat from other publications, that these psychoneuroses, as far as my experiences extend, are based on sexual drive-forces. I do not mean to say by this that the energy of the sexual drive contributes to the forces that maintain the pathological manifestations (the symptoms), but I wish expressly to stress that this contribution is the only constant energy source for neurosis, and the most important one. Consequently, the sexual life of the people in question is expressed exclusively, predominantly or only partially in these symptoms. The symptoms are, as I have said elsewhere, the patient's sexual activity. My proof for this claim has lain in a growing number of psychoanalyses of hysterics and others suffering from nervous disorders. I have given a detailed account of the results of these elsewhere and shall continue to do so.[30]

Psychoanalysis removes the symptoms of hysterics on the basis that they are substitutes – transcriptions, we might say – for a series of affect-laden mental processes, desires and strivings which, as the result of a particular psychical process (*repression*), have been denied the possibility of fulfilment in psychical activity that is capable of reaching consciousness. Hence these thought-formations, retained in a state of unconsciousness, strive for an expression appropriate to their affective value, a *discharge*, and find this in hysteria through the process of *conversion* to somatic phenomena – the hysterical symptoms. If a particular technique is skilfully employed to transform the symptoms back into conscious, emotionally invested ideas, we are in a position to learn something very precise about the nature and ancestry of these previously unconscious psychical formations.

(Results of Psychoanalysis)

Thus we have learned that symptoms are substitutes for strivings which draw their power from the source of the sexual drive. This fully accords with what we know of the character of hysterics – taken here as a model for all psychoneurotics – before they fall ill, and with what we know of the causes of their illness. The hysterical character exhibits a degree of *sexual repression* beyond that which we may consider normal, an intensification of those resistances to the sexual drive known to us as shame, disgust and morality, and an almost instinctive flight from intellectual preoccupation with the problem of sex, which in pronounced cases successfully preserves complete sexual ignorance into the age of sexual maturity.[31]

In many cases this character trait, essential to hysteria, is concealed from the untrained observer by the presence of the second constitutional factor involved in hysteria: the overwhelming formation of the sexual drive. Only psychological analysis can reveal this in every case, and solve the mystery of hysteria, with all its inconsistencies, by establishing the pair of opposites consisting of an excessive sexual need and an exaggerated aversion to sex.

The occasion for illness arises in the person with a predisposition to hysteria when, because of that person's own developing maturity or the external conditions of their life, they face real and serious sexual demands. Between the compulsions of the drive and the resistance of sexual refusal, the person then finds the solution of illness. It does not resolve the conflict, but seeks to elude it by transforming libidinal strivings into symptoms. It is only apparently exceptional if a hysterical person, a man, for example, falls ill under the influence of a banal emotion, a conflict without sexual interest at its centre. In all cases, psychoanalysis is then able to demonstrate that it is the sexual component of the conflict that has made the illness possible by removing the mental processes from their normal execution.

(Neurosis and Perversion)

Many objections to these findings are probably explained by the fact that sexuality, from which I deduce the psychoneurotic symptoms, is equated with the normal sexual drive. But psychoanalysis goes further than that. It shows that symptoms do not arise only at the expense of the so-called normal sexual drive (at least not exclusively or predominantly), but represent the converted expression of drives which would be described as *perverse* (in the broadest sense) if they could be expressed in fantasy intentions and actions undistracted by consciousness. The symptoms are thus formed partly at the expense of abnormal sexuality; *neurosis is, we might say, the negative of perversion.*[32]

The sexual drive of psychoneurotics exhibits all the deviations that we have studied as variations of the normal, and expressions of the pathological, sexual life.

a) In the unconscious mental life of all neurotics (without exception) we will find impulses of inversion, and the fixation of the libido on people of the same sex. The significance of this factor for an understanding of the illness cannot be properly assessed without deeper discussion. I can only assure the reader that the unconscious tendency towards inversion is never absent, and in particular that it provides great help in explaining male hysteria.[33]

b) Among psychoneurotics, all tendencies to anatomical transgressions are demonstrably present in the unconscious and in the formation of symptoms. Particularly frequent and intense among them are those that assign the role of the genitals to the mucous membrane of the mouth and the anus.

c) The partial drives play quite a prominent role in forming the symptoms of psychoneuroses. Mostly apparent in pairs of opposites, we have encountered them introducing new sexual goals, the drive to the love of looking and exhibitionism, and the drive to cruelty in both active and passive formations. The contribution of the latter is indispensable for an understanding of the presence of *suffering* in the symptoms, and in almost every case it controls part of the patient's social behaviour. Through this link between cruelty and the libido, love is also transformed into hatred, and tender impulses into hostile ones. This is entirely characteristic of a whole series of neurotic cases, indeed, it would appear, of paranoia in general.

Interest in these results is only heightened by certain special facts.

α) Where a drive of this kind is discovered in the unconscious, and is capable of pairing with an opposite, in almost every case the opposite can be shown to take effect as well. Each 'active' perversion is thus accompanied here by its passive counterpart: someone who is unconsciously an exhibitionist is also and at the same time a voyeur, and in anyone suffering the consequences of the repression of sadistic impulses we will encounter an additional influx of symptoms drawing on the sources of the tendency towards masochism. The complete agreement with what we have discovered about the corresponding 'positive' perversions is most worthy of note. In our understanding of the illness, however, one or the other of the opposing inclinations plays the predominant role.

β) In a more pronounced case of psychoneurosis we only rarely encounter one of these perverse drives on its own. More generally we find a larger number of these and usually traces of all of them; however, the individual drive is, in its intensity, independent of the formation of the others. Here, too, the study of positive perversions provides us with a precise counterpart.

5) *Partial Drives and Erogenous Zones*

Considering all that we have learned from our investigation of the positive and negative perversions, it seems reasonable to trace these back to a series of 'partial drives'. These are not primary, but they do permit further interpretation. At first the word 'drive' suggests nothing but the psychical representation of a continuously flowing, internal somatic source of stimuli, in contrast to 'stimulus', which is produced by individual external excitements. 'Drive' is thus one of the terms that separate the mental from the physical. The simplest and most obvious assumption about the nature of drives would be that they have no inherent quality of their own, and only come into consideration in so far as they give work to the mental life. What distinguishes the drives from one another and gives them specific qualities is their relationship to their somatic *sources* and their *goals*. The source of the drive is a process of excitement in an organ, and the immediate goal of the drive lies in the removal of that organic stimulus.[34]

A further provisional assumption in drive theory, and one which we are unable to escape, tells us that the physical organs provide two kinds of excitement, based in differences that are chemical in nature. One of these kinds of excitement we describe as specifically sexual, and the organ in question as the *'erogenous zone'* of the partial drive that issues from it.[35]

In the perverse tendencies which place a sexual significance upon the oral cavity and the anal orifice, the role of the erogenous zone is immediately clear. In all respects it behaves like a piece of the sexual apparatus. In hysteria, these body parts and their tracts of mucous membrane similarly become the site of new sensations and changes in innervation – indeed of processes that can be compared to penile erection – just as the genitals themselves do in response to the stimuli of normal sexual processes.

The significance of the erogenous zones as secondary apparatuses and surrogates for the genitals becomes most clearly apparent in the case of psychoneuroses, although this is not to claim that it is any less important for other kinds of illness. It is only less discernible here because in these illnesses (compulsive neurosis, paranoia) the symptoms are formed in regions of the mental apparatus which lie further from the individual centres responsible for physical control. In compulsive neurosis, the significance of the impulses that create new sexual goals, and which appear independent of erogenous zones, is the more striking. But with the love of looking and exhibitionism the eye corresponds to an erogenous zone, in the case of the pain and cruelty component of the sexual drive it is the skin that assumes the same role, having at particular points in the body become differentiated into sensual organs and modified into mucous membranes: the erogenous zone κατ' ἐξοχήν [*par excellence*].[36]

6) Explanation of the Apparent Predominance of Perverse Sexuality in Psychoneuroses

As a result of the above discussions, the sexuality of psychoneurotics may have been shown in a false light. It has come to appear as though psychoneurotics were brought, by their predisposition, very close to perversion in their sexual behaviour, and conversely removed equally far from normality. Now it may very well be that the constitutional predisposition of these patients, aside from an excessive degree of sexual repression and an overwhelmingly strong sexual drive, contains among other things an unusual tendency towards perversion in the broadest sense. However, the examination of less severe cases shows that we need not necessarily make this assumption, or at least that in our assessment of the pathological effects there is another factor moving in the opposite direction. Among most psychoneurotics, the illness only appears after puberty in the face of the requirements of normal sexual life. It is particularly at the latter that repression is directed. Or else later illnesses are generated when the libido cannot be satisfied in the normal way. In both cases the libido behaves like a stream the main bed of which is moved to a different place; it fills the collateral paths that might previously have been empty. In this way the inclination towards perversion among psychoneurotics, apparently so great (although negative), may also be collaterally conditioned, but must be collaterally intensified. The fact is that sexual repression as an internal element must be categorized along with those external elements such as restrictions on freedom, lack of access to the normal sexual object, dangers involved in the normal sexual act and so on, which create perversions in individuals who might otherwise have remained normal.

The situation may differ between different individual cases of neurosis: in one, the innate level of the inclination towards perversion may be made important, and in another its collateral intensification by the diversion of the libido from the normal sexual goal and sexual object. It would be unfair to construct an opposition in which a relationship of co-operation actually prevails. The greatest accomplishments of neurosis will always occur when constitution and experience co-operate in the same direction. A marked constitution, for example, will be able to manage without support from the impressions of life, while a substantial shock in life might bring the neurosis into being even in the case of an average constitution. These views, incidentally, apply equally to the aetiological significance of the innate and to accidental experience in other areas.

If one prefers to assume that a particularly well-developed tendency towards perversions is one of the peculiarities of the psychoneurotic constitution, one has a greater chance, depending on the innate preponderance of one erogenous zone or another, of differentiating between a great variety of such constitutions in one or other of the partial drives. The question of whether the perverse predisposition has a particular relationship to the choice of the form of illness has, like so much else in this field, not yet been investigated.

7) Reference to the Infantilism of Sexuality

By demonstrating the part played by perverse impulses in the formation of symptoms in psychoneuroses, we have increased the number of people who would count as perverts to a quite extraordinary level. Not only do neurotics themselves represent a very numerous class of people: it should also be borne in mind that all forms of neurosis shade off in uninterrupted series to health; Moebius was, after all, justified in saying: we are all a little hysterical. Consequently we are forced by the extraordinary distribution of perversions to assume that even the predisposition towards perversions must not be something rare and special but is part of the constitution that is considered normal.

We have heard that there is some contention about whether the perversions derive from innate conditions or arise as a result of chance experiences, as Binet assumed in the case of fetishism. Now we are presented with the decision that there is something innate underlying perversions, but that it is something *innate in everyone*, since a predisposition may vary in intensity, and waits to be brought to the fore by the influences of life. What is at issue are the innate roots of the sexual drive, which in many cases develop into the true vehicles of sexual activity (perversions), and in others are insufficiently suppressed (repression) so that they are indirectly able to draw to themselves a considerable share of sexual energy as symptoms of illness, while in the most favourable cases which fall between these two extremes, they bring about a so-called normal sex life by means of effective restriction and other forms of modification.

But we shall also note that the hypothetical constitution, containing the seeds of all perversions, will only be apparent in children, even if all drives appear only at modest intensities in the child. If we are becoming aware of the formula that the sexuality of neurotics has remained in an infantile state, or else has been returned to that state, our interest will turn towards the sexual lives of children, and we will want to pursue the interplay of those influences that dominate the developmental process of child sexuality to its outcome in perversion, neurosis or a normal sex life.

Notes

1. The data contained in the first essay are drawn from the well-known publications of Krafft-Ebing, Moll, Moebius, Havelock Ellis, von Schrenk-Notzing, Löwenfeld, Eulenburg, I. Bloch, M. Hirschfeld and the works in the *Jahrbuch für sexuelle Zwischenstufen*, edited by the latter. As these publications also list the rest of the literature on the subject, I have been able to spare myself detailed references. The insights gained from the psychoanalytic investigation of inverts are based on communications from I. Sadger, and on my own experience.

2. The only appropriate word in the German language, '*Lust*', is unfortunately too ambiguous and refers both to the feeling of the need and the feeling of its satisfaction.

3. For these difficulties and attempts to establish the proportionate number of inverts, cf. the work of M. Hirschfeld in the *Jahrbuch für sexuelle Zwischenstufen*, 1904.

4. This kind of resistance against the compulsion towards inversion might provide the conditions which would make it possible to exert an influence through suggestive treatment or psychoanalysis.

5. It has been rightly suggested from several quarters that the autobiographical data of inverts concerning the appearance of the tendency to inversion over time are unreliable, since they might have repressed from memory the proof of their heterosexual feelings. Psychoanalysis has confirmed this suspicion in those cases of inversion to which it has had access; it has crucially modified their anamnesis by filling in their childhood amnesia.

6. Moebius ('Über Entartung' ['On Degeneracy'], *Grenzfragen des Nerven- und Seelenlebens*, No. III, 1900) confirms how circumspect we should be about diagnosing degeneracy, and how little practical significance there is in such a diagnosis: 'If we survey the wide range of degeneracy that has been highlighted here, we can see without further ado that there is little value in diagnosing degeneracy at all.'

7. To be fair to the advocates of 'uranism', we must observe that some of the most eminent men of whom we are aware have been inverts, perhaps even absolute inverts.

8. In the understanding of inversion, pathological viewpoints have made

way for anthropological ones. That change is down to I. Bloch (*Beiträge zur Ätiologie der Psychopathia sexualis* [*Contributions to the Aetiology of Psychopathia sexualis*], 2 parts, 1902–3). The same author has also emphatically demonstrated the fact of inversion in the ancient civilizations.

9. Compare the last detailed accounts of somatic hermaphroditism: Taruffi, *Hermaphroditismus und Zeugungunfähigkeit* [*Hermaphroditism and Infertility*], German edition by R. Teuscher, 1903, and the works of Neugebauer in several volumes of the *Jahrbuch für sexuelle Zwischenstufen*.

10. J. Halban, 'Die Entstehung der Geschlechtscharaktere' ['The Origins of the Sexual Characteristics'], *Archiv für Gynäkologie*, vol. 70, 1903. This work also contains a bibliography on the subject.

11. The first writer to introduce bisexuality as an explanation of inversion is (according to an account of the literature in the sixth volume of the *Jahrbuch für sexuelle Zwischenstufen*) thought to have been E. Gley, who published an essay ('Les aberrations de l'instinct sexuel' ('The Aberrations of the Sexual Instinct') as early as January 1884 in *La Revue philosophique*. It is, incidentally, remarkable that the majority of authors who trace inversion back to bisexuality stress this element not only for inverts but also for all those who have turned out normally, and consequently see inversion as the result of a developmental disorder. Thus, one of the earliest of these, Chevalier (*Inversion sexuelle* [*Sexual Inversion*], 1893). Krafft-Ebing ('Zur Erklärung der konträren Sexualempfindung' ['On the Explanation of Contrary Sexual Sensation'], *Jahrbücher für Psychiatrie und Neurologie*, vol. 13) speaks of an abundance of observations 'that reveal at least the virtual continuing existence of this second centre (of the subordinate sex)'. One Dr Arduin ('Die Frauenfrage und die sexuellen Zwischenstufen' ['The Question of Women and the Intermediate Sexual Stages']) claims, in the second volume of the *Jahrbuch für sexuelle Zwischenstufen*, 1900: 'that in each person male and female elements are present (cf. this journal, vol. 1, 1899: 'The objective diagnosis of homosexuality' by Dr M. Hirschfeld, pp. 8–9 ff.), but – as a function of their membership of a sex – some are disproportionately more highly developed than others, where we are dealing with heterosexual people . . .' – For G. Herman ('Genesis, das Gesetz der Zeugung' ['Genesis, the Law of Procreation'], vol. 5, *Libido und Mania*, 1903) it is clear 'that every woman contains male germ-cells and properties, and every man female ones' etc. – in 1906 W. Fliess ('Der Ablauf des Lebens' ['The Course of Life']) claimed paternity of the idea of bisexuality (in the sense of *twofold sexuality*). In non-specialist circles, the positing of the idea of male bisexuality is considered to be one of the achievements of the philosopher O. Weininger, prematurely deceased, who made this idea the basis of a rather rashly written book (*Geschlecht und Charakter* [*Sex and Character*], Vienna, 1903). The above references may show how little foundation there is for this claim.

12. While it may be the case that psychoanalysis has so far provided no complete explanation of the origin of inversion, it has none the less revealed the psychical mechanism through which it arises, and considerably enriched the ways in which the questions relating to it are framed. In all the cases we have examined we have established that during early childhood future inverts pass through a phase of very intense but short-lived fixation on a woman (usually the mother). Once this has been overcome they identify with the woman and take themselves as their own sexual object; that is, narcissism leads them to seek out young men and men similar to themselves, whom they wish to love as their mother loved them. In addition, we have very often found that supposed inverts were by no means insensitive to the charms of women, but that they continually transferred the excitement provoked by women to a masculine object. Thus, throughout their whole lives, they repeated the mechanism through which their inversion had come about. Their compulsive striving after men proved to be determined by their ceaseless flight from women.

Psychoanalytic research most resolutely resists any efforts to set homosexuals apart from other people as a special group. By studying instances of sexual excitement other than those manifestly disclosed, it learns that all people are capable of same-sex object-choices, and that they have also made these choices in the unconscious. Indeed, libidinal emotional attachments to people of the same sex do not play a lesser role as factors in normal life, and play a greater role as motors of illness than do similar attachments to members of the opposite sex. In fact, where psychoanalysis is concerned, the independence of the object-choice from the sex of the object, the equally free availability of male and female objects which we may observe in childhood, in primitive conditions and in prehistoric times, seems to be the original basis from which both the normal and the inverted type are forced, by limitations in either direction, to develop. In psychoanalytical terms, then, men's exclusive sexual interest in women is a problem that requires explanation, and not something natural based on a fundamental chemical attraction. The decision concerning definitive sexual behaviour occurs only after puberty, and is the result of a series of factors which are not yet fully understood, but which are partly constitutional and partly accidental in nature. Certainly individual factors among these may appear so overwhelming that they influence the result in their own direction. Generally, though, the multiplicity of defining elements is reflected in the diversity of outcomes in the person's manifest sexual behaviour. Among inverted types we can confirm the predominance of archaic constitutions and primitive psychical mechanisms. The validity granted to the *narcissistic object-choice* and the *preservation* of the erotic significance of the *anal zone* appear to be their most essential characteristics. But nothing is to be gained by separating off the most extreme types of inversion from the others on the basis of such constitutional qualities. What appears to be the satisfactory basis for the explanation of these types can equally be demonstrated, albeit to a lesser degree of intensity, in the constitution of intermediary types and among those who are manifestly normal. Differences in the results may be qualitative in nature: analysis shows that differences in determining factors are always quantitative. Among the accidental influences on object-choice we have found failure (sexual intimidation in early life) to be noteworthy, and we have also become aware that the presence of both parents plays an important part. The loss of a strong father in childhood can often encourage inversion. Finally, it is important that the inversion of the sexual object should be most rigidly distinguished in conceptual terms from the mixture of the sexual characteristics. A certain degree of independence is also unmistakable in this relationship.

In an essay: 'On the Nosology of Male Homosexuality (Homoeroticism)' (*Internationale Zeitschrift für Psychoanalyse*, II, 1914) Ferenczi presents a series of significant points of view on the question of inversion. Ferenczi rightly objects that under the heading of 'homosexuality', which he wishes to replace with the better word 'homoeroticism', a number of very different conditions, of unequal status in both organic and psychical terms, are bundled together because they share the symptom of inversion. He calls for a sharp distinction at least between the two types of the *subject-homoeroticist*, who feels and behaves like a woman, and the *object-homoeroticist*, who is entirely masculine and has merely swapped the female object for an object of the same sex. He recognizes the former as the correct 'sexual intermediate stage' in the sense used by Magnus Hirschfeld, and the second he describes – less happily – as a compulsive neurotic. Resistance to the tendency towards inversion as well as the possibility of psychical influence are only held to be relevant in the case of the object-homoeroticist. Further, having acknowledged these two types, we might add that in many people a degree of subject-homoeroticism is found mixed with a proportion of object-homoeroticism.

Over the past few years works by biologists, chief among these the work of Eugen Steinach, have cast a clear light on the organic conditions of homoeroticism and of sexual characteristics in general.

The experimental procedure of castration, with the subsequent implanting of gonads of the opposite sex, has been successfully employed in various species of mammal to transform males into females and vice versa. The transformation more or less completely affected the somatic sexual characteristics and psychosexual behaviour (subject- and object-eroticism). The bearer of this sex-defining power is not seen as that part of the gonad that forms the sex cells, but the so-called interstitial tissue of the organ (the 'puberty gland').

In one case, sexual redefinition also occurred in a man who had lost his testicles through tubercular illness. In his sexual life he had adopted the feminine role as a passive homosexual, and showed very clearly pronounced secondary female characteristics (in body hair, growth of beard, accretions of fat on the breasts and hips). After the implantation of a cryptorchic human testicle this man began to act in a masculine way, and to direct his libido towards women in the normal manner. The somatic female characteristics vanished at the same time. (A. Lipschütz, *Die Pubertätsdrüse und ihre Wirkungen* [*The Puberty Gland and its Effects*], Bern, 1919.)

There would be no justification in claiming that these fine experiments establish a new foundation for the theory of inversion, or rashly expecting them to provide a path, in effect, to the general 'cure' of homosexuality. W. Fliess has rightly stressed that these experiments and what has been learned from them do not devalue the theory of the universal bisexual predisposition of the higher animals. Rather, it seems likely to us that further investigations of this kind will produce a direct confirmation of the bisexual hypothesis.

13. The most profound difference between love in the ancient world and in our own probably lies in the fact that antiquity placed the emphasis on the drive itself, while we transfer it to the object of the drive. The ancients celebrated the drive and were prepared to use it in the ennoblement even of an inferior object, while we think little of the activity of the drive as such, only excusing it through the merits of the object.

14. At this point I cannot help recalling the credulous submissiveness of people under hypnosis to their hypnotist, which suggests to me that the essence of hypnosis should be seen as the unconscious fixation of the libido upon the person of the hypnotist (via the masochistic components of the sexual drive) – S. Ferenczi has linked this characteristic of suggestibility to the 'parent complex' (*Jahrbuch für psychoanalytische und psychopathologische Forschungen*, I, 1909).

15. At the same time it should be observed that sexual over-valuation does not accompany all mechanisms of object-choice, and that we will later encounter another, more direct explanation for the sexual role of the other parts of the body. The element of the 'hunger for stimulation' used by

Hoche and I. Bloch to explain the spread of sexual interest to parts of the body other than the genitals does not seem to me to merit this significance. From the outset, the various changes in the libido behave towards one another like communicating tubes, and the phenomenon of collateral current must be taken into account.

16. In typical cases the woman fails to demonstrate a 'sexual over-valuation' of the man, but hardly ever does the same with the child to whom she has given birth.

17. This weakness could be said to be the prerequisite for the constitution. Psychoanalysis has identified as an accidental cause premature sexual intimidation, which drives the subject away from the normal sexual goal and towards a substitute for it.

18. Deeper psychoanalytic investigation has led to a justified criticism of Binet's claim. The content of all observations on this subject is an initial encounter with the fetish, in which it already appears to be in possession of sexual interest, although it is impossible to tell from the surrounding circumstances how it came into that possession. All of these 'premature' sexual impressions also occur in the period after the fifth or sixth year, despite the fact that psychoanalysis raises doubts about whether new pathological fixations can be formed at such a late stage. The true state of affairs is that behind the first memory of the appearance of the fetish there lies a submerged and forgotten phase of sexual development, represented by the fetish as a 'screen memory', the residues and imprint of which is therefore represented by the fetish. The transformation of this phase from early childhood into fetishism, and the choice of the fetish itself, are constitutionally determined.

19. Accordingly, the shoe or slipper becomes a symbol of the female genitals.

20. Psychoanalysis has filled one of the remaining gaps in the understanding of fetishism by referring to the significance of a coprophilic *olfactory pleasure* for the choice of the fetish. Feet and hair are strong-smelling objects that are elevated to fetishes after the sensation of smell, which is by now displeasing, has been abandoned. Another contribution to the explanation of the fetishistic preference for feet arises out of children's sexual theories (see below). The foot replaces the woman's sorely missed penis. In some cases of foot fetishism it has been shown that the drive to look, originally aimed at the genitals, which sought to approach its object from below, was obstructed along the way by prohibition and repression, and therefore clung on to the foot or the shoe as a fetish. In the process, the female genitals were, in accordance with the child's expectation, imagined as male genitals.

21. It seems to me to be beyond a doubt that the concept of the 'beautiful' has its roots in sexual excitement, and originally referred to that which was sexually stimulating ('*die Reize*' – 'charms' or 'stimuli'). Connected to this is the fact that while it is the sight of the genitals that provokes the strongest sexual excitement, we can never actually consider them 'beautiful'.

22. Analysis reveals this perversion – like most others – to have an unexpected diversity of motives and meanings. The exhibitionist compulsion, for example, is also highly dependent on the castration complex; it repeatedly stresses the integrity of the subject's own (male) genitals and repeats infantile satisfaction at the lack of the member in the female.

23. Later reflections based on certain assumptions concerning the structure of the mental apparatus and the different kinds of drive at work within it have largely modified my understanding of masochism. I have been led to acknowledge a *primary – erogenous* – masochism, out of which two later forms, *feminine* and *moral* masochism, develop. By turning the sadism that is unused in life against oneself, a *secondary* masochism arises, which is added to the primary version. (See 'Das ökonomische Problem des Masochismus' ['The Economic Problem of Masochism'], *Internationale Zeitschrift für Psychoanalyse*, 1924.)

24. On this subject, cf. later remarks concerning the pre-genital phases of sexual development in which this view is confirmed.

25. The research quoted assigns a special position, based on the source of the drive, to the pair of opposites, sadism and masochism, which separates them off from the series of the other 'perversions'.

26. Rather than supplying a great deal of evidence for this claim, I shall only quote one passage from Havelock Ellis: 'The investigation of histories of sadism and masochism, even those given by Krafft-Ebing (as indeed Colin Scott and Féré have already pointed out), constantly reveals traces of both groups of phenomena in the same individual.' [*Studies in the Psychology of Sex*, vol. III. *Analysis of the Sexual Impulse; Love and Pain; the Sexual Impulse in Women*, Philadelphia, 1913]

27. Cf. the later mention of 'ambivalence'.

28. We must, on the other hand, consider those forces which hamper sexual development – disgust, shame and morality – as historical imprints of the external inhibitions which the sexual drive has undergone in the psychogenesis of humanity. It has been observed that in the development of the individual these appear at the right moment as though spontaneously, in response to signals provided by education and external influence.

29. On the origin of perversions I shall observe, in anticipation, that we have cause to assume that before these became fixed – as in the case of fetishism – the beginnings of normal sexual development were present. In individual cases, analytical examination has been able to demonstrate that perversion is also the residue of a development towards the Oedipus complex; once this has been repressed, the strongest component of the sexual drive, in terms of the person's predisposition, has once again come to the fore.

30. My intention is to complement rather than diminish this statement in altering it to read as follows: Nervous symptoms are based on the demands of the libidinal drives, and also on the opposing demands of the ego, in reaction against them.

31. *Studien über Hysterie* [*Studies in Hysteria*], 1895, Vienna. J. Breuer says of the patient upon whom he first practised the cathartic method: 'The sexual element was astonishingly undeveloped in her.'

32. A few details aside, the clearly conscious fantasies of perverts, which can under favourable conditions be transformed into actions, the delusory anxieties of paranoiacs, projected upon others in a hostile sense, and the unconscious fantasies of hysterics that one can uncover behind their symptoms with the help of psychonalysis coincide in terms of their content.

33. Psychoneurosis is also very often associated with manifest inversion, and in the process the heterosexual current is completely suppressed. – It is only fair to point out that it was remarks made privately to me by W. Fliess in Berlin that first brought my attention to the inevitable universality of the tendency to inversion among psychoneurotics, after I had revealed this in individual cases. – This fact, which has not been given its due importance, should crucially influence all theories of homosexuality.

34. Drive theory is the most significant, but also the most incomplete piece of psychoanalytic theory. In my later works ('Jenseits des Lustprinzips' ['Beyond the Pleasure Principle'], 1921, 'Das Ich und das Es' ['The Ego and the Id'], 1920), I have developed further contributions to the theory of drives.

35. It is not easy to justify these hypotheses, drawn from the study of a particular class of neurotic illnesses, at this point. On the other hand, however, it is impossible to say anything conclusive about drives without mentioning these premises.

36. Here we must recall Moll's hypothesis, which breaks down the sexual drive into drives for contrectation and detumescence. Contrectation refers to a need for skin contact.

II

Infantile Sexuality

(Neglect of the Infantile)

Concerning the sexual drive, popular opinion is that it is absent in childhood and awakens during the period of life known as puberty. But this is not only a simple error, it is one that has severe consequences, since it is chiefly to this mistake that we owe our current ignorance of the basic relations of the sexual life. A thorough study of manifestations of sexuality in childhood would probably uncover the significant traits of the sexual drive for us, reveal its development and show its composition from various different sources.

It is remarkable that those authors who seek to explain the qualities and reactions of adult individuals should have paid so much more attention to the history supplied by the lives of the individual's ancestors, thus imputing so much more influence to heredity than to the other primeval history that lies within the life of the individual: childhood itself. One would have thought that the influence of this period of life would be easier to understand and would have a right to be considered before the influence of heredity.[1] Occasional notes are indeed found in the literature concerning early sexual activity among small children, erections, masturbation and even attempts at something like coitus, but only ever as exceptional events, as curiosities or alarming examples of precocious depravity. No author has, to my knowledge, clearly recognized the regular incidence of a sexual drive in childhood, and in writings about childhood development, so numerous these days, the chapter on 'sexual development' is usually passed over.[2]

(Infantile Amnesia)

I believe that the reason for this curious neglect lies partly in conventional caution, which the authors bear in mind because of their own upbringing, and partly in a psychical phenomenon which has not even been explained hitherto. I am referring to the curious *amnesia* which, in most people (not all!), casts a veil over their childhood up to the sixth or eighth year. It has never occurred to us to wonder about the fact of this amnesia; but we would have good reason to do so. For we are told that during those years, of which we later retain nothing but a few incomprehensible fragments of memory, we reacted vividly to impressions, we knew how to express pain and joy in a human way, we showed love, jealousy and other passions that moved us violently at the time, indeed we said things that adults noticed as good proof of insight and the beginning of a capacity for judgement. And as adults we ourselves know nothing of any of it. Why does our memory lag so far behind our other mental activities? We have reason to believe that no other period of our lives is more capable of reception and reproduction than the childhood years.[3]

On the other hand we must assume, or we may convince ourselves by the psychological examination of others, that the very impressions which we have forgotten have none the less left the deepest traces in our mental life, and have become defining factors in all of our subsequent development. It cannot, then, be a matter of a real decline in childhood impressions, but only an amnesia like that which we observe in relation to later experiences among neurotics, the essence of which consists merely in keeping them from the consciousness (repression). But what forces create this repression of childhood impressions? Anyone solving this mystery would also have explained hysterical amnesia.

None the less, we should not neglect to stress that the existence of infantile amnesia creates a new point of comparison between the mental state of the child and that of the psychoneurotic. We have encountered another such point before, when we were faced with the formula that the sexuality of psychoneurotics has preserved the child's point of view, or has been led back to it. Unless infantile amnesia itself can be linked to childhood sexual impulses!

It is, incidentally, more than a mere *jeu d'esprit* to link infantile and hysterical amnesia. The hysterical amnesia which serves the purpose of repression can only be explained if the individual already has a collection of memory traces that have withdrawn from conscious possession, and which now, through associative connection, draw to themselves the very thing that the forces of repression are working to repel from consciousness.[4] Without infantile amnesia, we might say, there would be no hysterical amnesia.

I now believe that it is because of infantile amnesia, which turns the childhood of each individual into what we might call a *prehistoric* past and screens from him the beginnings of his own sex life, that no importance is placed on childhood for the development of the sexual life in general. No single observer can fill the gap in our knowledge that is thus produced. As early as 1896 I stressed the importance of the childhood years for the origin of certain important phenomena dependent upon the sexual life, and since then I have ceaselessly stressed the important part played by the infantile element in sexuality.

1) The Period of Sexual Latency in Childhood and its Interruptions

The extraordinarily frequent findings of exceptional sexual impulses in childhood, supposedly in contravention of the rules, as well as the uncovering of previously unconscious childhood memories in neurotics, allow us to form more or less the following picture of sexual behaviour in childhood.[5]

It seems certain that the seeds of sexual impulses are already present in new-born babies, and that these continue to develop for a while before undergoing a progressive suppression, which can be interrupted by regular advances in sexual development and delayed by individual qualities. Nothing certain is known about the regularity and periodicity of this oscillating process of development. It appears, however, that the sexual lives of children are generally expressed around the third or fourth year in a form accessible to observation.[6]

(Sexual Inhibitions)

That period of total or partial latency sees the construction of mental forces which later appear as obstacles in the path of the sexual drive, and which will later narrow its direction much after the fashion of dams (disgust, the feeling of shame, the aesthetic and moral requirements of the ideal). Among children who have grown up in the civilized world one has a sense that the construction of these dams is the task of education, and certainly education does make a considerable contribution to it. In fact this development is organically conditioned and hereditarily fixed, and can sometimes be generated without any help from education. Education will remain within its assigned sphere if it limits itself to following the lines that have been sketched organically, and imprinting them rather more cleanly and deeply.

(Reaction Formation and Sublimation)

With what means are these constructions, so significant for later personal culture and normality, erected? Probably at the expense of the infantile sexual impulses themselves, whose influx has not stopped during this period of latency, but whose energy – either entirely or to a very large extent – is guided away from sexual application and led towards other purposes. Cultural historians seem to agree in their hypothesis that the distraction of sexual energies from sexual goals and their redirection towards new goals, a process that is called *sublimation*, represents a massive gain for all cultural achievements. We would therefore add that the same process is involved in the development of the individual, and shift its beginning to the childhood period of sexual latency.[7]

We might also hazard a hypothesis about the mechanism of this kind of sublimation: on the one hand the sexual impulses of these childhood years are unusable, since the functions of propagation are deferred, a fact that constitutes the chief characteristic of the latency period. On the other hand they are inherently perverse, which is to say that they emanate from the erogenous zones and are borne by drives which, in view of the direction in which the individual is developing, could only prompt sensations of displeasure. Consequently they arouse mental counter-forces (reaction impulses) which, in order effectively to suppress such displeasure, erect the psychical dams mentioned above: disgust, shame and morality.[8]

(Interruptions of the Latency Period)

Without deceiving ourselves about the hypothetical nature and inadequate clarity of our insights into the processes of childhood latency or deferral, we would like to return to reality to admit that such a use of infantile sexuality represents an ideal of education, from which the development of the individual generally deviates at some point and often to a considerable degree. Sometimes a sexual manifestation that has escaped sublimation breaks through, or else a sexual activity is preserved through the whole of the latency period up until the intensified irruption of the sexual drive in puberty. Educators, if they pay any attention to child sexuality at all, behave as though they shared our views on the formation of the moral defensive powers at the expense of sexuality, as though they knew that sexual activity makes the child impossible to educate, since they hunt out all the child's sexual manifestations, referring to them as 'vices', without being able to do much about them. But we have every reason to direct our interest towards these phenomena that are so feared by educators, because we expect that they may provide information about the original formation of the sexual drive.

2) The Manifestations of Infantile Sexuality

(Thumb-sucking)

For reasons that will later become clear, among infantile manifestations of sexuality we shall take as our model *thumb-sucking* (or rapturous sucking), to which the Hungarian paediatrician Lindner has devoted an excellent study.[9]

Thumb-sucking, which first appears in babyhood and may continue into the early years of adulthood or throughout the whole of a person's life, consists in a rhythmically repeated sucking contact with the mouth (the lips), and has nothing to do with the purpose of ingesting food. Part of the lip itself, the tongue, some other random piece of skin within reach – even the big toe – are taken as objects to be sucked. A clutching drive that makes its appearance at the same time is expressed in simultaneous tugging of the earlobes, and part of another person (usually their ear) can be used for a similar purpose. Passionate sucking consumes all the child's attention, leading either to sleep or even in some cases to a motor reaction in a kind of orgasm.[10] The rubbing of certain sensitive parts of the body, the breast, the outer genitals, is often combined with rapturous sucking. In this way many children move from sucking to masturbation.

Lindner himself clearly recognized the sexual nature of this activity, and stressed it without reservations. In the nursery, thumb-sucking is often equated with other sexual 'bad habits' on the child's part. Many paediatricians and neurologists have objected most vociferously to this conception of the activity, and to some extent their objection is doubtless based on a confusion between the 'sexual' and the 'genital'. This contradiction throws up the difficult and unavoidable question of the general characteristic that we are willing to acknowledge in expressions of the child's sexuality. In my view the context of the phenomena which we have come to understand through psychoanalytical examination justifies us in considering thumb-sucking as a form of sexual expression, and using it to study the essential traits of infantile sexual activity.[11]

(Auto-eroticism)

We are duty-bound to examine this example very thoroughly. Let us stress that the most striking characteristic of this sexual activity lies in the fact that the drive is not directed towards other people. It finds satisfaction in the child's own body; it is *auto-erotic*, to use a felicitous term coined by Havelock Ellis.[12]

It is also clear that the activity of the sucking child is determined by a quest for pleasure experienced in the past and now recalled. In the simplest case, the child finds satisfaction through rhythmic sucking on a place on the skin or mucous membrane. Neither is it difficult to guess on which occasions the child had its first experiences of this pleasure, which it now seeks to recover. The child's first and most important activity, sucking on the mother's breast (or its surrogate), must already have made the child familiar with this pleasure. We should say that the child's lips have acted as an *erogenous zone*, and the stimulus of the warm stream of milk was probably the source of the pleasurable sensation. The satisfaction of the erogenous zone was probably associated at first with the satisfaction of the need for nourishment. Sexual activity first attaches itself to one of the functions required for the maintenance of life, and only comes to depend upon it later on. If we see a child falling back into sleep, sated from the breast, with reddened cheeks and a blissful smile on its face, we cannot help thinking that this image also remains a definitive expression of sexual satisfaction in later life. Now the need for the repetition of sexual satisfaction is separated from the need to ingest food, a separation that is inevitable once the teeth appear and the food is not only sucked but chewed. The child does not use a foreign body for sucking, but instead uses a place on its own skin. This is more comfortable for the child, first because it makes it independent of the outside world, which it cannot yet control, and secondly because it enables it to create what we might call a second, albeit an inferior, erogenous zone. The inferiority of this second place explains why the child will later be led to seek a part of identical value, the lips of another person. ('A shame I can't kiss myself,' one might imagine the child saying.)

Not all children engage in thumb-sucking. We can assume that the children who do it are those in whom the erogenous significance of the labial zone is constitutionally intensified. If this significance is preserved, these children will, as adults, be connoisseurs of kissing, with a tendency towards perverse kissing or, in males, have a powerful impulse for drinking and smoking. But if repression intervenes, they will be disgusted by food, and produce hysterical vomiting. Because of the twofold nature of the labial zone, repression will affect the alimentary drive. Many of my female patients with eating difficulties, globus hystericus, lumps in the throat and vomiting, were energetic thumb-suckers in childhood.

In thumb-sucking, or 'rapturous sucking', we have already been able to observe the three essential characteristics of a manifestation of infantile sexuality. It *attaches itself* to one of three functions important to the preservation of life: it still has no sexual object, it is *auto-erotic* and its sexual goal is dominated by an *erogenous zone*. Let us say in advance that these characteristics also apply to most other activities of the infantile sexual drives.

3) *The Sexual Goal of Infantile Sexuality*

(Characteristics of Erogenous Zones)

From the example of thumb-sucking, we may deduce still more about what characterizes an erogenous zone. It is a place on the skin or mucous membrane where stimuli of a particular kind cause a sensation of pleasure of a particular quality. There is no doubt that the pleasure-creating stimuli are bound to certain conditions, and that we do not know what they are. The feature of rhythm must play some part in them, and the analogy with tickling comes immediately to mind. What seems less certain is whether we may describe the pleasure provoked by this stimulus as 'particular', and where in that particularity the sexual element resides. Psychology is still so much in the dark in matters of pleasure and displeasure that the most cautious hypothesis is the one most to be recommended. Perhaps we will later encounter reasons that seem to support the specific quality of the sensation of pleasure.

The erogenous property has an outstanding capacity to attach itself to individual parts of the body. There are predestined erogenous zones, as the example of thumb-sucking shows. The same example, however, also shows that any random place on the skin or mucous membrane can come to act as an erogenous zone, and must therefore have a certain aptitude to do so. The quality of the stimulus, then, has more to do with the production of the sensation of pleasure than the nature of the body part. The sucking child looks around his own body and chooses a part for pleasurable sucking, which then, through habit, becomes the preferred one; if the child happens to encounter one of the predestined parts (nipple, genitals), this will, of course, be the one chosen. The whole of the analogous capacity for displacement then reappears in the symptomatology of hysteria. Within this neurosis, repression has the greatest effect upon the actual genital zones, and these pass on their excitability to the other erogenous zones, normally disdained in adult life, which then behave wholly like genitals. In addition, though, any part of the body may be equipped with the excitability of the genitals, as the example of thumb-sucking reveals, and be elevated to the rank of erogenous zone. Erogenous and hysterogenous zones show the same characteristics.[13]

(Infantile Sexual Goal)

The sexual goal of the infantile drive lies in provoking satisfaction through the stimulation of the erogenous zone that has been chosen in one way or another. This satisfaction must first have been experienced if it is to create a need for repetition, and we may expect that nature has taken secure precautions not to leave this experience of satisfaction to chance.[14] We have already encountered the arrangement that accomplishes this goal in the labial zone; it is the simultaneous connection of this body part with the ingestion of food. We shall encounter other similar arrangements in the form of sources of sexuality. The state of the need for the repetition of satisfaction is revealed in two ways: in a curious feeling of tension that has more of the characteristics of displeasure, and in a *centrally originating* sensation of itching or stimulation projected on to the erogenous zone. So the sexual goal might also be formulated as follows: it is a matter of replacing the sensation of stimulation projected upon the erogenous zone with an external stimulus that abolishes the sensation of excitement by provoking the sensation of satisfaction. This external stimulus will generally consist in a manipulation that is analogous to sucking.

The fact that the need can also be aroused peripherally by a real change in the erogenous zone accords fully with our physiological knowledge. It only appears strange to us to some extent because it appears that, in order to be abolished, one stimulus seems to require a second applied to the same place.

4) Masturbatory Sexual Manifestations[15]

It can only be very encouraging for us to discover that there is not much more to learn about the child's sexual activity once we have come to understand the drive in relation to a single erogenous zone. The most distinct differences are to do with the process required for satisfaction, which, in the labial zone, consisted in sucking, and which must be replaced by other muscular actions according to the location and properties of the other zones.

(Activity of the Anal Zone)

Like the labial zone, the anal zone is suited by its location to act as intermediary for the *attachment* of sexuality to other bodily functions. We imagine the erogenous significance of this place in the body as having originally been very great. It is not without some astonishment, then, that we learn from psychoanalysis the transformations that sexual excitement normally undergoes, and how often it is that this zone preserves a considerable degree of genital excitability.[16] The digestive disorders that occur so frequently in childhood ensure that the zone is not without intensive stimuli. Intestinal catarrh at a very early age makes children 'nervous', in the common parlance; in later neurotic illness it has a determining effect on the symptomatic expression of the neurosis, placing at its disposal the full range of intestinal disorders. Taking into account the erogenous significance of the outlet zone of the intestinal canal, which it preserves at least in a modified form, we should not scoff at the influence of haemorrhoids, to which earlier forms of medicine attached such weight in the explanation of neurotic conditions.

Children who make use of the erogenous excitability of the anal zone reveal themselves by withholding their stools until these accumulate to the point of causing violent muscular contractions, and as they pass through the anus provide intense stimulation to the mucous membrane. In so doing they can create sensations of pleasure as well as of pain. One of the best signs of later eccentricity or nervousness is seen when a baby stubbornly refuses to evacuate its bowels when placed on the pot, in other words when the child's carer wishes it to do so, but chooses to perform the same function at its own whim. The child is, of course, not worried about soiling its bed; its sole concern is that it should not miss the subsidiary gain in pleasure through defecation. Educators are once again correct when they term as naughty those children who 'suspend' these tasks.

The content of the bowels, which, acting as an irritant on the surface of a sexually sensitive mucous membrane, behaves like the predecessor of another organ that is to become active only after childhood, has other kinds of important significance for the baby. It is clearly treated as a part of the child's own body, and represents its first 'gift': the child can use evacuation to express obedience, or retention to express defiance towards those around it. Starting out as a 'gift' it later acquires the significance of a 'child', which, according to one infantile sexual theory, is acquired by eating and born through the intestine.

The retention of the faecal mass – which is at first deliberate, with the intention of providing a quasi-masturbatory stimulus of the anal zone, or to be used in the child's relations with its educators – is incidentally one of the sources of the constipation that occurs so frequently among neuropaths. The whole significance of the anal zone is then reflected in the fact that we encounter very few neurotics who do not have their particular scatological customs, ceremonies and the like, which they keep assiduously secret.[17]

Actual masturbatory stimulation of the anal zone with the finger, prompted by itching that is either centrally determined or peripherally maintained, is by no means rare among older children.

(Activity of the Genital Zones)

Among the erogenous zones of the child's body there is one which may not play the primary role, and which cannot be the vehicle of the oldest sexual impulses, but which is destined for great things in future. In both the male and the female child it relates to urination (glans, clitoris), and in the former it is contained in a mucous sac, so that there can be no shortage of stimulations produced by secretions capable of prompting early sexual excitement. The sexual activities of this erogenous zone, which is among the real sexual parts, are the starting point for a sexual life that will later be 'normal'.

Because of its anatomical location, the secretions that flow over it, all the washing and rubbing involved in personal hygiene, and certain accidental excitements (such as the movement of intestinal worms in the case of girls), it is inevitable that the pleasurable sensation of which this place in the body is capable already becomes apparent to the child in infancy, and awakens a need for its repetition. If we consider the sum of these arrangements, and bear in mind that soiling something is bound to be similar in its effects to measures for keeping it clean, it is hard not to come to the conclusion that infantile masturbation, to which almost all individuals are prone, establishes the future primacy of this erogenous zone for sexual activity. The action that gets rid of the stimulus and releases satisfaction consists in a rubbing movement with the hand or in pressure, no doubt reflex in nature, either from the hand or as a result of the thighs being pressed together. The latter occurs far more frequently in girls. In boys, the preference given to the hand already suggests the important contribution that the drive to mastery will later supply towards male sexual activity.[18]

It can only clarify matters if I suggest that we can identify three phases of infantile masturbation. The first of these occurs in babyhood, the second in the brief blossoming of sexual activity around the fourth year, and only the third corresponds to the masturbation that takes place in puberty, and which is often the only phase to be acknowledged.

(The Second Phase of Childhood Masturbation)

Babyhood masturbation seems to disappear after a short time, but if it continues without interruption to puberty, it can lead to the establishment of the first major deviation from the development that a civilized human being should seek to attain. At some point in the childhood years after babyhood, and usually before the fourth year, the sexual drive of this genital zone appears to reawaken, and then to linger for a time until it becomes suppressed again, or else to continue without interruption. The possible forms of this are very diverse and can only be defined by more detailed examination of individual cases. But all the details of this *second* infantile sexual activity leave the deepest (unconscious) traces of impressions within the memory, determining the development of that person's character if he or she remains healthy, and the symptoms of neuroses of the person should he or she become ill after puberty.[19] In the latter case we find that this sexual period is forgotten, and the conscious memories producing it are displaced; – I have mentioned above that I would also wish to link infantile amnesia with this infantile sexual activity. With psychoanalytical research one can bring forgotten material to consciousness, and thus remove a compulsion emanating from the unconscious psychical material.

(Return of Early Infantile Masturbation)

The sexual excitement of early infancy returns during the years of childhood in the form of a tickling itch with a central source, which seeks satisfaction in masturbation, or in the form of a process similar to nocturnal emissions which, like the nocturnal emissions of adulthood, achieves satisfaction without the intervention of any kind of action. The latter case is more frequent among girls and during the second half of childhood. Its source is not entirely understandable, and it often – but not always – seems to be conditioned by a period of earlier active masturbation. The symptomatology of these sexual manifestations is poor; rather than the genital apparatus, which is still rudimentary, it is generally the urinary apparatus, acting as a kind of trustee, that presents the symptoms. Most illnesses attributed to the bladder during this period are sexual disorders; *enuresis nocturna*, where it does not represent an epileptic fit, corresponds to a nocturnal emission.

The reappearance of sexual activity is determined by internal and external causes which may, in cases of neurotic illness, be deduced from the configuration of symptoms and revealed with certainty by psychoanalytic inquiry. Below, we shall discuss internal causes; during this period, chance external causes assume a great and lasting significance. Chief among these is the influence of seduction, which prematurely treats the child as a sexual object and reveals to it, in circumstances that will inevitably make a great impression upon it, the satisfaction of the genital zones, which the child is then generally compelled to repeat through masturbation. This kind of influence can come from adults or even from other children; I cannot admit that I over-estimated its frequency or significance in my 1896 paper, 'On the Aetiology of Hysteria', although I was unaware at the time that some individuals who have remained normal may have had the same experiences, and therefore placed more stress on seduction than on the factors already present within the sexual constitution and development.[20] It is clear that seduction is not required for the awakening of the child's sexual life, and that such an awakening can also take place spontaneously, as a result of internal causes.

(Predisposition to Polymorphous Perversity)

It is telling that under the influence of seduction the child can become polymorphously perverse, and can be tempted into all kinds of possible transgression. This shows that the child already carries the appropriate aptitudes within its own predisposition; the implementation of these aptitudes encounters very little resistance, because depending on the age of the child the mental dams against sexual excess – shame, disgust and morality – have not yet been constructed or are still in the process of being formed. In this respect the child is not behaving any differently from the average uncultivated woman, in whom the same polymorphously perverse predisposition is maintained. Under ordinary conditions, such a woman can remain more or less sexually normal, while under the guidance of a skilled seducer she will develop a taste for all manner of perversions, and continue to call upon these in her sexual activity. Prostitutes exploit the same polymorphous, and consequently infantile predisposition in the exercise of their profession. Given the huge number of women working in prostitution, and those who must be said to possess aptitudes for prostitution without actually engaging in the profession, it becomes in the end impossible not to acknowledge that this same predisposition to all perversions is a universal and fundamentally human trait.

(Partial Drives)

In addition, the influence of seduction does not help to lift the veil on the origins of the sexual drive, but blurs our understanding of them by prematurely bringing the child into contact with the sexual object, for which the infantile sexual drive at first demonstrates no need. Nevertheless we must admit that the child's sexual life, however preponderant the dominance of the erogenous zones may be, also reveals certain components in which other people are considered, from the outset, as sexual objects. These include drives, relatively independent of the erogenous zones, to the love of looking and showing, and to cruelty, which only later emerge in intimate relation with genital life, but which already become apparent in childhood as autonomous tendencies, separate from erogenous sexual activity. Above all, the small child is without shame, and at certain periods in its early years shows an unambiguous pleasure in revealing its body, particularly emphasizing the sexual parts. The complement to this tendency, the curiosity to see other people's genitals, probably only becomes apparent rather later in childhood, when the obstacle of the feeling of shame has already become fairly well developed. Under the influence of seduction the perversion of voyeurism can become highly significant for the child's sexual life. But from my examinations of the childhoods of both healthy and neurotic patients I must conclude that the child's drive to look may appear as a spontaneous sexual expression. Small children, whose attention has been directed to their own genitals – usually by masturbation – generally discover the next step without external intervention, and develop a lively interest in the genitals of their playmates. As the opportunity to satisfy such curiosity is usually provided only by the satisfaction of the two excremental needs, such children become voyeurs, eager spectators at the urination and defecation of others. Once these inclinations have been repressed, the curiosity to see the genitals of others (either of one's own or the opposite sex) remains as a painful compulsion, which, in some cases of neurosis, then generates the most powerful drive force for the formation of symptoms.

The cruelty component of the child's sexual drive develops even more independently of other forms of sexuality related to the erogenous zones. Cruelty is close to the childish character in general, because the inhibition which makes the drive to mastery stop before it causes pain to the other – the capacity for pity – forms relatively late in life. No thorough psychological analysis of this drive has yet been satisfactorily carried out; we may assume that the impulse to cruelty emerges out of the drive to mastery, and appears in sexual life at a point when the genitals have not yet assumed the role they will later play. It then dominates a phase of sexual life which we will describe below as the pre-genital organization. Usually, children who distinguish themselves by showing particular cruelty to animals and playmates rightly raise the suspicion of intense and premature sexual activity in the erogenous zones, and in the case of simultaneous precocity of all sexual drives it would appear that erogenous sexual activity seems still to be primary. The suppression of inhibition in the form of pity means there is a danger that this connection of cruel drives with erogenous drives, formed in childhood, will prove impossible to break in later life.

Since Jean-Jacques Rousseau's *Confessions*, the painful stimulus of the skin of the buttocks has been known to all educators as one of the erogenous roots of the passive drive to cruelty. From this they have rightly deduced that corporal punishment, mostly applied to this part of the body, should be avoided in the case of those children whose libidos are susceptible to being forced into collateral channels by the later requirements of cultural education.[21]

5) *Infantile Sexual Research*

(The Drive to Knowledge)

The same period in which the child's sex life reaches its first blossoming, from the third to the fifth year, also sees the beginnings of the activity attributed to the drive to knowledge, or the research drive. The drive to knowledge can neither be counted among the elementary drive components nor placed exclusively under the heading of sexuality. On the one hand its action corresponds to a sublimated aspect of mastery, while on the other it works with energy derived from the love of looking. Its relations with sexual life, however, are particularly significant, for psychoanalysis has taught us that the drive to knowledge in children is drawn with an unsuspected precocity and an unexpected intensity to sexual problems, and indeed it may be awoken by those very problems.

(The Riddle of the Sphinx)

Practical rather than theoretical concerns set the child's research activity in motion. The threat, experienced or expected, to the child's conditions of life as a result of the arrival of a new child, and the fear associated with the loss of care and love associated with that event make the child thoughtful and alert. The first problem that the child deals with, in accordance with the story of the awakening of this drive, is not the question of sexual difference, but the riddle: Where do children come from? In a distortion that is easily rectified, this is also the riddle posed by the Theban Sphinx. On the contrary, the child accepts the fact of the two sexes without putting up any resistance or asking questions. It is obvious to the male child to assume that everyone he knows has genitals like his own, and impossible for him to reconcile the absence of such a thing with an idea of the genitals of others. The boy vigorously maintains this conviction, stubbornly defends it against the contradictions that observation will soon throw up, and abandons it only after serious internal struggles (castration complex). The substitute formations of the woman's lost penis play a large part in the formation of various perversions.[22]

(Castration Complex and Penis-envy)

The assumption that all people have a single form of (male) genitalia is the first of the notable and serious infantile sexual theories. It is of little use to the child that biological science is obliged to agree with his prejudice and acknowledge the female clitoris as a genuine substitute for the penis. The little girl does not succumb to similar errors when she sees the boy's differently shaped genitalia. She is immediately willing to acknowledge them, and succumbs to penis-envy, which culminates in the desire, significant in terms of its later effects, to be a boy herself.

(Theories of Birth)

Many people have clear memories of the intense interest they took, during the pre-pubertal period, in the question of where children come from. There were very different anatomical solutions: children come out of the breast, or are cut from the body, or else the navel opens up to let them through.[23] Outside of analysis one seldom recalls the research of early childhood into this subject; it has long since succumbed to repression, but its results were always similar. One gets children by eating something particular (as in a fairy tale) and they are then born from the bowel just as stools are passed. These childhood theories recall certain arrangements in the animal kingdom, particularly in the cloaca of sub-mammalian species.

(Sadistic Conception of Sexual Intercourse)

When children become spectators of sexual relations between adults at such a tender age – the adults being convinced that the child has no understanding of sexual matters – they cannot avoid seeing the sexual act as a kind of mistreatment or overpowering, in the sadistic sense. Psychoanalysis also teaches us that an infantile impression of this kind contributes considerably to the predisposition towards a later sadistic displacement of the sexual goal later in life. In addition, children are greatly preoccupied with the problem of what sexual intercourse or, as they understand it, marriage may consist in, and generally seek the solution to the mystery in a union accomplished by the agency of the functions of urination or defecation.

(The Typical Failure of Infantile Sexual Research)

Generally speaking, we may say of children's sexual theories that they are representations of the child's own sexual constitution and, despite their grotesque errors, they display a greater understanding of sexual processes than one would have expected of their creators. Children also perceive their mother's changes in pregnancy, and interpret them correctly; the fable of the stork is often told to an audience that responds with a profound but generally mute mistrust. But as two elements remain unknown to infantile sexual research, the role of the fertilizing semen and the existence of the female sexual orifice – the very points, incidentally, in which the infantile sexual organization still lags behind – the efforts of the infant researchers generally remain unproductive, and conclude in a renunciation that can often do lasting harm to the drive to knowledge. The sexual research of these early childhood years is always a solitary process; it signifies a first step towards the child's autonomous orientation in the world and significantly alienates the child from the people around him who previously enjoyed his complete trust.

6) Phases in the Development of Sexual Organization

So far we have stressed, among the characteristics of infantile sexual life, that it is significantly auto-erotic (it finds its object in the child's own body) and that overall its individual partial drives remain unconnected and independent of one another in their efforts to attain pleasure. The outcome of this development lies in the so-called normal sexual life of the adult, in which the acquisition of pleasure is placed at the service of the function of reproduction, and the partial drives, under the primacy of a single erogenous zone, have formed a solid organization in order to achieve the sexual goal with a sexual object other than one's own.

(Pre-genital Organizations)

The study, with the help of psychoanalysis, of the inhibitions and disorders within this development enables us to recognize the beginnings and the early stages of such an organization of the partial drives, which themselves produce a kind of sexual regime. These phases of sexual organization normally pass smoothly without being revealed through anything more than hints. Only in pathological cases are they activated and made identifiable to superficial observation.

Those organizations of sexual life, in which the genital zones have not yet attained their predominant role, we shall call *pre-genital*. So far we have encountered two of these, which resemble a regression to early animal states.

One first such pre-genital sexual organization is the *oral* or, if we prefer, the *cannibalistic*. Here, sexual activity is not yet separated from the ingestion of food, and opposites within it are not differentiated. The object of one activity is also that of the others, and the sexual goal consists in the *incorporation* of the object, the model for what will later have such a significant psychical part to play in the form of *identification*. One leftover of this fictitious organizational phase, imposed upon us by pathology, may be seen in sucking, in which sexual activity, freed from the activity of feeding, has abandoned the extraneous object in favour of an object situated in the child's own body.[24]

A second pre-genital phase is that of the *sadistic-anal* organization. Here the polar opposition running through the sexual life is already formed; the twin poles cannot yet be called *male* and *female*, however, but must be identified as *active* and *passive*. Activity is produced by the drive to mastery using the musculature of the body; above all it is the erogenous intestinal mucous membrane that presents itself as an organ with a passive sexual goal. Objects exist for both tendencies, but they are not identical. At the same time other partial drives are activated in an auto-erotic way. During this phase, then, sexual polarity and an extraneous object can already be observed. Organization and subordination to the function of reproduction are still absent.[25]

(Ambivalence)

This form of sexual organization can be maintained throughout a person's life, and can appropriate a large part of their sexual activity. The preponderance of sadism and the cloacal role of the anal zone give it a particularly archaic imprint. One of its other characteristics is the fact that in it pairs of opposite drives develop in an appreciably similar way, a phenomenon described by the felicitous term coined by Bleuler, *ambivalence*.

The hypothesis of pre-genital organizations of the sexual life is based on the analysis of neuroses, and its value can hardly be assessed without knowledge of them. We may expect that analytic efforts, as they progress, will provide us with more information about the construction and development of the normal sexual function.

To complete the picture of infantile sexual life we must add that an object-choice, analogous to that which we have suggested as being characteristic of the pubertal phase of development, is often or generally made during childhood, in such a way that all sexual efforts are directed towards a single person, with whom those efforts seek to attain their goals. This is, then, the closest approach to the definitive formation of sexual life after puberty that is possible during childhood. The only difference lies in the fact that the composition of the partial drives and their subordination to the primacy of the genitals has either not taken place at all during childhood, or has done so only very imperfectly. The establishment of this primacy in the service of reproduction is, therefore, the last phase that the sexual organization undergoes.[26]

(Dual-phase Object-choice)

It can be seen as a typical phenomenon that the object-choice occurs over two periods of time, in two phases. The first phase begins between the second and fifth years, and stagnates or is set back throughout the latency period; it is distinguished by the infantile nature of its sexual goals. The second phase begins with puberty and determines the definitive formation of sexual life.

The fact, essentially reduced to the effect of the latency period, that the object-choice occurs in two phases comes to have great significance for disturbances of that final outcome. The results of the infantile object-choice have consequences for the later period; either they have remained the same, or they may be revived during puberty. Because of the development of repression that occurs between the two phases, however, they prove to be unusable. Their sexual goals have been moderated, and they now represent what we might describe as the *affectionate* current of sexual life. Only psychoanalytical investigation is capable of demonstrating that this affection, veneration and respect masks the old sexual strivings, unusable now, of the infantile partial drives. The object-choice made in puberty must renounce the infantile objects, and start over again as a *sensual* current. Often enough, the failure of these two currents to coincide means that one of the ideals of sexual life, the unification of all desires in a single object, cannot be achieved.

7) Sources of Infantile Sexuality

In our attempt to trace the origins of the sexual drive, we have found so far that sexual excitement arises a) as the reproduction of a satisfaction experienced in the context of other organic processes; b) through the appropriate peripheral stimulation of the erogenous zones; c) as the expression of certain 'drives' whose origin we do not fully understand, such as the drive to look and the drive to cruelty. Psychoanalytic research, starting in a later period and extending back to childhood, and the observations of the child made simultaneously, now combine to show us still other regular sources of sexual stimulation. Observation of the child has the disadvantage of dealing with objects that can easily be understood, and psychoanalysis faces the obstacle that it cannot reach its conclusions except by making long detours. If the two methods are combined, however, they yield an adequate level of certain knowledge.

In our examination of the erogenous zones we have already discovered that these places on the skin are distinguished only by a special intensification of a kind of excitability which is present to a certain degree across the whole of the skin surface. So we will not be surprised to learn that certain kinds of general stimulation of the skin produce very clear erogenous effects. Among these we place particular emphasis on thermal stimuli; perhaps this may also contribute to our understanding of the therapeutic effect of warm baths.

(Mechanical Excitements)

To this we must also add the generation of sexual excitement by rhythmic mechanical agitation of the body. Here we can identify three kinds of stimulus acting respectively on the sensory apparatus of the vestibular nerves, on the skin and on the deep parts (muscles, joints). Because of the sensations of pleasure which result from this – it is worth stressing that for a considerable time we can use 'sexual excitement' and 'satisfaction' without distinction, and will be obliged to provide an explanation of this point later on – we are able to see proof of the pleasure generated by certain kinds of mechanical agitation of the body in the fact that children are so fond of games involving passive motion, such as rocking and being flown through the air, and incessantly demand that these actions be repeated. As everyone knows, rocking is regularly employed to put restless children to sleep.[27] The agitation produced by car journeys and later by train journeys has such a fascinating effect on older children that at some point in their lives all boys, at least, want to be engine-drivers and coachmen. They tend to take a mysterious interest, of extraordinary intensity, in everything to do with railways, and at the age of fantasy activity (shortly before puberty) to place them at the centre of a highly sexual symbolism. The compulsion to make such a connection between train travel and sexuality clearly derives from the pleasurable character of the sensations of motion. If repression, which turns many childhood preferences into their opposite, is afterwards added to this, the same people, once they are adolescents or adults, will react with nausea to rocking and swinging, will be exhausted when travelling by train or tend to suffer anxiety attacks during the journey, and protect themselves against any repetition of the painful experience with the help of *railway anxiety*.

To this we may add the fact – still not understood – that the coincidence of fear and mechanical shaking produces serious hysteriform traumatic neurosis. At the very least we may assume that these influences, which at low intensities become sources of sexual excitement, when they are excessively powerful produce a profound change in the sexual mechanism or chemistry.

(Muscle Activity)

It is well known that, in children, energetic and abundant muscle activity is a need from which they draw extraordinary pleasure. The question of whether that pleasure has anything to do with sexuality, whether it itself includes sexual satisfaction or can become an opportunity for sexual stimulation, may provide matter for critical consideration, which may also be used to contradict the earlier suggestion that the pleasure derived from sensations of passive motion is sexual in nature or sexually exciting. It is a fact, though, that many people say that they had their first sensations of excitement in their genitals while fighting or wrestling with their playmates, a situation which involves, aside from the general muscular exertion, abundant skin contact with one's opponent. The tendency towards muscular fighting with a particular person, as in later years towards verbal fighting ('Those who love one another, tease one another') is a sure sign that the object-choice is directed towards that person. We might recognize one of the roots of the sadistic drive in the fact that sexual excitement is encouraged by muscular activity. For many individuals the infantile connection between physical fighting and sexual excitement can be a determining factor in the later preferred direction of their sexual drive.[28]

(Affective Processes)

There is less doubt surrounding the child's other sources of sexual excitement. It is easy to establish, through simultaneous observation and subsequent examination, that all the more intense emotional processes, including the excitement associated with fear, encroach upon sexuality, and this can, incidentally, also contribute to our understanding of the pathogenic effect of emotions of this kind. In the case of the school pupil, the fear of being examined, the tension produced by a difficult piece of homework, can determine both the emergence of sexual manifestations and the pupil's relationship towards school, while in many cases such circumstances produce a feeling of stimulation which leads the child to touch its genitals, or a process resembling nocturnal emission with all its disturbing consequences. The behaviour of children in school, quite puzzling enough for their teachers already, deserves to be considered in relation to their budding sexuality. The sexually exciting effect of many inherently non-pleasurable emotions, such as fear, terror or shock, remains with many people throughout their adult lives, and probably explains why so many people pursue the opportunity for such sensations, although only if certain circumstances (belonging to an imaginary world, lectures, plays) temper the seriousness of the sensation of displeasure.

If we were correct in supposing that even intensely painful sensations produce the same erogenous effect, particularly when the pain is attenuated or kept at a distance by a subsidiary condition, then one of the roots of the sado-masochistic drive, whose diverse composition we are so slowly coming to understand, would lie in that correlation.[29]

(Intellectual Work)

Finally, it is impossible not to recognize that the concentration of attention upon an intellectual task and intellectual effort in general produces, in many adolescents and even adults, a concomitant sexual stimulation, which we should probably consider the sole justifiable basis for the view, otherwise so questionable, that nervous disorders derive from intellectual 'overwork'.

If, after these investigations and suggestions, which are neither exhaustive nor complete, we cast our eye over the sources of childhood sexual excitement, we may guess or recognize the following generalizations: things appear to combine in the broadest sense to set in motion the process of sexual excitement, the essence of which, it is true, has become most puzzling to us. Above all, this is achieved more or less directly by excitement of the sensitive surfaces – the skin and the sensory organs – and most directly by the effects of stimulation on certain places that are described as erogenous zones. In these sources of sexual excitement it is the quality of the stimuli that is most important, although the element of intensity (in the case of pain) is not completely irrelevant. But that aside, there are arrangements within the organism which mean that sexual excitement appears as a side-effect of many internal processes once the intensity of those processes exceeds certain quantitative boundaries. What we have called the partial drives of sexuality either derive directly from these internal sources of sexual stimulation, or are assembled from elements produced by those sources and by erogenous zones. It may be that nothing significant occurs within the organism that does not contribute to the excitement of the sexual drive.

I do not think it possible at present to give greater clarity and certainty to these general propositions, and I hold two elements responsible for this: first, the novelty of the whole way of seeing, and secondly, the fact that we know nothing about the essence of sexual excitement. None the less, I should like to make two further observations which promise to open up wider vistas.

(Different Sexual Constitutions)

a) Just as we saw, above, the possibility of establishing a multiplicity of innate sexual constitutions on the basis of differences in the development of the erogenous zones, we can now attempt to do this by taking into account the indirect sources of sexual excitement. We may assume that these sources flow into all individuals, but not equally strongly, and that in the privileged development of particular sources of sexual excitement an additional contribution will be made to the differentiation of the various sexual constitutions.[30]

(Reciprocal Paths of Influence)

b) If we abandon the figurative mode of expression that we have been using for such a long time, in which we spoke of the 'sources' of sexual excitement, we reach the idea that if paths of communication lead from other functions to sexuality, they must also be able to pass in the opposite direction. If, for example, the shared possession of the labial zone by two functions is a reason for the production of sexual satisfaction by the eating of food, the same factor also helps us to understand why it is that eating disorders arise when the erogenous functions of the shared zone are disturbed. If we know that concentration of the attention is capable of producing sexual excitement, we may easily suppose that, as the result of an effect occurring along the same path but in the opposite direction, the state of sexual excitement influences the availability of tractable attention. Much of the symptomatology of neuroses which I deduce from disorders of the sexual processes is manifested in disorders of the other, non-sexual bodily functions, and this previously incomprehensible effect becomes less puzzling once we see it as being merely the counterpart to the influences governing the production of sexual excitement.

But the same paths along which sexual disorders encroach upon the other bodily functions must also perform another major service in the healthy person. It is along these paths that the sexual drive-forces must pass if they are to reach goals other than sexual goals – what we term the sublimation of sexuality. In conclusion, we must admit that although these paths certainly exist, and although they may probably be travelled in both directions, very little that is certain is known about them.

Notes

1. Nor can we correctly appraise the proportion due to heredity before assessing the proportion that belongs to childhood.

2. Subsequently, the claim set down here seemed so daring even to me that I set about putting it to the test by going through the literature once again. As a result of this review, I left it unaltered. The scientific treatment of both physical and mental phenomena during childhood is in its earliest stages. One author, S. Bell ('A Preliminary Study of the Emotion of Love between the Sexes', *American Journal of Psychology*, XIII, 1902), says: 'I know of no scientist who has given a careful analysis of the emotion as it is seen in the adolescent.' Somatic sexual manifestations from the period before puberty have only attracted attention in the context of degenerative phenomena and as a sign of degeneration. – A chapter about the love-life of children is absent from all accounts of the psychology of this age that I have read, for example the well-known works of Preyer, Baldwin (*Die Entwicklung des Geistes beim Kinde und bei der Rasse* [*Mental Development in Children and in the Race*], 1895), Pérez (*L'enfant de 3–7 ans*, 1886), Strümpell (*Die pädagogische Pathologie* [*Pedagogical Pathology*], 1899), Karl Groos (*Das Seelenleben des Kindes* [*The Mental Life of the Child*], 1904), Th. Heller

(*Grundriss der Heilpädagogik* [*Outline of Medical Pedagogics*], 1904), Sully (*Studies of Childhood*, 1895) and others. The best impression of the contemporary situation in this field can be drawn from the journal *Die Kinderfehler* (from 1896 onwards). – But one reaches the conclusion that the existence of love in childhood is no longer in need of discovery. Pérez (loc. cit.) speaks up in its favour; in K. Gross (*Die Spiele der Menschen* [*The Games People Play*], 1899) it is mentioned as being generally known 'that some children are accessible to sexual impulses at an early age, and feel an urge for contact with the opposite sex' (p. 326); the earliest case of the appearance of sexual love impulses ('*sex-love*') in the series of observations by S. Bell concerned a child in the middle of its third year. On the same subject, compare Havelock Ellis, *Studies in the Psychology of Sex*, 1903, Appendix II.

Since the publication of Stanley Hall's extensive work (*Adolescence, its Psychology and its Relations to Physiology, Anthropology, Sociology, Sex, Crime, Religion and Education*, two volumes, New York, 1904) the above assessment of the literature of child sexuality need no longer prevail. – The recent book by A. Moll, *Das Sexualleben des Kindes* [*The Sexual Life of the Child*], Berlin, 1909, gives no cause for such a modification. On the other hand, see: Bleuler, 'Sexuelle Abnormitäten der Kinder' ['Sexual Abnormalities in Children'] (*Jahrbuch der schweizerischen Gesellschaft für Schulgesundheitspflege*, IX, 1908). A book by Frau Dr H. v. Hug-Hellmuth, *Aus dem Seelenleben des Kindes* [*From the Mental Life of the Child*, Leipzig and Vienna], 1913, has compensated since then for the neglected sexual factor.

3. I have attempted to solve one of the problems connected with the earliest childhood memories in my essay 'Über Deckerinnerungen' ['On Screen Memories'], (*Monatschrift für Psychiatrie und Neurologie*, VI, 1899) [cf. *The Psychopathology of Everyday Life*, Chapter IV].

4. The mechanism of repression cannot be understood if one takes into account only one of these two processes, which work in parallel. For the purposes of comparison, we might consider the way in which the tourist is helped to the tip of the great pyramid at Giza: he is pushed from one side and pulled from the other.

5. The latter material is rendered usable by the justified expectation that the childhood years of later neurotics do not deviate significantly in this respect from those who will later be healthy, but only in terms of intensity and clarity.

6. One possible anatomical analogy to my view of the behaviour of the child's sexual function might be provided by Bayer's discovery (*Deutsches Archiv für klinische Medizin*, vol. 73) that the internal sex organs (uterus)

of new-borns are generally larger than those of older children. However the view of this post-partum involution, also observed by Halban in other parts of the genital apparatus, has not been definitively established. According to Halban (*Zeitschrift für Geburtshilfe und Gynäkologie*, LIII, 1904) this retrogressive process comes to an end after a few weeks of life outside the womb. – Authors who consider the interstitial part of the gonad to be the sex-defining organ have been led by anatomical examinations to speak in turn of infantile sexuality and a period of sexual latency. I quote from Lipschütz's book mentioned on p. 150, note 12, writing of the puberty gland: 'We will come closer to the facts if we say that the maturity of the sexual characteristics which occurs in puberty is based only on a series of processes that accelerates, rapidly around this time, but which has begun much earlier – even, we believe, in the embryo.' (p. 168) – '*What has hitherto simply been described as puberty, is probably only a second major phase of puberty which begins around the middle of the second decade* . . . Childhood, calculated from birth to the start of the second major phase, could be described as the "*intermediate phase of puberty*".' (p. 170.) – This accord of anatomical findings with psychological observation, stressed in an essay by Ferenczi (*Internationale Zeitschrift für Psychoanalyse*, VI, 1920), is overturned by the statement that the '*first peak*' of the development of the sexual organ falls in the early embryonic period, while the childhood blossoming of sexual life should be shifted to the third and fourth year. There is, of course, no need for anatomical formation to be completely simultaneous with psychical development. The studies in question have been performed on the human gonad. Since animals do not have a latency period in the psychological sense, it would be very useful to know whether the anatomical findings on the basis of which the authors assume two peaks of sexual development can also be demonstrated in other higher animals.

7. I also borrow the term 'period of sexual latency' from W. Fliess.

8. In this case, the sublimation of sexual drives follows the path of reaction formation. In general, however, sublimation and reaction formation should not be separated conceptually and seen as two different processes. Sublimations can also occur through other, simpler mechanisms.

9. In *Jahrbuch für Kinderheilkunde*, N.F., XIV, 1879.

10. Here we first see something that will remain valid throughout the whole of life: the fact that sexual satisfaction is the best soporific. Most cases of nervous insomnia can be traced back to sexual dissatisfaction. It is well known that unscrupulous nannies put crying children to sleep by stroking their genitals.

11. In 1919, in issue 20 of the *Neurologisches Zentralblatt*, under the title

'Das Lutscherli', one Dr Galant published the confession of a young woman who had not given up this childhood activity and described the satisfaction she derived from sucking as completely analogous to sexual satisfaction, particularly from her beloved's kiss. 'Not all kisses are like a *Lutscherli*: no, no, far from it! You can't describe the lovely feeling that runs through your whole body when you suck. You're simply out of this world, you're quite contented and blissfully happy. It's a wonderful feeling; you require nothing but peace, peace that mustn't be interrupted. It's just inexpressibly beautiful: you feel no pain, no sorrow, you're transported to another world.'

12. However, H. Ellis defined the term 'auto-erotic' rather differently, in the sense of a stimulus that is not provoked from without but arises from within. For psychoanalysis, what is essential is not the genesis of the excitement but its relationship with an object.

13. Further considerations and the evaluation of other observations lead to the attribution of an erogenous quality to all body parts and internal organs. Cf. below, narcissism.

14. In biological discussions it is hardly possible to avoid using teleological ways of thinking, even when we know that in individual cases there is no guard against error.

15. Cf. the literature about masturbation – very abundant, but often confused in its views – for example Rohleder, *Die Masturbation*, 1899, and the 2nd volume of the *Diskussionen der Wiener Psychoanalytischen Vereinigung*, 'Die Onanie' ['Masturbation'], Wiesbaden, 1912.

16. Cf. the essays 'Charakter und Analerotik' ['Character and Anal Eroticism'] and 'Über Triebsumsetzungen insbesondere der Analerotik' ['On the Translation of Drives Especially in Anal Eroticism'] (*Gesammelte Werke*, vols. VII and X).

17. In a work that deepens our understanding of the significance of anal eroticism to an extraordinary degree ('"Anal" und "Sexual"', *Imago*, IV, 1916), Lou Andreas-Salomé has written that the history of the first prohibition which the child encounters, the prohibition on deriving pleasure from anal activity and its products, is influential upon the whole of its development. On this occasion the little creature must first become aware of an environment that is hostile to the impulses of its drive, learn to distinguish its own essence from this extraneous presence, and then carry out the first 'repression' of its opportunities for pleasure. From that point on the 'anal' remains the symbol for everything that is to be rejected, to be set apart from the rest of life. The clear distinction that will later have to be made, between anal and genital processes, encounters resistance in the close anatomical and functional analogies and relations between the two.

The genital apparatus remains a neighbour of the cloaca, 'and in woman is only sublet from it'.

18. Unusual techniques in the practice of masturbation in later years seem to relate to the influence of a prohibition on masturbation that has been overcome.

19. The question of why the sense of guilt in neurotics is almost always, as Bleuler recently acknowledged, connected with remembered masturbatory activity, usually from the time of puberty, still calls out for an exhaustive analytic explanation. The most general and effective factor in this conditionality must be that masturbation is the executive agency of the whole of infantile sexuality, and is for that reason empowered to take over the feeling of guilt attached to it.

20. In an appendix to his *Studies in the Psychology of Sex* (1903), Havelock Ellis lists a number of autobiographical accounts by individuals who were later predominantly normal, concerning their first sexual impulses in childhood and the causes of those impulses. These accounts suffer from one shortcoming, which is that they do not take into account the primeval past of sexual life that is screened by infantile amnesia and can only be completed by psychoanalysis with an individual who has become neurotic. But they are none the less valuable in more than one respect, and information of this kind has led me to those modifications of my aetiological assumptions which are mentioned in the text.

21. When I made the above claims about infantile sexuality in 1905, I based them to a large extent on the results of psychoanalytic studies of adults. At that time, direct observation of children could not be used to its full extent, and had only produced individual suggestions and valuable confirmations. Since then it has become possible, through the analysis of individual cases of nervous illness in early childhood, to gain a direct insight into infantile psycho-sexuality. It is gratifying to be able to point out that direct observation fully confirms the conclusions drawn from psychoanalysis and has thus provided good evidence for the dependability of this last method of research. – The 'Analysis of a Phobia in a Five-year-old Boy' (vol. VII of the *Gesammette Werke*) has also taught us much that is new, for which we would not have been prepared by psychoanalysis: for example, the fact that sexual symbolism – a representation of the sexual by non-sexual objects and relations – extends into the first years of possession of the power of language. In addition, my attention was drawn to a shortcoming in the account I have given above, which, in order to give a clear account, describes the conceptual separation of the two phases of *auto-eroticism* and *object-love* as a separation in time. But from the analyses quoted (and from the writings of Bell, see

above), we can tell that children at the age of three to five are capable of a very clear *object-choice*, accompanied by strong affects.

22. We may legitimately talk about a castration complex among women as well. Both male and female children form the theory that the woman originally had a penis which has been lost through castration. The conviction that the woman does not possess a penis often leaves a lasting contempt for the other sex in the male individual.

23. A great abundance of sexual theories is characteristic of these later years of childhood. Only a few examples of these are mentioned in the text.

24. As regards residues of this phase among adult neurotics, see the work of Abraham, 'Untersuchungen über die früheste prägenitale Entwicklungsstufe der Libido'. ['Studies in the Earliest Pre-Genital Stage of Libido Development'] (*Internationale Zeitschrift für Psychoanalyse*, IV, 1916). In a later work ('Versuch einer Entwicklungsgeschichte der Libido' ['Attempt at a History of the Development of the Libido'], 1924), Abraham has broken down both this oral and the later sadistic-anal phase into two subdivisions, characterized by a different attitude towards the object.

25. Abraham draws our attention (in the essay quoted above) to the fact that the anus develops out of the *primal mouth* of the embryonic predispositions, which appears to be a biological prototype for psychosexual development.

26. I later (1923) altered this account, to introduce a third phase in childhood development, which follows on from the pre-genital organizations, and which already merits the name 'genital', which shows a sexual object and a degree of convergence in sexual strivings towards this object, but which differs in one significant respect from the definitive organization of sexual maturity. It knows, in fact, only one kind of genital, the male. For that reason I have called it the *phallic* stage of organization ('Die infantile Genitalorganisation' ['Infantile Genital Organization'] *Internationale Zeitschrift für Psychoanalyse*, IX, 1923; *Gesammelte Werke*, vol. XIII). The biological model for this is, according to Abraham, the identical genital formation of the embryo in both sexes.

27. Some people claim to remember that when being rocked they felt the impact of the fanned air on their genitals as a direct sexual pleasure.

28. The analysis of cases of neurotic walking disorders and agoraphobia raises doubts concerning the sexual nature of the pleasure of motion. Modern civilized education, as everyone knows, employs a wide range of sports to distract young people from sexual activity; it would be more correct to say that it replaces sexual enjoyment with the pleasure of movement, and forces sexual activity back to one of its auto-erotic components.

29. So-called 'erogenous' masochism.

30. The inevitable conclusion we may draw from the above considerations is that each individual must be identified as having an oral, anal, urinary eroticism, and so on, and that the observation of the corresponding mental complexes does not amount to a diagnosis of abnormality or neurosis. The differences separating the normal from the abnormal can lie only in the relative strength of the individual components of the sexual drive, and in the use made of them in the course of their development.

III

The Transformations of Puberty

The onset of puberty sees the beginning of those transformations which should lead infantile sexual life to its definitive, normal shape. The sexual drive has so far been primarily auto-erotic, and now it finds its sexual object. Hitherto it has been activated by individual drives and erogenous zones which, independently of one another, had a certain pleasure as their sole sexual goal. Now there is a new sexual goal, and all partial drives combine to contribute to its attainment, while the erogenous zones are subordinated to the primacy of the genital zone.[1] As the new sexual goal assigns very different functions to the two sexes, their sexual development now diverges widely. That of the male is more consistent, more easily intelligible, while that of the female may even be seen to undergo a certain regression. The normality of sexual life is now achieved by the precise convergence of the two currents aimed towards the sexual object and the sexual goal, the affectionate and the sensual currents, the former of which contains a residue of the early blossoming of sexuality in infancy. It is like completing the building of a tunnel from both sides at the same time.

In men, the new sexual goal consists in the discharge of sexual products; it is by no means remote from the older goal, the attainment of pleasure; in fact, the peak of pleasure is connected with this final act of the sexual process. The sexual drive now puts itself at the service of reproduction; it becomes altruistic, so to speak. If this transformation is to be successful, the original predispositions and all the particularities of the drives must be taken into account.

Here, too, as in all cases in which new connections and assemblages leading to complicated mechanisms are to be formed, the opportunity also arises for pathological disorders to occur where these new arrangements are not attained. All pathological disorders of the sexual life may rightly be seen as inhibitors of development.

1) The Primacy of the Genital Zones and Pre-pleasure

The starting point and the final goal of the development described here are clearly apparent. We are still largely in the dark where the intermediate passages are concerned; we will have to leave them with more than one of their mysteries.

The most conspicuous feature of the processes of puberty has been selected as their most essential: the manifest growth of the external genitals, the period of latency in childhood having been expressed by the relative inhibition of that growth. At the same time the development of the internal genitals is so far advanced that they are capable of emitting sexual products, or accepting them in order to form a new life. Thus an extremely complicated apparatus has been produced, waiting to be put into operation.

This apparatus has to be set in motion by stimuli, and observation now shows us that it can be assailed by stimuli travelling along three paths: from the external world, through excitement of the erogenous zones, with which we are already familiar; from within the organism, along paths still to be examined; and from the life of the mind, which itself represents a storehouse for external impressions and a reception area for internal excitements. These three paths all lead to the same state, which is characterized as 'sexual excitement', and which is manifested in two kinds of signs, the mental and the somatic. The mental indication consists in a curious feeling of tension, of pressing urgency; prime among the various physical signs is a series of changes in the genitals, which have an indubitable significance, that of readiness, of preparation for the sexual act (the erection of the male member, the moistening of the vagina).

(Sexual Tension)

Associated with the characteristic of tension within sexual excitement is a problem that is just as difficult to solve as it is important for an understanding of the sexual processes. In the face of differences of opinion within the field of psychology, I maintain that a feeling of tension must bear within itself the characteristic of displeasure. What strikes me as crucial is that such a feeling brings with it a compulsion to change the psychical situation, and that it acts with a drive-force that is entirely remote from the essence of the pleasure that has been felt. But if we include the tension of sexual excitement among the feelings of displeasure, we encounter the objection that it is indubitably felt to be pleasurable. There is always pleasure in the tension produced by the sexual process; a feeling of some kind of satisfaction is clearly apparent even in the preparatory changes in the genitals. So how can we reconcile the displeasing feeling of tension with this feeling of pleasure?

Everything to do with the problem of pleasure and displeasure touches upon one of the sorest points in contemporary psychology. We shall try to learn as much as possible from the conditions of the present case, and avoid approaching the problem as a whole.[2] Let us first cast a glance at the way in which the erogenous zones fall into line with the new order. They are assigned an important role in the initiation of sexual excitement. The one that is perhaps the most remote from the sexual object, the eye, is the one that most often has, within the context of the quest for the object, the potential to be stimulated by that particular quality of excitement whose cause is the sexual object we identify as beauty. For this reason too, the merits of the sexual object are called 'attractions'. On the one hand, pleasure is associated with this attraction, while on the other its consequence is an intensification of sexual excitement, or a provocation of it where it is not already present. If the excitement of another erogenous zone, such as a caressing hand, is added to this, the effect is the same: a sensation of pleasure, soon intensified by the pleasure derived from the preparatory changes, and a further intensification in sexual tension, which soon becomes the most distinct displeasure if it is not permitted to bring about further pleasure. More transparent, perhaps, is another case: if, for example, in someone who is not sexually excited, an erogenous zone, such as the skin of a woman's breast, is stimulated by touch. The touch itself provokes a feeling of pleasure, but at the same time it is better suited than anything else to provoke a sexual excitement that demands an increase in pleasure. The problem is: how can that experience of pleasure produce a need for greater pleasure?

(Mechanism of Pre-pleasure)

But pleasure is the role assigned to the erogenous zones in this situation. What held true for one holds true for all. All the erogenous zones are used to provide a certain amount of pleasure through the stimulation suited to them, which generates the intensification of tension, which in turn has to summon up the necessary motor energy to bring the sexual act to its conclusion. The penultimate part of this, in turn, is the appropriate stimulation of an erogenous zone, the genital zone itself, around the glans penis, with the most appropriate object, the mucous membrane of the vagina; and from the pleasure produced by this excitement, this time along a reflex path, comes the motor energy that supplies the emission of sexual matter. This final pleasure is the greatest, and it differs in its mechanism from those preceding it. It is provoked entirely through discharge, it is entirely the pleasure of satisfaction, and with it the excitement of the libido temporarily subsides.

There seems to me to be some justification in capturing this difference in the essence of the pleasure acquired through the stimulation of the erogenous zones and the other kind, which accompanies the evacuation of the sexual matter, by giving them a name. The former may appropriately be called *pre-pleasure*, in contrast with *final pleasure* or the pleasure of satisfaction from sexual activity. Pre-pleasure is, then, the same as that which the infantile sexual drive produced, albeit to a lesser degree; final pleasure is new, and hence probably linked to conditions that only came into being with puberty. The formula for the new function of the erogenous zones might now be expressed as follows: they are used, through the pre-pleasure that is to be had from them as it was to be had from them in infancy, to bring about the production of the pleasure of greater satisfaction.

I was recently able to explain another example, from a quite different area of mental activity in which, similarly, a greater effect of pleasure is achieved by means of a less intense sensation of pleasure, which acts as a premium of enticement. This also provided an opportunity to take a closer look at the essence of pleasure.[3]

(Dangers of Pre-pleasure)

But the connection of pre-pleasure with infantile sexual life is intensified by the pathogenic role that can be assigned to it. The mechanism that receives pre-pleasure clearly presents a threat to the accomplishment of the normal sexual goal, and this occurs if at some point in the preparatory sexual processes the pre-pleasure is too great, and its component of tension too small. The drive-force for the further continuation of the sexual process is absent, and the trajectory as a whole becomes shorter, the preparatory action in question replacing the normal sexual goal. Experience tells us that this harmful case comes about when the erogenous zone or the corresponding partial drive has contributed to an unusual degree to the gain of pleasure during infancy. If additional elements arise and contribute to fixation, a compulsion may easily come into being in later life, resisting the reclassification of that single pre-pleasure into a new context. One instance of this, in fact, is present in the mechanism of many perversions which represent a lingering over the preparatory acts of the sexual process.

The failure of the function of the sexual mechanism, when it is the fault of pre-pleasure, is most easily avoided when the primacy of the genital zones has already been sketched out in infancy. It seems in fact that all preparations in this direction have actually been made during the second half of childhood (from eight years of age to puberty). During these years the genital zones already behave as they do in adulthood, they become the seat of sensations of stimulation and preparatory changes, if pleasure is felt as a result of the satisfaction of other erogenous zones. This effect still remains pointless, however, which is to say that it contributes nothing to the continuation of the sexual process. During childhood, then, a certain degree of sexual tension is produced alongside the pleasure of satisfaction, although it is less constant and less intense. We can now understand why, when discussing the sources of sexuality, we were equally right in saying both that the process in question was sexually satisfying and that it was sexually exciting. We become aware that on the road towards knowledge we have at first exaggerated the differences between infantile and adult sexual life, and are now correcting that exaggeration. Not only deviations from normal sexual life, but also its normal formation, are determined by the infantile manifestations of sexuality.

2) *The Problem of Sexual Excitement*

We have not had any explanation of the origin or the nature of the sexual tension which arises simultaneously with pleasure along with the satisfaction of erogenous zones.[4] The immediate assumption, that this tension is somehow generated by pleasure itself, is not only inherently unlikely, but is also shown to be flawed, since no tension is produced with the greatest pleasure linked to the evacuation of sexual products; on the contrary all tension is erased. So pleasure and sexual tension must only be indirectly related to one another.

(Role of the Sexual Materials)

Apart from the fact that sexual excitement normally only comes to an end with the discharge of sexual materials, there are also other grounds for linking sexual tension to the sexual products. In a continent life, the sexual apparatus tends, at varying but not random intervals, to discharge the sexual materials, accompanying this with a sensation of pleasure and a dreamed hallucination of a sexual act, and where this process – nocturnal emission – is concerned, it is hard to dismiss the view that the sexual tension, that is able to make the brief hallucinatory journey to a substitute for the act is a function of the accumulation of semen in the reservoirs for the sexual products. Experience tells us something similar about the exhaustibility of the sexual mechanism. Once the supply of semen is evacuated, not only does it become impossible to perform the sexual act, but the erogenous zones, and the appropriate excitement of them, fails to produce any pleasure. We note in passing that a certain degree of sexual tension is required even for the excitability of the erogenous zones.

We would thus be driven towards the hypothesis – fairly universally widespread, if I am not mistaken – that it is the accumulation of sexual materials which creates and maintains sexual tension, more or less through the pressure of those products on the walls of their reservoir, acting as a stimulus to a centre in the spine. This state is perceived by higher centres and then delivers the familiar sensation of tension to the consciousness. If stimulation of the erogenous zones heightened sexual tension, this would necessarily imply that the erogenous zones have a pre-formed anatomical connection with those centres, that they raise the tonus of the excitement, put the sexual act in motion if the sexual tension is sufficient, and stimulate the production of sexual materials if it is insufficient.

The weakness of this theory, which we find accepted, for example, in Krafft-Ebing's depiction of sexual processes, lies in the fact that, having been established in relation to the sexual activity of the adult male, it barely takes into account three conditions which it should also serve to explain. These are conditions as they relate to children, women and castrated men. In none of these three cases can we speak of an accumulation of sexual products as we might do with men, and this makes the simple application of the pattern more difficult; none the less it should also be conceded that information could be found that might cover these cases as well. At any rate, the warning remains: we should take care not to burden the factor of the accumulation of sexual products with tasks that it appears unable to perform.

(Importance of the Internal Sexual Organs)

That sexual excitement can be to a remarkable degree independent of the production of the sexual materials seems to be suggested by the observation of male castrati; sometimes their libidos escape the effects of the operation, even though the opposite behaviour, which was the reason for the operation, is the rule. In addition, we have known for a long time that illnesses which have destroyed the production of the male sex-cells leave intact the libido and potency of the now sterile individual. It is by no means all that surprising, then, as C. Rieger suggests, that the loss of the male gonads during adulthood may have no further effect on the individual's mental behaviour. It is true that castration performed at a tender age, before puberty, does effectively tend to erase the sexual characteristics, but at the same time it is possible that, apart from the loss of the sexual glands, an inhibition of the development of other factors associated with their absence might be involved.

(Chemical Theory)

Experiments on animals involving the removal of the gonads (testicles and ovaries) and various forms of implantation of new such organs among vertebrates (see the work of Lipschütz quoted above, p. 150, note 12) have already cast a partial light on the origin of sexual excitement and in so doing have reduced the significance of the accumulation of cellular sexual products even further. Experiments have shown (E. Steinach) that a male can be transformed into a female and, conversely, a female into a male, and that in consequence of this the psychosexual behaviour of the animal changed according to its somatic sexual characteristics, and did so simultaneously with them. It would appear that this sex-determining influence, however, is not the result of the contribution of the gonad, which produces the specific sexual cells (spermatozoa and egg), but of its interstitial tissue, which is for that reason given emphasis by the authors, who refer to it as a 'puberty gland'. It is highly possible that further investigations will show that the puberty gland is normally hermaphroditic in nature, which would provide an anatomical explanation of the theory of the bisexuality of the higher animals, and even now it appears likely that it is not the only organ involved in the production of sexual excitement and the sexual characteristics. At any rate, this new biological finding accords with what we have already learned about the role that the thyroid gland plays in sexuality. It seems likely that certain chemical materials are produced in the interstitial parts of the gonads which, once absorbed into the bloodstream, cause certain parts of the central nervous system to be charged with sexual tension, in analogy with those cases, with which we are already familiar, in which a toxic stimulation is turned into a specific organic stimulation by the introduction of other toxins alien to the body. The question of how sexual excitement arises out of the stimulation of erogenous zones, the central apparatuses having been previously charged, and what complicated combinations of purely toxic and physiological stimulation are produced when these sexual processes occur, cannot be dealt with even hypothetically at the present time. What we should maintain, however, as being essential to this conception of the sexual processes, is the hypothesis of particular materials deriving from the sexual metabolism. For this apparently random proposition is supported by an insight to which little attention is generally paid, but which is very much worthy of note. Those neuroses that can be traced back to disorders of the sexual life show the greatest clinical similarity with the phenomena of intoxication and abstinence produced by the habitual ingestion of pleasure-producing toxins (alkaloids).

3) The Libido Theory

The conceptual structure that we have created with a view to mastering the psychical manifestations of sexual life accords well with these hypotheses concerning the chemical basis of sexual excitement. We have defined the concept of the *libido* as a quantitatively changeable force enabling us to measure processes and transformations within the realm of sexual excitement. In view of its particular origin, we distinguish this libido from the energy that must be supposed to be at the root of the mental processes in general, and thus we also grant it a qualitative character. In distinguishing between libidinal and other psychical energy, we are expressing the presumption that the sexual processes of the organism differ from the nutritional processes because of a particular chemistry. The analysis of perversions and psychoneuroses has led us to the insight that this sexual excitement comes not only from the so-called sexual organs, but from every organ in the body. In this way we form the image of a quantum of libido, whose psychical representation we shall call the *ego-libido*, whose production, increase or reduction, distribution and displacement should help us to explain observed psychosexual phenomena.

This *ego-libido* only becomes comfortably accessible to analytic study, however, once it has discovered its psychical application in the *investment* of sexual objects, and thus become an *object-libido*. We then see it concentrating on objects, fixating on them or abandoning them, moving on from one object to another and, from those situations, directing the sexual activity of the individual to lead to satisfaction: that is, to the partial and temporary extinction of the libido. The psychoanalysis of what are called transference neuroses (hysteria and compulsive neurosis) gives us a sure insight into these matters.

As regards the vicissitudes of the object-libido, we can tell that it is kept remote from its objects, suspended in particular states of tension and finally brought back into the ego, so that it once again becomes the *ego-libido*. To distinguish it from the object-libido we might also call the ego-libido the *narcissistic* libido. From the viewpoint of psychoanalysis we look out over a boundary that we may not cross, into the mechanisms of the narcissistic libido, and form an idea of the relationship between the object-libido and the narcissistic libido.[5] The narcissistic or ego-libido appears to us as a large storehouse from which the object-investments are dispatched and into which they are reincorporated, the investment of the ego by the libido as the primal state occurring in childhood, which is only masked by the later effusions of the libido, but has basically been preserved behind them.

It should be the task of a libido theory of neurotic and psychotic disorders to express all observed phenomena and inferred processes in terms of the libido economy. It is easy to guess that greater importance will be placed on the vicissitudes of the ego-libido, particularly where it comes to explaining deeper psychotic disorders. The difficulty, then, lies in the fact that for the time being the instrument of our investigation, psychoanalysis, provides us only with certain information about the metamorphoses taking place in the object-libido,[6] but is incapable of distinguishing, without a great deal of difficulty, the ego-libido from the other energies at work in the ego.[7] For this reason, libido theory can for the time being only be pursued speculatively. But we will sacrifice all we have gained from earlier psychoanalytic observation if, following the example of C. G. Jung, we dilute the very concept of the libido, by making it coincide with the psychical drive-force *per se*.

The distinction of the sexual drive impulses from the others, and thus the restriction of the concept of the libido to the former, is strongly supported by the hypothesis, mentioned above, of a particular chemistry at work within the sexual function.

4) *Differentiation Between Men and Women*

We know that it is not until puberty that a sharp distinction between the male and female characteristics is produced, an opposition which then crucially influences the shapes of the lives of human beings more than any other. The masculine and feminine dispositions, however, are easily identified, even in childhood; the development of inhibitions concerning sexuality (shame, disgust, pity and so on) appears earlier in little girls, among whom it encounters less resistance than among boys; the tendency towards sexual repression generally appears greater; where partial drives of sexuality are apparent, they tend to choose the passive form. The auto-erotic activity of the erogenous zones, however, is the same in both sexes, and because of this conformity the possibility of a difference between the sexes, such as that which occurs after puberty, is suppressed throughout childhood. As regards the auto-erotic and masturbatory sexual manifestations, we might put forward the proposition that the sexuality of little girls is entirely masculine in character. Indeed, if we wished to give the terms 'masculine and feminine' a more definite content, we might state that the libido is, universally and in accordance with certain laws, masculine in nature, whether it occurs in the male or the female, and irrespective of whether its object is a man or a woman.[8]

Since I became familiar with the idea of bisexuality, I have come to consider this element to be the crucial factor, and believe that, without taking bisexuality into account, one would hardly be able to reach an understanding of the sexual manifestations of both men and women that one is able to observe in practice.

(Leading Zones in Men and Women)

Apart from this, I can only add the following: the leading erogenous zone of the female child lies in the clitoris, and the male genital zone is therefore homologously in the glans. Everything I have been able to learn about masturbation in little girls has related to the clitoris rather than the parts of the external genitals which will be important for the later sexual functions. I myself doubt that under the influence of masturbation the female child can achieve anything other than clitoral masturbation, apart from certain exceptional cases. Spontaneous discharges of sexual excitement, so frequent among little girls, are expressed in spasms of the clitoris, and its frequent erections enable the girl to assess the sexual manifestations of the other sex correctly without instruction, simply by transferring the sensations of her own sexual processes to boys.

If we wish to understand how it is that the little girl becomes a woman, we must pursue the subsequent vicissitudes of this clitoral susceptibility to stimulation. While puberty brings boys a great advance of the libido, to girls it brings a fresh wave of repression, which particularly affects clitoral sexuality. What succumbs to repression is a piece of masculine sexual life. The intensification of sexual inhibitions occurring as a result of this pubertal repression of the woman then generates a stimulus for the man's libido and obliges it to heighten its performance: as the libido rises, so too does sexual over-valuation, which only attains its full measure when faced with the self-denying woman, who is also denying her own sexuality. If the clitoris is itself excited by the sexual act, once this is finally permitted, it preserves the role of passing this excitement on to the adjacent female parts, just as a piece of kindling can be used to light the harder logs. It often takes a certain amount of time before this transfer can take place, and during that time the young girl experiences a loss of sensation. This anaesthesia can become lasting if the clitoral zone refuses to pass on its susceptibility to stimulation, which is prepared by ample activity in childhood. It is well known that anaesthesia among women is often only apparent and local. They experience loss of feeling at the entrance to the vagina, but this does not mean that they cannot feel excitement in the clitoris or even in other zones. To these erogenous causes of anaesthesia we must add psychical causes, which are also determined by repression.

If the erogenous susceptibility to stimulation of the clitoris has been successfully transferred to the vaginal orifice, the woman will have changed her subsequent zone of sexual activity, while the man's has been unaltered from childhood onwards. Within this change in the leading erogenous zone, as in the phase of repression in puberty – which, we might say, sets aside infantile masculinity – lie the main conditions for women's particular predisposition towards neuroses and particularly towards hysteria. These conditions are therefore most profoundly connected to the essence of femininity.

5) The Discovery of the Object

While primacy of the genital zones is established by the processes of puberty, and the man's erect member points imperiously towards its new sexual goal, that of penetrating a bodily cavity which stimulates the genital zone, the discovery of the object – preliminary work on which has been done since earliest childhood – is being accomplished in the psychical sphere. When the very first sexual satisfaction was still connected with the ingestion of food, the sexual drive had a sexual object outside the child's own body, in the mother's breast. It lost this only later, perhaps at the very point when it became possible for the child to form an overall idea of the person to whom this organ, which provided it with satisfaction, belonged. As a general rule, the sexual drive then generally becomes auto-erotic, and only once the latency period is past is the original situation reconstituted. Not without good reason has the sucking of the child at the mother's breast become the model for every loving relationship. The discovery of the object is in fact a rediscovery.[9]

(The Sexual Object in Early Infancy)

However, an important part survives of this first and most important of all sexual relationships, even after the separation of sexual activity from the ingestion of nourishment has taken place, and this part helps to prepare the object-choice, and thus to re-establish lost happiness. Throughout the whole of the latency period the child learns to *love* other people who alleviate its helplessness and satisfy its needs, following the pattern and acting as a continuation of the child's relationship to its wet-nurse during early infancy. There will perhaps be some resistance to the identification of the tender feelings and high regard shown by a child to its carers with sexual love, but I believe that a more precise psychological examination will be able to establish that identity beyond a doubt. Contact between the child and its carer is, for the child, an endlessly flowing source of sexual stimulation and satisfaction of erogenous zones, particularly since the carer – more generally the mother – bestows upon the child feelings derived from her sexual life, stroking, kissing and rocking the child, and quite clearly taking it as a substitute for a fully valid sexual object.[10] The mother would probably be horrified if it were explained to her that with all her caresses she was awakening her child's sexual drive and preparing its later intensity. She considers her actions to be asexual, 'pure' love, since she carefully avoids giving the child's genitals any more stimulation than is unavoidable in the pursuit of hygiene. But the sexual drive is not only aroused by stimulating the genital zone, as we know; what we call affection will inevitably one day have its effect on the genital zones. If the child's mother had a fuller understanding of the great significance of the drives for mental life as a whole, for all ethical and psychical tasks, she would also be able to spare herself any self-reproach even after the situation had been explained to her. She is only fulfilling her duty in teaching the child to love; it is supposed, after all, to become a competent adult with energetic sexual needs and accomplish everything in life that the drive compels the individual to do. An excess of parental affection will, of course, be harmful, by accelerating sexual maturity, and also by 'spoiling' the child, and making it incapable in later life of doing without love or of being satisfied with a smaller degree of it. It is one of the best indicators of later nervousness if the child proves insatiably demanding on the affection of its parents, while, conversely, neuropathic parents, who have a tendency towards boundless affection, are most likely to awaken the child's predisposition to neurotic illnesses with their caresses. This example also tells us that neurotic parents can pass on their disorder to their children along paths more direct than heredity.

(Infantile Anxiety)

Children themselves behave from an early age as though their affection for their carers were the same as sexual love. Anxiety among children is originally nothing but a manifestation of the fact that they miss the beloved person; for that reason they respond with fear when they meet strangers; they are afraid of the dark, because in the dark one cannot see the beloved person; and they are calmed down if they can hold that person's hand in the darkness. We overestimate the effects of childhood terrors and frightening nursery-tales told by carers if we hold them responsible for making children anxious. Only children with a tendency towards anxiety are affected by these stories, which make no impression on others; and only children whose sexual drive is excessive or prematurely developed, or whose sexual drive has been rendered demanding through pampering, tend towards anxiety. The child is behaving like an adult in turning its libido into anxiety because it is unable to satisfy it, and adults who have become neurotic as the result of an unsatisfied libido will in their anxiety behave like children, and begin to be frightened once they are on their own, that is, without someone on whose love they think they can depend, and will seek to conquer that anxiety by taking the most childlike measures.[11]

(The Barrier Against Incest)[12]

It may be that the parents' affection for the child has so successfully managed to avoid arousing its sexual drive prematurely, before the physical conditions of puberty have appeared, that mental excitement penetrates unmistakably through to the genital system. If this is the case, that affection will be able to accomplish its task of guiding the child, once it has reached the age of maturity, in the selection of its sexual object. Certainly, the most natural thing for the child to do is to select as sexual objects the very people whom it has loved since childhood with what might be called an 'attenuated' libido.[13] But as a result of the postponement of sexual maturity, the time has been gained to erect the barrier against incest along with the other sexual inhibitions, and for the child to absorb those moral proscriptions which expressly exclude the loved ones of childhood, as blood relations, from object-choice. Respect for this barrier is above all a cultural requirement of society, which must defend itself against the absorption by the family of those interests that it requires in order to establish superior social units, and for that reason uses all available means to loosen the tie that binds every individual, but particularly the adolescent, to the family and which, during childhood, is the sole defining connection.[14]

But object-choice is first accomplished in the imagination, and the sex life of the maturing adolescent has hardly any other space in which to expend itself than in fantasies, that is, in ideas that are not destined to be carried out.[15] The infantile tendencies, now reinforced by somatic emphasis, recur in these fantasies. Among them, primarily and with a frequency governed by laws, is the sexual impulse, in most cases already distinguished by sexual attraction, of the child for the parents, the son for the mother and the daughter for the father.[16] At the same time, once these clearly incestuous fantasies have been overcome and rejected, one of the most significant, but also the most painful, psychical accomplishments of puberty has been effected: the break from parental authority, which must occur before the opposition of the new generation to the old, so important for the advance of civilization, can be put into effect. At each stage along the journey of development that individuals must travel, a number of them are held back, so that there are some individuals who have not overcome parental authority, and have never withdrawn their affection from the parents, or have only done so incompletely. They are generally girls, who thus, to the delight of their parents, linger on in a state of childish love far beyond puberty. It is highly instructive to discover that when they later marry, these girls lack the ability to give their husbands what is due to them. This tells us that the apparently non-sexual love of the parents and sexual love are nourished from the same source, which amounts to saying that the former corresponds only to an infantile fixation of the libido.

The closer we come to the deeper disorders of psychosexual development, the more unmistakably the significance of incestuous object-choice comes to the fore. In psychoneurotics, following sexual rejection, much or all of the psychosexual activity devoted to the discovery of the object remains in the unconscious. In girls with an excessive need for affection and a matching horror of the real requirements of sexual life, it becomes irresistibly tempting for them to realize the ideal of the asexual love in life, while at the same time being able to conceal their libido behind an affection which they can express without self-reproach, by clinging on to the infantile affection, refreshed in puberty, for parents or siblings. Psychoanalysis can easily show such people that they are, in the generally understandable sense of the word, *in love* with these blood relations, by using symptoms and other pathological manifestations, seeking out their unconscious thoughts and translating them into conscious ones. Similarly, when a previously healthy person has fallen ill after an unhappy experience in love, one can reveal with certainty that the mechanism that has caused this illness is the direction of the libido back towards those individuals who were preferred in childhood.

(After-effect of the Infantile Object-choice)

Even a person who has successfully avoided the incestuous fixation of his or her libido does not totally escape its influence. It is clearly an echo of that phase of development if the object of a young man's first passionate love is, as so often, a mature woman, and a girl's is an older man invested with authority, both of whom bring to life the image of the mother and the father.[17] In all likelihood, object-choice is generally made according to these models. Above all, a man will seek his remembered image of his mother, which has dominated him since earliest childhood; it is entirely in accord with this if his mother, should she still be alive, resists this renewal of herself and responds to it with hostility. Given the significance of the childhood relationship with the parents for the later choice of sexual object, we will easily understand that any disorder in these childhood relationships has the most serious consequences for sexual life in adulthood; the lover's jealousy never lacks an infantile root, or at least an infantile reinforcement. Arguments between the parents themselves, or their unhappy marriage, determine the most serious predisposition to disorders in sexual development or neurotic illness in their children.

Infantile affection for one's parents is probably the most important, but not the only one of those traces which, refreshed during puberty, point the way for the object-choice. Other elements from the same source allow the man, still taking his lead from his childhood, to develop more than one single *sexual series*, to form very different conditions for his object-choice.[18]

(Prevention of Inversion)

One task implicit in the object-choice is to ensure that one finds the opposite sex. As is well known, this problem is not solved without a certain amount of fumbling. The first impulses after puberty go wrong often enough, although without doing lasting harm. Dessoir has rightly pointed out the regularity with which boys and girls have crushes on their peers. The strongest force countering a lasting inversion of the sexual object is certainly the attraction that the opposite sexual characteristics express for each other; we cannot explain this in this context.[19] But this factor is not in itself sufficient to exclude inversion: all kinds of secondary elements are probably involved. Above all, society's authoritative inhibition; where inversion is not seen as a crime, we can see that it fully corresponds to the sexual inclinations of many individuals. In addition, we may assume, where men are concerned, that childhood memory of the affection of the mother and other female individuals who looked after him when he was a child helps to direct his choice energetically towards women, while the sexual intimidation that he experienced from his father early in life, and his competitive attitude towards him, leads him away from his own sex. But these two elements also apply to the girl, whose sexual activity is subject to the particular attention of her mother. As a result of this a hostile relationship is generated towards her own sex, which crucially influences the object-choice in the direction that is considered normal. The upbringing of boys by males (slaves, in the ancient world) seems to encourage homosexuality; the employment of male servants as well as the lesser involvement of the mother in bringing up her children help us to understand the frequency of inversion among the contemporary aristocracy. In some hysterics the premature disappearance of one parent (as the result of death, divorce, estrangement), following which the remaining parent had drawn all of the child's love to him- or herself, established the condition for the sex of the person later chosen as a sexual object, and thus simultaneously made a lasting inversion possible.

Notes

1. The schematic representation given in the text seeks to stress differences. Above (pp. 174–5) we have examined the extent to which infantile sexuality, through its object-choice and the formation of the phallic phase, approaches the definitive sexual organization.

2. Cf. an attempted solution to this problem in the introductory remarks to my essay 'Das ökonomische Problem des Masochismus' ['The Economic Problem of Masochism'] 1924. (*Internationale Zeitschrift für Psychoanalyse*, X; *Gesammelte Werke*, vol. XIII.)

3. See my 1905 study, *Der Witz und seine Beziehung zum Unbewussten* [*The Joke and Its Relation to the Unconscious*, translated by Joyce Crick, London, 2002] (vol. VI of the *Gesammelte Werke*). The 'pre-pleasure' gained by joke technique is used to free a greater pleasure by dissolving internal inhibitions.

4. It is highly telling that the German language gives an account of the role of the preparatory sexual excitements mentioned here, which simultaneously supply a proportion of satisfaction and a contribution to sexual tension, in the use of the word '*Lust*'. '*Lust*' is ambiguous, and refers both to the sensation of sexual excitement ('*Ich habe Lust*' – I would like to, I feel compelled to) and to that of satisfaction.

5. This restriction is no longer as valid as it once was, since neuroses other than 'transference neuroses' have become accessible to psychoanalysis in greater numbers.

6. Cf. the previous note.

7. See 'Zur Einführung des Narzissmus' ['On the Introduction of Narcissism' in *Beyond the Pleasure Principle* and *Other Writings*, translated by John Reddick, London, 2003], *Jahrbuch der Psychoanalyse*, VI, 1914 (vol. X of the *Gesammelte Werke*). The term 'narcissism' was not created by Näcke, as I erroneously state there, but by H. Ellis.

8. It is indispensable that we be aware that the terms 'masculine' and 'feminine', whose content seems so unambiguous to ordinary opinion, are considered to be among the most confused in science, and can be broken down in at least *three* directions. Masculine and feminine are used now in the sense of *activity* and *passivity*, now in the *biological* and now, too, in the *sociological* sense. The first of these three meanings is the essential one, and the one most useful in psychoanalysis. It is this that is meant when the libido is described above in the text as male, because the drive is always active, even when it has set itself a passive goal. The second, biological meaning of masculine and feminine is the one that permits the clearest definition. Here masculine and feminine are characterized by the presence of semen or ova and the functions arising from them. Activity and its subsidiary manifestations, stronger muscle development, aggression, greater intensity of the libido, are generally associated with biological masculinity, but are not necessarily connected with it, since there are species of animals in which these qualities are more readily assigned to the female. The third, sociological meaning derives its content from the observation of really existing male and female individuals. In human beings, this creates a situation whereby neither pure masculinity nor femininity is to be found in the psychological or in the biological sense. Rather, each individual person displays a mixture of his or her own biological sexual characteristics, with biological traits of the other sex, and an amalgamation of activity and passivity, both where these psychical character traits depend on the biological, and where they are independent of them.

9. Psychoanalysis teaches that there are two paths of object-discovery, first

the one described in the text, which draws its support from early infantile models, and secondly the *narcissistic* path, which seeks the subject's own self and finds it in the other. This latter is of particular importance for pathological outcomes, but does not fit within the context being examined here.

10. Should this idea strike the reader as 'blasphemous', he should consult the similar account of the mother-and-child relationship in Havelock Ellis (*Sexual Inversion*, p. 16).

11. I owe the explanation of the origin of childhood anxiety to a three-year-old boy I once heard pleading from a dark room: 'Auntie, talk to me; I'm frightened because it's so dark.' His aunt called to him: 'What good would that do? You can't see me.' 'It doesn't matter,' replied the child, 'if someone speaks the light comes on.' So he was not afraid because of the dark but because he missed a beloved person, and could promise to calm down as soon as he had received proof of her presence. – The discovery that neurotic anxiety arises from the libido and is the product of its transformation, and therefore stands in more or less the same relation to it as vinegar does to wine, is one of the most significant results of psychoanalytical research. For a further discussion of this problem, see my *Vorlesungen zur Einführung in die Psychoanalyse* [*Introductory Lectures on Psychoanalysis*], 1917 (vol. XI of the *Gesammelte Werke*), although this does not accomplish a definitive explanation.

12. [This marginalium was missing, clearly in error, from 1924 onwards.]

13. Cf. what I have said on pp. 174–5 about the child's object-choice: the 'affectionate current'.

14. The barrier on incest is probably one of humanity's historical acquisitions, and like other moral taboos it may already be fixed through organic inheritance in many individuals. (Cf. my paper: *Totem und Tabu* [*Totem and Taboo* in *On Murder, Mourning and Melancholia*, translated by Shaun Whiteside, London 2005], 1912–13, vol. IX of the *Gesammelte Werke*.) But psychoanalytic examination shows how intensely the individual battles with the temptation to incest during his periods of development, and how often he transgresses it in fantasies and even in reality.

15. The fantasies of puberty follow on from the infantile sexual research abandoned in childhood, and may extend some way back into the latency period. They may be considered entirely or largely unconscious, and for that reason elude precise dating. They are highly important for the origin of many symptoms, by directly providing their primary stages and producing the forms in which the repressed libido components find satisfaction. Equally they are the models for those nocturnal fantasies that become conscious as dreams. Dreams are often nothing but the revivification of such fantasies, influenced by and borrowing from residual stimuli from the waking day ('the day's residues'). – Among the sexual fantasies of puberty some stand out, distinguished by their most universal occurrence and their being largely independent of the experience of the individual. These include fantasies of eavesdropping on parental sexual intercourse, of early seduction by loved ones, of the threat of castration, fantasies concerning the womb, whose content concerns lingering, and even having experiences, in the womb, and the so-called 'family romance' or 'family saga' in which the adolescent is reacting to the differences between his attitude to his parents now and in childhood. O. Rank, for example, has demonstrated the close relationships of these fantasies to myth in his essay 'Der Mythus von der Geburt des Helden' ['The Myth of the Birth of the Hero'], 1909.

It is correctly said that the Oedipus complex is the core complex among neuroses, and that it represents the essential part in the content of the neurosis. Infantile sexuality reaches its peak in it, and, through its after-effects, has a crucial influence on the adult's sexuality. Each new human arrival faces the task of overcoming the Oedipus complex; anyone who fails to do so will succumb to neurosis. The advance of psychoanalytical work has stressed this meaning of the Oedipus complex ever more emphatically; the acknowledgement of its existence has become the shibboleth distinguishing the devotees of psychoanalysis from its opponents.

In another book (*Das Trauma der Geburt* [*The Trauma of Birth*], 1924) Rank traced the bond with the mother back to embryonic prehistory, and thus demonstrated the biological basis of the Oedipus complex. In contrast to what we have said above, he deduces the barrier against incest from the traumatic impression of the terror of birth.

16. Compare my examination of the inevitability of fate in the Oedipus fable in *The Interpretation of Dreams*, Chapter V, Section D (β).

17. See my essay 'Über einen besonderen Typus der Objektwahl beim Manne' ['On a Particular Type of Object-choice in Men'], 1910 (vol. VIII of the *Gesammelte Werke*).

18. Countless peculiarities of the human love life, such as the compulsive nature of passionate love itself, can only be understood by referring back to childhood, when they will be seen as its residual effects.

19. This would be the right place to refer to a book by Ferenczi (*Attempt at a Genital Theory*, 1924), in which the sex lives of the higher animals are deduced from the history of their biological development.

Recapitulation

It is time to attempt a recapitulation. We began with the deviations of the sexual drive in relation to its object and its goal, and came upon the question of whether these are the products of an innate predisposition or are acquired as a result of the influences of life. The answer to this question came to us from our understanding, gained through psychoanalytic investigation, of the workings of the sexual drive among psychoneurotics, a large group of people not far removed from healthy people. We thus learned that among these people inclinations towards all perversions are demonstrable as unconscious forces and reveal themselves as formers of symptoms, and we were able to say that neurosis was, so to speak, a negative of perversion. In view of what is now recognized to be the very widespread nature of tendencies towards perversions, we were compelled to the view that the predisposition towards perversions is the fundamental and universal predisposition of the human sexual drive, from which normal sexual behaviour develops as the result of organic changes and psychical inhibitions along the road to adulthood. We hoped to be able to demonstrate that fundamental predisposition in childhood; among the forces which restricted the orientation of the sexual drive we included shame, disgust, pity and the social constructions of morality and authority. This led us to see all fixated deviations from normal sexual life as representing inhibited development and infantilism. We had to stress the great variations in the original predisposition, positing, however, a relationship of cooperation rather than opposition between that predisposition and the influences of life. On the other hand, it seemed to us that the original predisposition must be a complex one, and the sexual drive must itself be something composed of many different factors, which in the perversions breaks down, so to speak, into its component parts. Consequently the perversions proved on the one hand to be inhibitions, and on the other to be dissociations, of normal development. The two views combined in the assumption that the adult's sexual drive comes into being through the combination of diverse stimuli from childhood into a unit, a tendency with a single goal.

We added an explanation for the predominance of perverse tendencies among psychoneurotics, likening it to a collateral filling of tributary channels after the main river bed was blocked by 'repression', and then turned our attention towards the contemplation of the sexual life in childhood.[1] We found it regrettable that the sexual drive had been denied in childhood, and that the sexual manifestations of children had been described as exceptions to the rule. Rather, it seemed to us that children came into the world with the seeds of sexual activity already present, and even while taking nourishment they enjoyed sexual satisfaction, which they then tried repeatedly to achieve for themselves in the well-known activity of 'thumb-sucking'. The child's sexual activity does not develop at the same pace as its other functions, however, but, after a first blossoming period from the second to the fifth year, enters the so-called latency period. During this time, the generation of sexual excitement is by no means suspended, but continues, delivering a supply of energy that is largely used for other than sexual purposes; on the one hand contributing sexual components for the formation of social feelings, and on the other (as a result of repression and reaction formations) helping to construct the later sexual inhibitions. In this way the forces designed to keep the sexual drive on certain tracks are constructed in childhood at the expense of largely perverse sexual impulses, and with the help of education. Another part of infantile sexual impulses escapes being put to these uses, and may be expressed as sexual activity. In that case we are able to learn that the child's sexual stimulation flows from many different sources. Above all, satisfaction arises out of the appropriate sensitive stimulation of what are called the erogenous zones; any part of the skin and any sensory organ, indeed probably any organ, could have this function, although there are certain privileged erogenous zones whose excitement is ensured by certain organic arrangements. Sexual stimulation can also emerge, so to speak, as a by-product of many processes within the organism once these attain a certain intensity, most particularly out of intense emotions, even those that are painful in nature. The excitements arising from all these sources do not yet come together, but each pursues its goal individually, which is merely the acquisition of a certain pleasure. The sexual drive, then, is *not centred* in childhood and is initially object-less, *auto-erotic*.

During childhood the erogenous zone of the genitals becomes apparent, either by virtue of the fact that, like all other erogenous zones, it produces satisfaction in response to appropriate sensitive stimulation, or, in a way that we do not yet fully understand, a sexual excitement with a particular relationship to the genital zone is produced simultaneously with satisfaction from other sources. We regretted that we were unable to achieve an adequate explanation of the relationship either between sexual satisfaction and sexual excitement, or between the activity of the genital zone and that of other sources of sexuality.

Through the study of neurotic disorders we have been able to observe that in the child's sexual life, from the very first, the beginnings of an organization of the sexual drive components are apparent. During the first, very early phase, *oral* eroticism is the most prominent; a second of these *'pre-genital'* organizations is characterized by the predominance of *sadism* and *anal* eroticism, and only in the third phase (which in the child only develops to the primacy of the phallus) do the actual genital zones contribute to the partial determination of sexual life.

We then established – and this was one of our most surprising discoveries – that this early blossoming of infantile sexual life (between the ages of two and five) also effects an object-choice, with the whole range of rich mental achievements that this entails, so that the related phase corresponding to this period, despite the imperfect synthesis of the individual drive components and the uncertainty of the sexual goal, should be considered a major predecessor of the definitive sexual organization.

The fact that sexual development in human beings *begins in two phases*, by which we mean that it is interrupted by the latency period, seemed worthy of particular attention. It seems to contain one of the preconditions for man's aptitude to develop a higher culture, but also for his inclination towards neurosis. As far as we know, nothing analogous can be demonstrated in animals related to man. In order to discover the origin of this human quality, we would have to return to the prehistory of the human species.

We cannot say what level of sexual activity in childhood can be considered normal, and not injurious to later development. The character of sexual manifestations proved to be primarily masturbatory. We also established through experience that the external influences of seduction can cause premature interruptions of the latency period, even leading to its cessation, and that in the process the child's sexual drive proves actually to be polymorphously perverse; and further, that any such early sexual activity hampers the child's receptivity to education.

Despite the lacunae in our insights into infantile sexual life, we then attempted to study those changes in it that are imposed by puberty. We selected two of these which appeared to be particularly significant: the subordination of all other sources of sexual stimulation to the primacy of the genital zones, and the process of object-choice. Both of these are already preformed during childhood. The former is achieved through the mechanism of the exploitation of pre-pleasure, whereby previously autonomous sexual acts, connected with pleasure and stimulation, become preparatory acts for the new sexual goal: this is the emission of sexual products, accomplishment of which, occurring with extreme pleasure, brings sexual excitement to an end. In the process we had to bear in mind the differentiation of the sexual essence into masculine and feminine, and found that in order to become a woman an additional repression is required, one which abolishes a part of infantile masculinity and prepares the female for the change in the leading genital zone. Finally, we found that object-choice was guided by the infantile hints, refreshed during puberty, of the child's sexual affection for its parents and carers, and was steered away from those people and towards individuals resembling them by the barrier against incest that had been erected in the meantime. Let us finally add that during the transition of puberty the somatic and the psychical development processes move side by side and unconnected for a while, until, with the irruption of an intense mental impulse of love into the innervation of the genitals, the normally required unity of the amorous function is produced.

(Factors Interfering with Development)

Each step on this long path of development can become a point of fixation, every joint in this complex assemblage can bring about a dissociation in the sexual drive, as we have shown with reference to various examples. It remains to us to provide a survey of the various internal and external elements which interfere with development, and to add at which point within the mechanism the disorder emanating from them occurs. The elements that we shall present are not of equal importance, and we must expect difficulties in assigning to each element the value that is its due.

(Constitution and Heredity)

First we should mention the innate *diversity of sexual constitutions*, which probably plays the major role, but which can, understandably, be deduced only from its later manifestations, and then not always with great certainty. By this, we mean the predominance of one or other of the various sources of sexual excitement, and we believe that such diversity among predispositions is at any rate expressed in the final result, even if this remains within the bounds of normality. Certainly, such variations in the original predisposition are imaginable, and this must necessarily and without further assistance lead to the formation of an abnormal sexual life. We may call these variations 'degenerative', and consider them the manifestation of hereditary deterioration. In this context I must report a curious fact. In more than half of the serious cases of hysteria, compulsive neurosis and so on that I have treated psychotherapeutically, I was able to demonstrate with certainty that the patients' fathers had suffered and recovered from syphilis, whether they had suffered from tabes or progressive paralysis, or whether their syphilitic illness could be established by anamnesis. I should like to make it clear that children who will later be neurotic bear no physical signs of hereditary syphilis, so that the abnormal sexual constitution may be seen as the last sign of the syphilitic inheritance. Although I have no wish to identify descent from syphilitic parents as a regular or inevitable aetiological condition of the neuropathic constitution, I do not consider the coincidence that I have observed to be arbitrary or insignificant.

The hereditary conditions of positive perverts are less well known, because they are able to escape investigation. But we have reason to suppose that similar things may be said of both the perversions and the neuroses. Often, in fact, we encounter perversion and psychoneurosis within the same family, distributed between the sexes in such a way that the male members – or one of them – are positively perverse, while the females, in accordance with the inclination of their sex towards repression, are negatively perverse, hysterical, which is good evidence for the essential connections that we have discovered between the two disorders.

(Further Modification)

At the same time one cannot suggest that the form of sexual life is defined unambiguously according to the emergence of the various components of the sexual constitution. Rather, the determining process continues, and other possibilities are generated according to the fate experienced by the sexuality emanating from the individual sources. This *further modification* is clearly the one that determines the final outcome, while the constitutions described as identical can lead to three different final outcomes. If the relationship between all the different predispositions, a relationship which we may assume to be abnormal, remains constant and is reinforced in adulthood, the only possible final result can be a perverse sexual life. The analysis of such abnormal constitutional predispositions has not yet been properly undertaken, but we are already familiar with cases which can be easily explained by hypotheses of this kind. Writing about a whole series of perverse fixations for example, authors have said that the necessary precondition for these is an innate weakness of the sexual drive. This view strikes me as untenable in this form; but it does become meaningful if it is taken to refer to a constitutional weakness in one of the factors of the sexual drive, the genital zone, the one which later assumes as its function the combination of the individual sexual activities towards the goal of reproduction. This combination, which needs to take place in puberty, is bound to fail, and the strongest of the other components of sexuality will impose its activity as a perversion.[2]

(Repression)

A different outcome is produced if, in the course of development, certain components of the disposition that have an excessive force undergo the process of *repression*, which we must stress is not to be equated with abolition. In this case, the excitements in question are produced in the normal way, but held back by psychical inhibition from the attainment of their goal, and compelled on to many different kinds of other paths, until they have manifested themselves as symptoms. The result can be an almost normal sexual life – usually a restricted one – but one that is complemented by psychoneurotic illness. It is precisely these cases that have become familiar to us through psychoanalytic investigation. The sexual lives of such people have begun like those of perverts: a whole part of their childhood is filled with perverse sexual activity which can extend far beyond early adulthood; then, as a result of internal causes – usually still before puberty, but sometimes even long after – a reversal due to repression occurs, and from this point onwards, without the old impulses being extinguished, neurosis takes the place of perversion. One will recall the proverb 'Young whore, old nun', except that in the present case this means that youth is too summarily dealt with. This replacement of perversion by neurosis in the life of a single individual, like the distribution of perversion and neurosis among various members in the same family, accords with the insight that neurosis is the negative of perversion.

(Sublimation)

The third outcome in the case of an abnormal constitutional predisposition is made possible by the process of '*sublimation*', in which excessively powerful excitements can be drained away from individual sources of sexuality and employed in other areas, producing a not inconsiderable intensification of psychical productivity from an essentially dangerous predisposition. This is one of the sources of artistic activity, and according to the completeness or otherwise of this kind of sublimation, an analysis of the character of highly gifted individuals, especially those with an artistic predisposition, may reveal a mixture, in various proportions, of productivity, perversion and neurosis. One sub-species of sublimation is probably suppression by *reaction formation* which, as we have found, begins in the child's latency period, in ideal circumstances to continue throughout the whole of life. What we call a person's 'character' is to a large extent constructed from the material of sexual excitements and assembled from drives that are fixated from childhood, from those constructions that are achieved by sublimation and others destined effectively to suppress those perverse stimuli that are recognized as unusable.[3] Thus the generally perverse sexual predisposition of childhood may be considered as the source of many of our virtues, in so far as it initiates them by reaction formation.[4]

(Accidental Experience)

No influences are nearly as significant as instances of sexual release and the phases of repression and sublimation, the latter two being processes whose internal conditions are absolutely unknown to us. However, anyone who considers repression and sublimation to be parts of the constitutional predisposition, seeing them as manifestations of its life, can justly claim that the definitive structure of the sexual life is above all a product of the innate constitution. Meanwhile no one with any insight will dispute the idea that such a collaboration between the different factors also leaves space for the modifying influences of accidental experience in childhood and later on. The relative effectiveness of the constitutional and accidental elements is not easily measured. In theory, one always tends to overestimate the former; therapeutic practice stresses the significance of the latter. On no account should one forget that the relationship between the two is one of co-operation rather than exclusivity. The constitutional element needs experiences to bring it out, and the accidental requires the support of the constitution if it is to achieve an effect. We might imagine most cases as a 'complementary series' in which declining intensities in one factor are balanced by rising intensities in the other, but there is no reason to deny the existence of extreme cases at either end of the series.

It accords more fully with psychoanalytical research if we assign the most important place among the accidental elements to the experiences of early childhood. A single aetiological series thus separates into two, which we may call the *dispositional* and the *definitive*. In the former, constitution and accidental childhood experiences work together just as much as disposition and later traumatic experiences do in the latter. All elements deleterious to sexual development manifest their effects by provoking a *regression*, a return to an earlier phase of development.

We shall now continue our task of listing the elements that we have come to know as being influential over sexual development, whether they represent effective forces or merely the manifestations of those forces.

(Precocity)

One such element is spontaneous sexual *precocity*, which can at least be demonstrated with certainty in the aetiology of neuroses, although it is no better equipped than other elements to institute a cause on its own. It is expressed in the interruption, abbreviation or abolition of the infantile latency period, and becomes the cause of disorders by prompting sexual manifestations that have the character of perversions, first because of the incomplete state of the sexual inhibitions, and also because the genital system is undeveloped. These inclinations towards perversion may now be preserved as such or, after instances of repression have occurred, become drive-forces of neurotic symptoms. In any case, sexual precocity obstructs the path of the subsequent desirable domination of the sexual drive by the higher mental agencies, and increases the compulsive character that already attaches to the agency of the drive. Precocious sexuality is often accompanied by precocious intellectual development; it occurs in this way in the stories of the childhoods of the most eminent and capable individuals; in these cases it does not appear quite as pathogenic in its effects as it does when it appears in isolation.

(Temporal factors)

Other elements which we could, along with precocity, define as *'temporal'* demand to be taken into account. The sequence in which the individual drive impulses are activated, and the length of time during which they can manifest themselves, appears to be phylogenetically established, until they are subjected to the influence of a fresh impulse or a typical repression. But both within this temporal sequence and its duration variations seem to appear, which must exert a defining influence upon the final result. It cannot be a matter of indifference whether a certain current appears sooner or later than the counter-current, for the effect of a repression is not reversible: in almost every case a temporal deviation in the configuration of the components gives rise to a change in the final result. On the other hand, drive motions, which begin particularly intensely, often come to an end remarkably rapidly, as we can see for example in the heterosexual attachments of future manifest homosexuals. Those childhood strivings which begin most violently do not justify the fear that they will exert a lasting domination upon the character of the adult; we might just as well expect them to vanish, to make way for their opposite. (Despots do not rule for long.) We cannot even hint at what such temporal confusions in the developmental processes might be traced back to. Here a vista opens up on to a deeper phalanx of biological and perhaps historical problems, with which we are not yet ready to do battle.

(Tenacity)

The significance of all early sexual manifestations is intensified by a psychical factor of unknown origin, which for the time being, it must be admitted, we can only posit with any assurance as a provisional psychological concept. I am referring to the greater *tenacity* or *susceptibility to fixation* of these impressions of the sexual life, which must be taken into account if we are fully to understand the situation among future neurotics or perverts. Among other people, the same premature sexual manifestations cannot have such a deep impact that they compel repetition or that they are able to dictate the paths of the sexual drive throughout the whole of the person's life. This tenacity may perhaps be partially explained with reference to another psychical element, which we cannot avoid encountering in the causation of neuroses: the greater importance assigned to memory traces in mental life as against impressions. This element is clearly dependent on intellectual education, and grows along with the level of personal culture. In contrast to this, primitive man has been characterized as the 'unhappy child of the moment'.[5] Because of the antagonistic relationship between culture and the free development of sexuality, the consequences of which can be pursued far into the structure of our lives, the way in which the child's sexual life has been lived has little importance for later life when the social and cultural level is low, and more when it is higher.

(Fixation)

The support of the psychical elements mentioned above provides a favourable basis for accidentally experienced stimulations of childhood sexuality. The latter (primarily seduction by other children or adults) contribute the material that can be fixated with the former into a lasting disorder. Many later observed deviations from normal sexual life are thus established in both neurotics and perverts by the impressions received during childhood, which is supposed to be free of sexuality. Causes are divided between the compliance of the constitution, precocity, the property of increased tenacity and the random stimulation of the sex drive by external influences.

But the unsatisfactory conclusion that we must draw from these investigations into the disorders of the sexual life is that we do not know nearly enough to turn our individual insights into a satisfactory theory which would help us to understand both the normal and the pathological.

(1905)

Notes

1. This applies not only to those tendencies to perversion which appear 'negatively' in neurosis, but equally to positive perversions worthy of the name. These latter, then, must be traced back not only to the fixation of the infantile tendencies, but also to a regression to those same tendencies as a result of the obstruction of other channels of the sexual current. For that reason even positive perversions are accessible to psychoanalytic therapy.
2. At the same time we often see a normal sexual current beginning during puberty, but then collapsing because of its internal weakness, in the face of the first external obstacles, before being replaced by regression to the perverse fixation.
3. In some character traits a connection with certain erogenous components has even been recognized. Thus defiance, thrift and order derive from the use of anal eroticism. Ambition is determined by a strong urethral-erotic disposition.
4. Such a connoisseur of humanity as Émile Zola describes, in *La Joie de vivre*, a girl who, with serenity and self-abnegation, sacrifices everything she owns and everything that she could lay claim to, her fortune and her wishes for her own life, to those she loves. This girl's childhood is dominated by an insatiable need for affection, which she allows to decline into cruelty when she is abandoned for another.
5. The increase in tenacity may also be the consequence of a particularly intense somatic sexual expression of earlier years.

On the Sexual Theories of Children

The material on which the following survey is based comes from a number of different sources. First, from direct observation of the remarks and actions of children, secondly, from the statements of adult neurotics, who in the course of psychoanalytic treatment relate what they consciously remember about their childhood, and thirdly, from the conclusions, constructions and unconscious memories translated into consciousness which emerge from psychoanalysis of neurotics.

The fact that the first of these three sources has not on its own delivered everything worth knowing is explained by the attitude of adults towards the sexual lives of children. Children are assumed not to engage in any sexual activity, and for that reason no effort is made to observe that activity. At the same time there is a tendency to suppress any manifestations of sexual activity that might be worthy of attention. The opportunity to draw on this clearest and most productive of sources is thus very limited. What comes from the uninfluenced communications of adults about their own conscious childhood memories raises at best the objection that those memories will have been retrospectively falsified, and also needs to be assessed in terms of the fact that the sources of the information have developed neuroses later in life. Material from the third source will be subject to all the challenges that tend to be brought against the dependability of psychoanalysis and the certainty of the conclusions drawn from it. Hence I cannot attempt to test the validity of this judgement here. I wish only to give the assurance that anyone who knows and practises psychoanalytic technique develops a profound trust in its results.

I cannot vouch for the completeness of my own results, only for the care with which I have striven to acquire them.

It is difficult to decide the extent to which we may legitimately take what we are reporting here as universally applicable to all children, to each individual child. The pressure of education and differences in the intensity of the sexual drive must certainly cause large individual variations in the child's sexual behaviour. For that reason I have not arranged my paper according to successive periods of childhood, but have brought together things which have happened either earlier or later in different children. It is my conviction that no child – no child fully in possession of its senses, or at least no intellectually gifted child – can help being preoccupied with sexual problems in the years *before* puberty.

I do not attach a great deal of importance to the accusation that neurotics are a particular class of people marked by a degenerative predisposition, and that we must beware of drawing conclusions about other people's childhoods on the basis of theirs. Neurotics are people like anyone else, not to be sharply distinguished from normal people, and are not always easily differentiated in childhood from those who remain healthy in later life. One of the most valuable results of our psychoanalytical investigations is that their neuroses do not have any particular content unique to them alone, but that, as C. G. Jung has put it, they succumb to the same complexes that we healthy people also struggle against. The only difference is that healthy people are able to conquer those complexes without suffering any major or practically demonstrable harm, while neurotics can only successfully suppress them at the cost of expensive substitute formations, which is to say that they effectively fail. Neurotics and normal people are, of course, even closer to one another in childhood than they are in later life, so I cannot see it as methodologically mistaken to use the statements of neurotics about their childhoods to draw analogical conclusions about normal childhoods. But since those who will later become neurotics very often have within their constitution an unusually high sexual drive and a tendency towards precocity, towards a premature manifestation of that drive, they help us to recognize many aspects of infantile sexual activity more vividly and distinctly than our otherwise dull observational abilities would enable us to do. We will, however, only be able to assess the true value of these statements from adult neurotics once we have also, following the method of Havelock Ellis, taken the trouble to collect the memories of healthy adults.

As a result of both external and internal relations, the statements below primarily refer only to the sexual development of one sex, the male. But the value of a collection like the one that I am attempting does not have to be merely descriptive. The knowledge of infantile sexual theories formed in the thinking of children can be interesting in various ways, including, surprisingly, the understanding of myths and fairy tales. But it is actually indispensable for the conception of neuroses themselves; these childhood theories are still valid within neuroses, and have a certain influence on the formation of symptoms.

If we could escape our physical existences and, as merely thinking beings – from another planet, for example – see the things of this earth with a fresh eye, perhaps nothing would strike us as much as the existence of two sexes among human beings who, otherwise so *similar* to one another, nevertheless stress the outward signs of their difference. Now it does not appear that children choose this fundamental fact as the source of their investigations into sexual problems. Since they have known their father and mother for as long as they can remember, they consider their presence to be a reality that requires no further examination, and a boy responds similarly to a little sister from whom he is separated only by a very small age difference of one or two years. Children's urge for knowledge in this area does not awaken spontaneously, out of an innate need for causality, for example, but is spurred on by the id-controlling drives, if – once the child is over the age of two, say – those drives are affected by the arrival of a new child. Children who have not seen a new arrival taking up lodging in their own nurseries can still imagine themselves in the same situation on the basis of their observations in other houses. The loss of the parents' devoted care, either actually experienced or justly feared, the sense that all of one's possessions will henceforth and for ever have to be shared with the new child, have an awakening effect on the child's emotional life and sharpen its ability to think. The older child manifests unconcealed hostility towards its competitor, expressed in unkind judgements about the newcomer, in the desire that 'the stork can take him away again' and the like, and sometimes even in minor attacks on the baby as it lies helplessly in the cradle. A larger age difference generally weakens the manifestation of this primary hostility; similarly, in rather later years, if there are no brothers and sisters, the desire for a playmate, such as the child has been able to observe elsewhere, can get the upper hand.

Stimulated by these feelings and concerns, the child comes now to occupy itself with the first great problem of life, and asks itself the question *where has children come from*, a question which probably means initially: where has this individual, upsetting child come from. We think we can hear an echo of this first riddle in countless riddles in myth and legend; the question itself is, like investigations of all kinds, a product of vital necessity, as though the task were imposed upon thought processes in order to prevent the recurrence of such feared events. Let us assume, in the meantime, that the child's thinking soon frees itself from its original stimulus, and goes on working as an autonomous investigative drive. Where the child is not already too intimidated, it sooner or later sets off on the nearest path, demanding answers from its parents and carers, whom it identifies as the source of knowledge. But this path is a misleading one. The child either receives evasive replies or a reprimand for its hunger for knowledge, or else is fobbed off with the mythologically significant information which, in Germany, runs: 'the stork brings the children, and fetches them out of the water'. I have reason to assume that far more children are dissatisfied with this solution than parents imagine, and that they respond to it with energetic doubt, although this is not always openly expressed. I know of one three-year-old boy who, having received this explanation, went missing, to the horror of his nurse, and was rediscovered on the bank of the great castle pond, to which he had hurried to see the children in the water; and another who was able to manifest his disbelief only by insisting that he knew better, and that it wasn't the stork that brought the children, it was the heron. Many communications appear to me to suggest that children reject the stork theory, but from this first deception and dismissal onwards they nurture within themselves a mistrust of adults, they come to suspect something forbidden that must be withheld from them by the 'grown-ups', and for that reason they shroud their subsequent investigations in mystery. But at the same time they have also experienced their first instance of a 'psychical conflict', in which opinions for which they feel a compulsive preference, but which do not find favour with the grown-ups, are opposed to those which are maintained by the authority of the 'grown-ups' but are not acceptable to the children themselves. This psychical conflict can soon turn into a 'psychical split': an opinion which is connected with good behaviour but also with the suspension of reflection becomes the dominant, conscious one; the other, for which the child's investigations have meanwhile supplied new proof that is not supposed to be valid, becomes the suppressed, 'unconscious' opinion. The core complex of neurosis is constituted in this way.

Recently, in the course of the analysis of a five-year-old boy, which his father had first begun and then passed to me with a view to publication, I was given irrefutable proof of an insight on the trail of which the psychoanalytic treatment of adults had put me some time before. I now know that the change undergone by the mother during pregnancy does not escape the sharp eyes of the child, and that the child is fully capable of establishing the correct connection between the mother's physical increase and the arrival of the child. In this case the boy was three and a half years old when his sister was born, and four and three quarters when he revealed his superior knowledge through the most unmistakable allusions. But this early knowledge is always kept secret and later repressed and forgotten with the subsequent vicissitudes of children's sexual researches.

The 'fable of the stork', then, is not to be counted among infantile sexual theories; on the contrary, it is the observation of animals, which do so little to conceal their sexual life and to which the child feels so closely related, that reinforces the child's disbelief. With the knowledge that it grows in the mother's body, which the child acquires independently, it would be on the right path towards the solution of the problem on which it is putting its powers of thought to the test. But the child is hampered in its further developments by an ignorance that cannot be assuaged, and by incorrect theories thrown up by the state of the child's own sexuality.

These false sexual theories, which I shall now discuss, all share one very curious characteristic. Although they are grotesquely incorrect, each of them none the less contains a piece of genuine truth. In this respect they are similar to those attempts by adults – termed strokes of genius – to solve universal problems beyond human understanding. The correct and valid aspect of these theories is explained by their source in the components of the sexual drive, which are already stirring within the child's organism. For these hypotheses have not been brought into being by arbitrary psychical forces or chance impressions, but by the needs of the psychosexual constitution, and it is for this reason that we can talk about typical sexual theories of children, and that we encounter the same mistaken opinions among all children to whose sexual lives we have access.

The first of these is linked to the neglect of sexual differences, which we initially stressed as being characteristic of children. It involves *the attribution to all people, including females, of a penis* like the one that the boy knows from his own body. Within this sexual constitution, which we are obliged to acknowledge as 'normal', in childhood the penis is already the leading erogenous zone, the most important auto-erotic sexual object, and the esteem in which it is held is logically reflected in the child's inability to imagine a personality similar to him without that significant component. If the small boy catches a glimpse of a little sister's genitals, his remarks show that his prejudice is already strong enough to bend his perception; he does not observe anything like the absence of the member, but says *regularly*, as though to provide comfort and information: 'the (. . .) is only small yet; but it'll grow when she gets bigger.' The idea of a woman with a penis recurs later in the dreams of the adult: during nocturnal sexual arousal the man throws down a woman, strips her naked and prepares for coitus, only to interrupt the dream and the arousal at the sight of the well-formed member in place of the female genitals. The many hermaphrodites of classical antiquity faithfully replicate this formerly universal infantile idea; we can observe that it does not have a harmful effect on most normal people, while the hermaphroditic formations of the genitals really allowed by nature almost always provoke the greatest repulsion.

If this idea of a woman with a penis becomes 'fixated' in the child, resisting all the influences of later life and making the man incapable of having a sexual object without a penis, such an individual, however normal his sexual life may be in other respects, will inevitably become a homosexual, and seek his sexual objects among men who in other physical and mental respects resemble women. A real woman, as is subsequently acknowledged, remains an impossible sexual object for him, as she lacks the significant sexual attraction, indeed, in the context of another impression from childhood, she can become an object of abhorrence to him. The child principally dominated by the arousal of the penis has usually given himself pleasure by stimulating it with his hand, and will have been caught doing this by parents or carers, and scared with the threat that he will have his member cut off. The effect of this 'castration threat' is, in correct proportion to the esteem in which this part of the body is held, quite extraordinarily profound and lasting. Sagas and myths testify to the turmoil of the child's emotional life, to the horror linked to the castration complex, which is later recalled to consciousness with a corresponding degree of revulsion. The woman's genitals, seen later in life and regarded as mutilated, recall this threat, and for that reason they cause a feeling of horror rather than pleasure in the homosexual. Nothing about this reaction is altered when the homosexual learns from science that the child's hypothesis that women also have a penis is not as incorrect as might be thought. Anatomy has recognized the clitoris in the female as the organ homologous to the penis, and the physiology of sexual procedures has added that this small penis, which has ceased to grow, actually behaves like a real and proper penis in the childhood of the female, that it becomes the site of those stimuli which appeal to the touch, that its sensitivity gives a masculine character to the little girl's sexual activity, and that it takes a phase of repression during puberty to allow the female to come into being by clearing away this masculine sexuality. As the sexual functions of many women atrophy, either because the excitability of the clitoris is stubbornly maintained, or because its repression is too intense, the result is that its effect is partly annulled by hysterical compensation. All of this suggests that there may be some substance to the infantile sexual theory that women, like men, have a penis.

It is easy to observe that the little girl fully shares her brother's assessment. She develops a great interest in this part of the boy's body, and her interest is immediately commanded by envy. She feels disadvantaged, she tries to urinate in the position that the boy is enabled to do by his possession of a large penis, and if she expresses the desire that she would rather be a boy, we know what lack this desire is supposed to fill.

If the child were able to follow the suggestions prompted by the excitement of the penis, it would get a good deal closer to the solution of its problems. The fact that the child grows in the mother's body is clearly not enough of an explanation. How does it get there? What is it that initiates its development? It is likely that the father has something to do with it; after all, he declares that the child is also his child.[1] On the other hand, the penis also has its part to play in these mysterious procedures, and reveals as much by its co-excitement as a result of all this thinking. This excitement is connected to drives that the child is unable to interpret, dark impulses to perform violent actions, to penetrate, to smash, to open up a hole somewhere or other. But if this suggests that the child seems on the way to postulating the existence of the vagina, and attributing to the father's penis just such a penetration of the mother, the act through which the child comes into being in the mother's body, the investigation is interrupted at this point amid much bafflement, obstructed by the theory that the mother has a penis as a man does, and the existence of the cavity that receives the penis remains undiscovered by the child. We will happily accept that the lack of success of this intellectual effort makes it easier to reject and forget. But this brooding and doubt becomes the prototype for all later intellectual problem-solving, and the first failure has a paralysing effect that lasts for ever.

Ignorance of the vagina also means that the child can be convinced of the second of its sexual theories. If the child grows in the mother's body and is removed from it, the only possible conduit through which this can take place is the intestinal orifice. *The child must be evacuated like an excrement, a stool*. If this question becomes the object of solitary reflection, or of discussion between two children, the information will doubtless emerge that the child comes out of the opening navel, or the belly is cut open and the child removed from it, as in the story of Little Red Riding-Hood. These theories are expressed out loud and later consciously remembered; there is nothing abhorrent about them. The same children have completely forgotten that in earlier years they believed in another theory of birth, which now obstructs the repression of the anal sexual components that has occurred in the interim. At that time, stools were something that could be discussed openly and without shame in the nursery, and the child was not yet so far from its constitutional coprophilic inclinations. There was nothing degrading about coming into the world like a heap of dung that was not yet condemned by disgust. The cloacal theory that correctly applies to many animals was the most natural and the only one that the child would consider likely.

In that case, though, it was only consistent for the child to refuse the woman's painful privilege of having children. If children are born through the anus, a man can give birth just as well as a woman. So the boy is also able to fantasize that he himself will have children, and we do not need to accuse him of feminine tendencies for that reason. He is only manifesting the continuing vivid presence of his anal eroticism.

If the cloacal theory of birth persists in the consciousness of the later childhood years, as sometimes happens, it also brings a solution to the question of where children come from, although one that can no longer be considered original. Things happen as in a fairy tale. One eats a particular thing, and that gives one a child. The mentally ill person then reactivates this infantile theory of childbirth. A maniac, for example, will lead the visiting doctor to a little pile of excrement that she has deposited in a corner of her cell, and tell him with a laugh: that's the child I gave birth to today.

The third of the typical sexual theories presents itself to children when, through some chance domestic event, they witness parental sexual intercourse, of which they can have only very incomplete perceptions. Whatever part of this process they happen to observe, whether it is the position of the two people in relation to each other or the sounds or some attendant circumstance, in all cases they come to the same, as we might say, *sadistic view of coitus*, and see it as something that the stronger partner does violently to the weaker, and compare it, particularly the boys, with scrapping of the kind that is familiar to them from their dealings with other children, and which is itself not without a component of sexual excitement. I have not been able to establish that children diagnose this procedure, which they have observed between their parents, as the final clue leading to the solution of the problem of where children come from. More often they have appeared to misjudge this relationship, precisely because they have interpreted the act of love as an act of violence. But this conception of coitus itself gives the impression of a return of that dark impulse to an activity of cruelty, which, when they first thought about the riddle of where children come from, was linked with the excitement of the penis. Neither should we dismiss the possibility that the early sadistic impulse, which would almost have enabled the child to guess the fact of coitus itself, appeared under the influence of the darkest memories of parental intercourse, memories for which the child gathered material during the first years of life, when it still shared its parents' bedroom, although it did not use the material at the time.[2]

The sadistic theory of coitus which, in its isolation, misleads where it could have brought confirmation, is in turn the manifestation of an innate sexual component, which may be more or less strongly pronounced in the individual child, which is consequently to a large extent true, and which partly guesses the essence of the sexual act and the 'battle of the sexes' that precedes it. In many cases the child is also in a position to support this conception, which it has produced on the basis of an accidental perception that it has grasped in part correctly, in part wrongly, and in a contradictory manner. In many marriages the woman really does regularly resist the conjugal embrace, which gives her no pleasure and means the risk of a new pregnancy, and as a result she may give the child who is believed to be asleep (or is pretending to be sleeping) an impression that can be interpreted only as resistance to an act of violence. On other occasions, the marriage as a whole presents the attentive child with the drama of a constant argument expressed in loud words and hostile gestures, so that the child sees nothing surprising in the idea that this argument should continue through the night, and is finally conducted using the same methods as the child is accustomed to using with its brothers and sisters or its playmates.

But the child also sees it as a confirmation of its conception of intercourse when it discovers traces of blood in the bed or on its mother's linen. These are taken as proof that the father has once again attacked the mother in the same way during the night, while we would interpret the same fresh trace of blood as a pause in sexual intercourse. Sometimes this connection can explain an otherwise inexplicable 'fear of blood' among nervous patients. The child's error in turn conceals a grain of truth; in certain well-known circumstances the trace of blood should indeed be acknowledged as a sign of instituted sexual intercourse.

In a broader context of the insoluble problem of where children come from, the child deals with the issue of the essence and content of the condition called 'being married', and provides different answers according to whether chance perceptions gathered from around the child's parents coincide with the child's own drives, which still place the emphasis on pleasure. But what all these answers appear to have in common is the idea that being married promises a satisfaction of pleasure and an overcoming of shame. The version that I have encountered most frequently is that '*you urinate in front of each other*', a revision which sounds as though it seeks symbolically to suggest that the speaker knows more than he is saying: that *the husband urinates in the wife's pot*. On other occasions the meaning of marriage shifts into: *showing your bottom to each other* (without being ashamed). In one case, in which upbringing had managed to postpone sexual experience for a particularly long time, the fourteen-year-old girl, who was already menstruating, came, via the stimulus of reading, upon the idea that being married consisted in a '*mingling of the blood*', and as her own sister had not yet had a period, the concupiscent girl attempted an assault on a visiting friend, who had admitted that she was currently menstruating, to force her to 'mingle blood' in that way.

Children's opinions about the essence of marriage, which are in many cases retained by the conscious memory, are of great importance for the symptoms of later neurotic illness. These initially find expression in children's games, in which the players act out with each other what being married consists of, and later the desire to be married can choose the infantile form of expression to appear in an initially unintelligible phobia or a corresponding symptom.[3]

These, I suggest, are the most important of the typical sexual theories produced spontaneously in the child's earliest years, influenced only by the sexual drive-components. I know that I have achieved neither a complete collection of material nor a perfect connection with other areas of the child's life. I might add some supplements here, whose absence any informed person would have noticed. Thus, for example, there is the significant theory that one has a child by kissing, which reveals, as though it is quite obvious, the predominance of the erogenous oral zone. In my experience this theory is exclusively feminine, and is sometimes encountered pathogenically among girls whose sexual investigations in childhood have had the most inhibitions placed in their way. One of my patients came via a chance perception to the theory of the 'couvade', which, as is well known, is a universal custom among some peoples, and the intention of which is probably to contradict doubts about paternity which can never be quite conquered. As a rather curious uncle of the patient stayed at home for days after the birth of his child and received visitors in his dressing-gown, she concluded that both parents were involved in childbirth, and that they both had to go to bed.

Around the tenth or eleventh year, sexual information begins to reach children. A child who has grown up in uninhibited social conditions, or has otherwise had happier opportunities for observation, tells others what it knows, because this makes it feel mature and superior. What children learn in this way is generally correct, that is, they find out about the existence of the vagina and its purpose, but otherwise these explanations, which they borrow from one another, are in many cases mixed with inaccuracies, and tainted with residues of older infantile sexual theories. They are hardly ever complete or adequate to the solution of the ancient problem. Where ignorance of the vagina prevented an understanding of the process, ignorance of semen now does the same. The child cannot guess that a substance apart from urine is evacuated through the male sexual member, and sometimes an 'innocent girl' will still be outraged on her wedding night to discover that her husband 'urinates into her'. This information from the pre-pubertal period is now joined by a new upturn in the child's sexual investigations; but the theories which children produce now no longer have the typical and original flavour of the primal and characteristic theories of early childhood, a time when the infantile sexual components can carry their expression through into theories without inhibition or transformation. Later intellectual efforts aimed at the solution of sexual mysteries do not seem to me to be worth collecting, and they can lay little claim to pathogenic significance. Their diversity is of course primarily dependent on the nature of the explanations given; their significance lies more in the fact that they reawaken the traces of that first period of sexual interest, now unconscious, so that in many cases they are connected to masturbatory sexual activity and a piece of emotional separation from the parents is connected with them. Hence the damning judgement of educators that such enlightenment at this age 'corrupts' children.

A few examples may show which elements often enter these late ruminations by children about the sexual life. A girl has learned from her schoolmates that the man gives the woman an egg which she hatches in her body. Somebody who has also heard about the egg identifies it with the testicle – the testicles are vulgarly known as '*Eier*', or 'eggs', in German – and racks his brains to imagine how the contents of the scrotum could repeatedly replenish themselves. Explanations are seldom so far-reaching that they prevent significant uncertainties concerning sexual processes. Thus girls can come to expect that sexual intercourse takes place on only one occasion, but that it takes a very long time, twenty-four hours, and from that single occasion all children come, one by one. We might be inclined to think that this child had acquired knowledge of the reproductive process in certain insects; but this supposition is not confirmed, and the theory appears to be an independent creation. Other girls ignore the gestation period, life in the mother's body, and assume that the child appears immediately after the night during which the first intercourse takes place. Marcel Prévost has taken this young girl's error and turned it into a funny story in one of his *Lettres de femmes*. Almost inexhaustible, and perhaps not without interest in a general sense, is the theme of this later sexual investigation among children or among adolescents who have remained in a childish stage, but it is further removed from my interest, and I need only stress that children bring to light much that is incorrect, the purpose of which is to contradict older and better knowledge, but knowledge which has been repressed and kept unconscious.

The way in which children react towards the information that reaches them is also important. In some children, sexual repression has been so extensive that they refuse to listen to anything, and these individuals manage to remain ignorant, or at least apparently ignorant, until late in life when, in the psychoanalysis of neurotics, knowledge from early childhood makes its appearance. I also know of two boys between the ages of ten and thirteen who listened to the sexual explanation, but gave the messenger the dismissive reply: 'It may well be that your father and other people do something like that, but I know very well that my father never would.' Whatever the diversity of this later behaviour of children as regards the satisfaction of the sexual thirst for knowledge, we may assume an entirely uniform attitude for the first years of childhood, and we believe that at that time they were all most eagerly striving to learn just what it is that parents do with each other that finally results in children.

(1908)

Notes

1. Cf. the analysis of the five-year-old boy in the *Jahrbuch für psychoanalytische und psychopathologische Forschungen*, 1st half-volume, 1909.

2. In the autobiographical book *Monsieur Nicolas*, Restif de la Bretonne confirms this sadistic misunderstanding of coitus in the story of an impression made upon him when he was three years old.

3. The children's games with the greatest significance for subsequent neurosis are 'doctors and nurses' and 'mummies and daddies'.

Contributions to the Psychology of Erotic Life

I

Concerning a Particular Type of Object-choice in Men

In the past, we have left it to the poets to depict for us the 'conditions of love', according to which people make their object-choices, and how they reconcile the demands of their fantasy with reality. Poets have certain qualities that enable them to solve such a task, in particular a great sensitivity in the perception of hidden mental impulses in others, and the courage to make their own unconscious speak. But one factor reduces the value of their communications. Poets are bound to the condition of achieving intellectual and aesthetic pleasure as well as certain emotional effects, and for that reason they cannot represent the stuff of reality unaltered, but are obliged to isolate fragments of it, dissolve obstructive connections, soften the whole and fill any gaps. These are the privileges of what is known as 'poetic licence'. In addition, they can express only a small degree of interest in the origin and development of such mental states, which they describe as complete. As a result, however, it is inevitable that science should use a heavier hand, bringing a smaller gain in pleasure, when dealing with the same material, whose poetic treatment has been delighting people for thousands of years. These observations may also serve to justify a strictly scientific treatment of human erotic life. Science is, in fact, the most complete renunciation of the pleasure principle of which our psychical work is capable.

During psychoanalytic treatment one has ample opportunity to glean impressions from the erotic life of neurotics, while at the same time bearing in mind that one has also observed or experienced similar behaviour among people of average health, or even among exceptional people. When favourable material permits the accumulation of impressions, individual types clearly emerge. Here I should first like to describe one such type of male object-choice, both because it presents itself as a series of 'conditions of love', whose co-existence is not comprehensible – in fact it is frankly alarming – and because it permits simple psychoanalytical explanation.

1) The first of these conditions of love should be identified as being effectively specific; as soon as one comes across it, one can seek the presence of the other characteristics of this type. One might refer to it as the condition of the '*damaged third*'; its content leads the person concerned never to choose as a love object a woman who is free, a girl or a single woman, but only a woman to whom another man can apply property rights, whether as husband, fiancé or friend. In some cases this condition proves so potent that the same woman can at first be ignored or even despised as long as she does not belong to anyone, while she immediately becomes the object of passionate love as soon as she enters one of the aforementioned relationships with another man.

2) The second condition is perhaps less constant, but none the less striking. This type is only fulfilled by its coincidence with the first, while the first also appears to occur in great frequency on its own. According to this second condition, the modest and unimpeachable woman never exerts the charm that raises her to become a love object; that charm will only be exerted by a woman who has somehow acquired a bad sexual reputation, and about whose fidelity and dependability there might be some doubt. This latter characteristic may vary significantly, from the faint shadow cast upon the reputation of a wife who is not disinclined to flirt to the openly polygamous conduct of a coquette or an adept in the art of love; at any rate, it is something of this kind that men belonging to our type cannot do without. To put it a little coarsely, we might call this condition 'love of whores'.

Just as the first condition gives rise to the satisfaction of agonistic and hostile impulses against the man from whom one is seizing the beloved woman, the second condition, which requires the woman to behave in some way like a prostitute, is related to the activation of *jealousy*, which seems to be a need for lovers of this type. Only if these men can be jealous does the passion reach its peak and the woman attain her full value, and the men never miss an opportunity to experience these most intense sensations. Curiously, the jealousy is directed not at the rightful owner of the beloved, but at newly arriving strangers who might cast suspicion upon the beloved. In extreme cases, the lover shows no desire to possess the woman for himself alone, and appears to feel entirely at ease in the triangular relationship. One of my patients, who had suffered terribly as a result of his lady's indiscretions, had no objections to her getting married, in fact he did all he could to encourage it. Then for years he never showed a sign of jealousy. Another typical case, however, had in his earliest love relationships been very jealous of the husband, and had demanded that the lady cease marital intercourse with him; in his many later relationships, however, he behaved like others and no longer saw the legitimate husband as a disturbance.

The following paragraphs do not describe the conditions required of the love object, but the behaviour of the lover towards the object of his choice.

3) In normal love-life the value of the woman is determined by her sexual integrity, and reduced by her approach to the character of the prostitute. So it seems to be a striking deviation from the normal if lovers of our type treat women with this character as *love objects of the highest value*. Relationships of love with these women are carried on by the greatest psychical expenditure, to the point of consuming all other interests; these women are the only people one could love, and the requirement of fidelity that the subject imposes on himself is renewed each time it can be broken down in reality. Within these traits of relationships of love we can see with extreme clarity the *compulsive* character that is always to a certain degree a part of passionate love. But the fidelity and intensity of the connection do not allow us to infer that such a love relationship fills the erotic life of the person in question, or even that it occurs only once. On the contrary, passions of this kind are repeated, with the same curious qualities – one the precise image of the other – several times during the life of a man belonging to this type; indeed, depending upon outward conditions, such as a change of residence or

surroundings, love objects can be replaced so often that they finally form *a long series*.

4) The most surprising thing for the observer, among lovers of this type, is the manifest tendency to '*rescue*' the loved one. The man is convinced that the woman needs him, that without him she will lose all moral control and rapidly descend to a deplorable level. So he is saving her by not letting her out of his sight. In individual cases, the intention of saving can be justified by the invocation of sexual unreliability and the socially threatened position of the lover; but it appears no less clearly where such supports are absent in reality. One man of this type, who was able to win his ladies through artful seduction and a subtle dialectics, spared himself no efforts in the relationship to keep his chosen one on the path of 'virtue' by means of self-penned treatises.

If we were to consider all the individual traits of the picture described here – the condition decreeing that the woman should not be free, or that she should behave like a prostitute, the high value placed upon the woman in question, the need for jealousy, the fidelity that is none the less compatible with a long series of objects, and the intention of saving the woman – we would consider it unlikely that they could all derive from a single source. And yet, if we consider the life histories of the people in question, immersing ourselves psychoanalytically in them, we will easily reach such a conclusion. The curious definition of object-choice, and the strange amorous behaviour, have the same psychical source as in the erotic life of normal people; they arise out of the infantile fixation of tenderness upon the mother and represent one of the outcomes of that fixation. Normal love-life contains only a few residual traits which unmistakably reveal the maternal model of the object-choice, such as the love of young men for more mature women; the libido was detached from the mother relatively quickly. In our type, on the other hand, the libido has lingered so long with the mother, even after the onset of puberty, that the love objects chosen subsequently possess the imprint of maternal characteristics, and all become easily recognizable maternal surrogates. Here we might make the comparison with the skull formation of the new-born; after a protracted birth the child's skull must represent the cast of the maternal pelvic canal.

Our task now is to justify the idea that the characteristic traits of our type, both the conditions of love and amorous behaviour, really do emerge from the maternal constellation. This might be most easily accomplished in relation to the first condition – the woman's un-freedom – or the condition of the damaged third party. One sees immediately that for a child who has grown up in a family, the fact that the mother belongs to the father becomes an inseparable part of the maternal essence, and the injured third party is none other than the father. Equally easy to identify as being related to the infantile connection is the supplementary trait of over-valuation: the loved one is the only one, she is irreplaceable. For no one has more than one mother, and the relationship with the mother is based on an unrepeatable event that is beyond any doubt.

If the love objects in our type are above all supposed to be mother surrogates, the formation of series, which so directly contradicts the condition of fidelity, becomes comprehensible. Psychoanalysis also teaches us, with reference to other examples, that the notion of something irreplaceable in the unconscious often announces its presence by breaking down into an infinite series – infinite because no surrogate possesses the required satisfaction. So the insatiable desire to ask questions, seen in children at a certain age, is explained by the fact that they have only a single question to ask, and it is one that they cannot utter. Similarly, the loquacity of some neurotically damaged people is produced by the pressure of a secret that demands to be communicated, but which, in the face of all temptation, they will still not betray.

On the other hand, the second condition of love, requiring the chosen object's resemblance to a prostitute, seems energetically to resist inference from the mother complex. To the adult's conscious thought the mother tends to appear a person of unimpeachable moral purity, and hardly anything can be so insulting, if it comes from without, or so tormenting if it comes from within, as doubt of this characteristic in her. This relationship of the keenest opposition between the 'mother' and the 'whore', however, will prompt us to examine the unconscious relationship between these two complexes, since we learned long ago that what is split in two in consciousness joins into one in the unconscious. Our investigation then leads us back to the time when the boy begins to acquire a more complete knowledge of sexual relationships between adults, in the years just before puberty. At this point, brutal pieces of information, tending undisguisedly to provoke contempt and rebellion, familiarize him with the mystery of the sexual life, destroying the authority of adults, which proves to be irreconcilable with the revelation of their sexual activity. The greatest impression made on the new initiate is in the connection between this information and his own parents. That relationship is often categorically rejected, with words along the lines: 'Maybe your parents and other people do things like that with each other, but with my parents it's quite impossible.'

It is a rarely absent corollary to 'sexual enlightenment' that, at the same time, the boy becomes aware of the existence of certain women who perform the sexual act in return for money, and who are for that reason universally despised. This contempt must be far from the boy's mind; all he can muster for these unfortunates is a mixture of longing and horror, once he knows that they could introduce him, too, into sexual life, which he hitherto considered the exclusive preserve of the 'grown-ups'. If he can then no longer maintain the doubt that his parents are an exception to the ugly norms of sexual activity, he tell himself with the perfect reasoning of the cynic that the difference between the mother and the whore is not so great after all, that they basically do the same thing. The explanations have in fact awoken trace memories of the impressions and desires of his early childhood, and have reactivated certain psychical impulses on the basis of those traces. The boy begins to desire his mother in a new way, and begins to hate his father again, as a rival standing in the way of his desire; he comes, as we say, under the control of the Oedipus complex. He does not forget this about his mother and considers it an act of infidelity that she has bestowed the favour of sexual intercourse not upon him but upon his father. If these impulses do not pass quickly, they inevitably lead to fantasies whose content is the mother's sexual activity in the most diverse forms, and the tension accompanying them is particularly easily resolved in the act of masturbation. As a result of the constant collaboration of these two driving motives, desirability and the desire for revenge, fantasies of the mother's infidelity are by far the most common; the lover with whom the mother commits infidelity almost always bears the traits of the subject's own self, or more properly those traits in an idealized form, as an adult and elevated to the level of the father. What I have described elsewhere as the 'family romance' (or 'family saga')[1] encompasses the various formations of this fantasy activity and its interweaving with the various egoistic interests of this age. Once we have understood this piece of mental development, however, we can no longer find it contradictory and incomprehensible that the condition of the lover's resemblance to a prostitute is derived directly from the mother complex. The type of masculine erotic life that we have described bears the traces of this evolution, and can be simply understood as a fixation on the boy's pubertal fantasies, which have later found an outlet in the reality of life. It is not difficult to assume that the eagerly practised masturbation of the years of puberty has made its contribution to the fixation of those fantasies.

The tendency to *save* the loved one seems to have only a loose and superficial connection with these fantasies, which have come to dominate real erotic life, and one that can be reduced to a conscious explanation. The loved one puts herself in danger by being inclined towards inconstancy and infidelity, so it is understandable that the lover should try to protect her against those dangers by guarding her virtue and working against her bad inclinations. In the meantime the study of screen memories, fantasies and nocturnal dreams reveals that what we have here is an eminently successful 'rationalization' of an unconscious motive, which might be equated with a highly successful secondary elaboration in the dream. In fact, the *saving motive* has a meaning and history of its own and is an independent descendant of the mother complex or, more correctly, the parent complex. When the child hears that he *owes* his life to his parents, that his mother '*gave him life*', affectionate impulses unite with impulses struggling towards adult manhood, towards independence; these yield the desire to return this gift to the parents, to give them something of equal value. It is as though the boy wished to say in defiance: I need nothing from my father, I want to give him back everything I have cost him. He then forms the fantasy of *rescuing his father from life-threatening danger*, thus leaving things even between them. In many cases this fantasy is displaced on to the emperor, the king or some other great man, and after this displacement has taken place it becomes capable of reaching consciousness, and is even usable to the poet. As applied to the father, the defiant meaning of the rescue fantasy is greatly predominant; when applied to the mother it generally assumes its affectionate meaning. The mother has given life to the child, and that unique gift cannot easily be replaced with something of equal value. With one of those small changes of meaning facilitated in the unconscious – and which we might, for example, equate with the flowing of one concept into another in the consciousness – the rescue of the mother assumes the meaning: give or make her a child, of course a child as one is oneself. The distance from the original meaning of rescue is not terribly great, and the shift in meaning is not arbitrary. One's mother has given one a life, one's own, and in return one is giving her another life, that of a child, highly similar to one's own self. The son proves his gratitude by wishing to have a son with his mother, who is equal to himself; in the rescue fantasy, that is to say, he identifies completely with his father. All drives, whether affectionate, grateful, lustful, defiant or self-glorifying, are satisfied by the single desire *to be his own father*. The moment of danger is not lost in the change of meaning; the act of birth, in fact, is the very first danger from which one was rescued by one's mother's efforts. Equally, birth is the first life-threatening danger, since it is the model of everything that will afterwards cause us to feel fear, and the experience of birth has probably left us with the affective expression that we call fear. The Macduff of Scottish legend, who was not born of his mother, but cut from his mother's womb, was unacquainted with fear for the same reason.

The ancient interpreter of dreams, Artemidorus, was certainly right in claiming that a dream changes its meaning according to the person of the dreamer. According to the rules for the expression of unconscious thoughts, 'rescue' can vary its meaning, according to whether it is fantasized by a woman or a man. It can mean either: to make a child = to cause to be born (for the man) or: to have a child oneself (for the woman).

Particularly when they are associated with water, the various meanings of rescue in dreams and fantasies make themselves clearly apparent. If a man in a dream rescues a woman from water, it means he is turning her into a mother, which means, according to the above reflections, he makes her his own mother. If a woman rescues someone else (a child) from the water, she is thus declaring herself, like the king's daughter in the legend of Moses,[2] to be the mother who brought him into the world.

Sometimes the rescue fantasy may have an affectionate meaning when it involves the father. In that case it seeks to express the desire to have the father as a son, that is, to have a son who resembles the father. Because of all these relationships between the rescue motif and the parent complex, the tendency to rescue the loved one constitutes an essential trait of the type of love described here.

I do not deem it necessary to justify my working method, which, as in my presentation of *anal eroticism*, at first stresses extreme and sharply circumscribed types from the observed material. In both cases there are far more individuals in whom these traits can only be identified in smaller numbers or in an indistinct form, and it is obvious that only the interpretation of the entire context in which these types are received makes possible their proper evaluation.

(1910)

Note

1. [In:] O. Rank, *Der Mythus von der Geburt des Helden* [*The Myth of the Birth of the Hero*], [Leipzig and Vienna] 1909. (*Schriften zur angewandten Seelenkunde*, vol. 5.) 2nd edition, 1922.

2. Ibid.

II

Concerning the Most Universal Debasement in the Erotic Life

1

If the psychoanalyst asks himself for which illness he is most frequently approached for help – apart from the various forms of anxiety – he must reply: psychical impotence. This strange disorder affects men of a highly libidinous nature, and is expressed in the refusal of the executive organs of sexuality to perform the sexual act, despite the fact that they can be demonstrated to be intact and properly functioning both before and after, and that there is a strong psychical inclination to the performance of the act. The patient himself takes his first step towards an understanding of his state when he learns that such a failure only occurs during his attempts with certain people, while with others it is never a problem. Then he knows that the inhibition of his masculine potency arises from some quality of the sexual object, and he will sometimes describe having the sense of an obstacle within himself, the perception of a counter-volition successfully obstructing the conscious intention. But he cannot guess what that internal obstacle is and what property of the sexual object it is that puts it into effect. If he has repeatedly experienced such failure, by making a familiar erroneous connection he will probably conclude that the memory of the first occasion has prompted the repetitions as a disturbing anxiety. As to the first occasion, he will connect it with an impression that he has had 'by chance'.

A number of authors have written and published psychoanalytical studies into psychical impotence. Any analyst can confirm the explanations offered on the basis of his own medical experience.[1] It is really a matter of the inhibiting effect of certain psychical complexes outside the knowledge of the individual. What emerges as the most general content of this pathogenic material is the incestuous fixation on mother and sister which has not been overcome. Otherwise, one should bear in mind the influence of accidental impressions of embarrassment connected with infantile sexual activity, and the elements that generally reduce the libido that is to be directed at the female sexual object.[2]

If one subjects cases of harsh psychical impotence to deep psychoanalytic study, one obtains the following information about the psychosexual processes at work. Once again, the basis of the illness is here – as it is most probably in all neurotic disturbances – an inhibition in the evolution of the libido towards what we would call its normal final formation. Here we have two currents that have failed to coincide, which can be brought together only by a completely normal loving relationship, and which we can identify as the *affectionate* and the *sensual*.

Of these two currents the affectionate is the older. It derives from the earliest years of childhood, was formed on the basis of the interests of the drive to self-preservation and is aimed at the members of the family and those with the responsibility of caring for the child. From the very outset it has admitted contributions from the sexual drives, components of erotic interest that are already more or less clearly apparent in childhood, and which, in neurotics, are revealed in every case by later psychoanalysis. This corresponds to the *primary infantile object-choice*. It tells us that when the sexual drives find their first objects, they are supported by the evaluations of the ego-drives, just as the first sexual satisfactions take their support from the bodily functions necessary for the preservation of life. The 'affection' of parents and carers, which rarely denies its erotic character ('the child is an erotic toy'), does a great deal to increase the contributions of eroticism to the investments of the child's ego-drives, and to take them to a level which one will have to take account of in subsequent development, particularly if certain other conditions lend their assistance.

These affectionate fixations on the part of the child continue through childhood and repeatedly bring with them eroticism which, in consequence, is distracted from its sexual goals. During puberty the powerful 'sensual' current is added to this, and it no longer fails to recognize its goals. It apparently never avoids following earlier paths, and then invests the objects of the primary infantile choice with much stronger libidinal charges. But since it there encounters the obstacle of the barrier against incest that has been erected in the meantime, it will manifest the tendency to find, as soon as possible, the passage away from these objects, which are unsuitable in reality to other, extraneous objects, with which a real sexual life can be led. These extraneous objects will still be chosen according to the model (the imago) of the infantile objects, but over time they will attract the affection that was attached to the earlier objects. The man will leave his father and mother – according to the biblical prescription – and pursue his wife: affection and sensuality will be reunited. The highest levels of sensual passion will imply the highest psychical valuation of the object (the normal over-valuation of the sexual object by the man).

Two factors will be crucial in deciding whether this advance in the development of the libido is to fail. First, the degree of *frustration in reality* that will oppose the new object-choice and devalue it for the individual. There is no sense in setting out to make an object-choice if one is not permitted to choose, or if one has no prospect of being able to choose anything suitable. Secondly, there is the degree of *attraction* that can be manifested by the infantile objects that are about to be abandoned, which is proportional to the erotic investment assigned to them in childhood. If these two factors are strong enough, the general mechanism of neurosis formation comes into play. The libido turns away from reality, is absorbed by fantasy activity (introversion), intensifies the images of the first sexual objects and becomes fixated on those. The prohibition on incest, however, forces the libido turned towards these objects to remain in the unconscious. The masturbatory activity of the sensual current that now belongs to the unconscious plays its own part in the reinforcement of that fixation. If progress that has failed in reality is now accomplished in the fantasy, and if, in fantasy situations leading to masturbatory satisfaction, imaginary sexual objects are replaced by different objects, nothing has been altered in this state of affairs. By virtue of this substitution, fantasies become capable of reaching consciousness, while no progress is made in the real placement of the libido.

Thus it can happen that the whole of a young person's sensuality is bound, in the unconscious, to incestuous objects or, we might say, fixated on unconscious incestuous fantasies. The result is then absolute impotence, which may be further ensured by a real weakening – acquired at the same time – of the organs that perform the sexual act.

For psychical impotence, properly so-called, to come into existence, less severe conditions are required. The whole of the sensual current need not succumb to the fate of having to hide behind the affectionate current; it must have remained strong enough, or resistant enough, to inhibition, to force its way partially out into reality. But the clearest signs show that the sexual activity of such people does not have the complete psychical drive-force behind it. This activity is capricious, easily disturbed, often incorrect in its performance, and provides little enjoyment. Most importantly, however, it must make way for the affectionate current. So a limitation in the object-choice has been generated. The sensual current that has remained active seeks only objects that do not recall the forbidden incestuous people; if a person emanates an impression that might lead to a high psychical valuation, it does not lead to an excitement of sensuality, but to affection without erotic effects. The erotic life of such people remains split in the two directions that are characterized in art as heavenly and earthly (or animal) love. Where they love they do not desire, and where they desire they cannot love. They seek objects that they do not need to love, in order to keep their sensuality far from their beloved objects, and the strange failure of psychical impotence recurs according to the laws of 'complex sensitivity' and the 'return of the repressed', when, in the object chosen to avoid incest, one feature, and usually an inconspicuous one, recalls the object that is to be avoided.

The chief means of protection against such a disturbance that a person can employ in this division of love consists in the psychical *debasement* of the sexual object, while the over-valuation normally applied to the sexual object is reserved for the incestuous object and its substitutes. As the condition of debasement is fulfilled, sensuality can express itself freely, allowing significant sexual achievements and a high degree of pleasure. Another connection contributes to this result. People in whom the affectionate and the sensual currents have not properly converged also generally have a love-life that is not especially refined; perverse sexual goals have been preserved there, the non-fulfilment of which is felt to be a severe deprivation of pleasure, but fulfilment of which appears possible only with the debased, despised sexual object.

We can now understand the motives behind the fantasies of a boy, mentioned in the first of our 'contributions', which reduced his mother to the status of a prostitute. They are efforts to bridge the gulf between the two currents of the love-life, in fantasy at least, and to acquire the mother as an object of sensuality by debasing her.

2

So far we have examined psychical impotence from a medicinal and psychological point of view, which is not justified by the title of this essay. But we shall see that we needed this introduction in order to have access to our actual theme.

We have reduced psychical impotence to the non-convergence of the affectionate and the sensual currents in erotic life, and we have explained this inhibition of development with reference to the influences of powerful childhood fixations and the later frustration that came about with the arrival of the barrier against incest in the meantime. There is one chief objection to this theory: it gives us too much, it explains to us why certain people suffer from psychical impotence, but makes it seem mysterious to us that others are able to escape that illness. Since all manifest elements under consideration – the strong infantile fixation, the prohibition on incest, and frustration in the years of development after puberty – must be acknowledged by almost all civilized people, we would be justified in expecting that psychical impotence was a universal illness of the civilized, and not an illness of certain individuals.

The obvious way to escape this conclusion would be to point to the quantitative factor of the cause of the illness, to the greater or lesser contributions of the individual causal elements responsible for whether or not a recognizably successful illness results from them. But although I must acknowledge this answer to be the correct one, I do not intend to use it to dismiss the conclusion. On the contrary, I wish to posit the assertion that psychical impotence is far more widespread than we imagine, and that a certain degree of it actually characterizes the erotic life of the civilized human being.

If, rather than restricting psychical impotence to the failure of coital action, where the intention of pleasure is present and the genital apparatus is intact, we extend the concept, we may add those men who are described as psychoanaesthetics, in whom the action itself never fails, but is performed without any particular pleasure: a condition that occurs more frequently than one would wish to think. Psychoanalytic examination in such cases reveals the same aetiological elements that we have encountered with psychical impotence in the narrower sense, although the symptomatic differences are not at first explained. From psychoanaesthetic men we are led by an easily justifiable analogy to the very large number of frigid women, whose behaviour in love cannot actually be better described or understood than by being equated with the more conspicuous psychical impotence of the man.[3]

But if, rather than extending the concept of psychical impotence, we consider the nuances of its symptomatology, we cannot rule out the insight that men's behaviour in love in our contemporary civilized world generally bears the stamp of psychical impotence. The affectionate and the sensual currents converge as they should only in a very small minority of civilized people; in almost every case the man almost feels restricted in his sexual activity by respect for the woman, and only develops his full potency if he has a debased sexual object before him. This in turn is partly explained by the fact that his sexual goals include perverse components, which he does not dare satisfy with the women he respects. He can only have complete sexual pleasure if he is able to abandon himself unreservedly to satisfaction, and he does not dare do this with his lawful wife. Hence his need for a debased sexual object, a woman who is ethically inferior to himself, to whom he does not have to ascribe aesthetic considerations, who does not know him, who is not able to judge him with reference to the other circumstances of his life. He is happiest devoting his sexual power to such a woman, even if all of his affection belongs to a superior woman. It may be that the tendency, which we so often observe, of men of the highest social classes to choose a woman of a lower class as a long-term lover or even a wife, is merely the consequence of the need for a debased sexual object, psychologically connected to the possibility of complete satisfaction.

I have no hesitation in holding the elements at work in true psychical impotence – the intense incestuous fixation of childhood and the real frustration of adolescence – responsible for this so frequent attitude of civilized men in their love-life. It is rather unpleasant to say so, and it is also paradoxical, but nevertheless it must be said: in order to feel truly free in one's erotic life and, thus also happy, one must overcome respect for the woman, and become familiar with the idea of incest with one's mother or sister. Anyone who subjects himself to serious self-examination in regard to this demand will doubtless find within himself that he considers the sexual act as basically something debasing, something that stains and sullies, not only in the physical sense. He will only be able to seek the origin of this appreciation, which he will certainly not be happy to admit, during that time of his youth when his sensual current was already strongly developed, but when its satisfaction was forbidden almost equally with an extraneous as with an incestuous object.

In our civilization women also undergo the after-effects of their upbringing and, at the same time, the repercussion of men's behaviour. The damage to the woman is, of course, the same if the man does not come to them with his full potency, as if the initial over-valuation of passionate love dissolves when contempt sets in once he has possessed her. Women show little sign of a need for debasement in the sexual object; this certainly has something to do with the fact that they do not generally display anything resembling the sexual over-valuation that occurs in men. But the fact that the woman spends a long time away from sexuality, and her sensuality lingers in the fantasy, has another significant consequence for her. Often she is then no longer capable of severing the connection between sensual activity and prohibition, and she proves to be psychically impotent, frigid, once such activity is finally permitted to her. This is the source, in many women, of the tendency to keep even permitted relationships a secret for some time, and in others of the capacity to experience normal sensations as soon as the condition of prohibition is reintroduced in a secret love affair.

I think the condition of prohibition in the erotic life of women may be assimilated to the need for the debasement of the sexual object in the man. Both are the consequences of the long delay between sexual maturity and sexual activity that is required, for cultural reasons, by education and upbringing. Both seek to abolish psychical impotence, which results from the non-confluence of the affectionate and the sensual impulses. If the same causes have a very different result in women and men, this may derive from another difference in the behaviour of the two sexes. Civilized women tend not to transgress the prohibition on sexual activity during the period of waiting, and consequently establish an internal connection between prohibition and sexuality. Men usually transgress that prohibition under the condition of the debasement of the object, and thus carry that condition with them into their later erotic life.

In view of such active efforts in the contemporary civilized world to reform the sexual life, it is not superfluous to recall that psychoanalytic research makes no more claims in this direction than any other. It seeks merely to uncover connections by tracing that which is manifest back to that which is hidden. Psychoanalysis will be content if these reforms use its discoveries to replace that which is harmful with that which is more advantageous. But it cannot predict whether other institutions will not have other, perhaps more serious sacrifices as a result.

3

The fact that the curbs placed by civilization on erotic life lead to the most universal debasement of the sexual object may divert us from the objects to the drives themselves. The harm done by the initial frustration of sexual pleasure is expressed in the fact that when it is later freely given in marriage it is no longer completely satisfying in its effects. But even unlimited sexual freedom from the very first does not produce better results. It is easy to establish that the psychical value of the need for love immediately declines once satisfaction becomes a matter of comfort. An obstacle is required if the libido is to be heightened, and where natural resistance is inadequate to satisfaction, people have in all ages introduced conventional forms of resistance in order to be able to enjoy love. That is equally true of individuals and of whole peoples. In times when no difficulties were placed in the way of the satisfaction of love, as for example during the decline of the ancient civilizations, love became worthless, life became empty, and stronger reaction formations were needed in order to re-establish the indispensable affective values. In this context we might claim that the ascetic current within Christianity created a set of psychical values for love which pagan antiquity could never give it. It assumed its supreme significance among the ascetic monks, whose life was filled almost entirely by the struggle against libidinous temptation.

At first, of course, one will certainly be tempted to trace back the difficulties outlined here to universal features of our organic drives. In general it is certainly also true to say that the psychical significance of a drive rises in proportion to its frustration. We might imagine exposing a number of very different people to starvation under the same conditions. As the imperious need for nourishment grew, all individual differences would blur and instead make way for the uniform manifestations of a single unsatisfied drive. But is it also true that the psychical value of a drive generally declines to a similar extent with its satisfaction? We might think, for example, of the drinker's relationship to wine. Is it not the case that wine always offers the drinker the same toxic satisfaction that has been so often compared with the erotic in poetry, and which may also stand comparison with it from the scientific point of view? Has anyone ever heard of a drinker being forced to keep changing his drink because if he drinks the same one all the time it loses its flavour for him? On the contrary, habit forges the bond between the man and the sort of wine that he drinks ever more strongly. Are we aware of the drinker needing to go to a country where wine is more expensive, or where the drinking of wine is forbidden, in order to stimulate his declining satisfaction by interposing such difficulties? We are not. If we listen to the statements of our great alcoholics, such as Böcklin, concerning their relationship with wine,[4] it sounds like the purest harmony, a model for a happy marriage. Why is the lover's relationship to his sexual object so very different?

Surprising as it may sound, I think that one would have to deal with the possibility that there is something in the nature of the sexual drive itself that is unfavourable to the achievement of complete satisfaction. Within the long and difficult history of the development of the drive two elements immediately stand out which might be responsible for this difficulty. First, because of the dual-phase beginning of object-choice, with the barrier against incest coming in between, the definitive object of the sexual drive is no longer the original one, merely a surrogate for it. But psychoanalysis has taught us this: if the original object of an impulse of desire has been lost through repression, it is often represented by an infinite series of substitute objects, none of which, however, is completely satisfying. This may explain the inconstancy in the object-choice, the 'hunger for stimuli', which so often characterizes the erotic life of adults.

Secondly, we know that the sexual drive at first breaks down into a large series of components – or rather that it emerges from such a series – not all of which can be absorbed into its later formation, but must first be suppressed or put to some other use. Most important among these are the coprophilic parts of the drive, which have probably proved incompatible with our aesthetic culture since we raised our olfactory organ from ground level by walking upright; and also a high proportion of the sadistic drives belonging to love-life.

But all such developmental processes affect only the upper layers of the complex structure. The fundamental processes supplying erotic excitement remain unchanged. The excremental has grown too deeply and inseparably intertwined with the sexual, the position of the genitals – *inter urinas et faeces* – remains the defining and unalterable element. Here, to modify a well-known saying of the great Napoleon, we might say: anatomy is destiny. The genitals themselves did not participate in the development of the forms of the human body as it became beautiful, they remained bestial, and consequently love is basically just as animal as it has always been. The erotic drives are difficult to educate, their education achieves now too much, now too little. That which civilization seeks to turn them into appears impossible to accomplish without a significant loss of pleasure, and the persistence of unused impulses becomes apparent in sexual activity as dissatisfaction.

We should, then, perhaps familiarize ourselves with the notion that it is impossible to balance the demands of the sexual drive with the requirements of civilization, that renunciation and illness, and, more remotely, the threat of the extinction of the human race because of its cultural development cannot be averted. This gloomy prognosis, however, is based only on the supposition that cultural dissatisfaction is the inevitable consequence of certain particularities that the sexual drive has developed under the pressure of civilization. The same incapacity of the sexual drive to yield complete satisfaction once it is subjected to the first demands of civilization becomes the source of the greatest cultural achievements, which are brought about as the result of a sublimation, pushed ever further onwards, of its drive components. For, what reason would people have for putting the sexual drive-forces to other uses if, by some distribution of those forces, they could have provided complete satisfaction of desire? People would be unable to break away from that desire, and would accomplish no further progress. So it seems that it is the irreducible differences between the demands of the two drives – the sexual and the egoistic – that make people capable of ever higher accomplishments, although there is always the constant danger to which weaker individuals are at present subject in the form of neurosis.

The intention of science is neither to frighten nor to console. But I myself am willing to admit that such far-reaching conclusions as those set out above should be established on a broader basis, and that perhaps other modes of development for humanity will be able to correct those that are treated here in isolation.

(1912)

Notes

1. M. Steiner, 'Die funktionelle Impotenz des Mannes und ihre Behandlung' ['Functional Impotence in Men and its Treatment'], 1907 [*Wiener medizinische Presse*, vol. 48, Sp. 1535]. W. Stekel, in *Nervöse Angstzustände und ihre Behandlung* [*Nervous Anxiety and its Treatment*], [Berlin and] Vienna, 1908 (2nd edition, 1912). – Ferenczi, 'Analytische Deutung und Behandlung der psychosexuellen Impotenz beim Manne' [correctly: des Mannes] ['Analytical Interpretation and Treatment of Psychosexual Impotence in Men'], *Psychiatrische-neurologische Wochenschrift*, 1908.
2. W. Stekel: loc. cit., p. 191ff.
3. And it should be freely admitted that frigidity in women is a complex subject, and one that is also approachable from another direction.
4. G. Floerke: *Zehn Jahre mit Böcklin* [*Ten Years with Böcklin*], 2nd edition [Munich], 1902, p. 16.

III

The Virginity Taboo

Few details of the sexual life of primitive peoples have such a surprising effect on our emotions as their assessment of virginity, the intact state of the woman. To us, the high regard placed upon virginity by the suitor is so solidly established and self-evident that we almost become embarrassed if called upon to explain it. The requirement that the girl should not bring into marriage to one husband a memory of sexual intercourse with another is of course nothing but the consistent continuation of the exclusive property right to a woman which constitutes the essence of monogamy, and the extension of this monopoly to include the past.

So it is not difficult for us to justify what at first seemed to us to be a prejudice, on the basis of our opinions about a woman's erotic life. The person who is first able to satisfy the virgin's longing for love, arduously contained over a long period of time, and who has thus overcome the resistances erected in her by the influences of milieu and her education, will be drawn by her into a lasting relationship that will no longer be possible with anyone else. On the basis of this experience the woman enters a state of dependence which guarantees the untroubled permanence of her possession and makes her capable of resisting new impressions and the temptations of strangers.

The expression 'sexual bondage' was chosen in 1892 by Krafft-Ebing[1] to describe the fact that individuals can acquire an unusually high degree of bondage with, and a lack of autonomy towards, another person with whom they are having sexual intercourse. This bondage can sometimes extend very far, as far as the loss of all autonomous will and the toleration of the most severe sacrifices of the person's own interests; the author, however, has not neglected to observe that a certain degree of such bondage is 'entirely necessary if the connection is to be of some duration'. Such a degree of sexual bondage is in fact indispensable to the maintenance of the civilized marriage and the curbing of the polygamous tendencies that threaten it, and in our social community this factor is regularly taken into account.

An 'unusual degree of passionate love and weakness of character' on the one hand, boundless egoism on the other: Krafft-Ebing deduces the origin of sexual bondage from the coincidence of these two factors. Analytic experiences, however, mean that we cannot content ourselves with this simple attempt at an explanation. Rather, it becomes apparent that the crucial factor is the amount of sexual resistance that is overcome, along with the concentration and uniqueness of the process of overcoming it. Accordingly, bondage is incomparably more frequent and intense in women than in men, although in our own times it is more frequent in men than it was in antiquity. Where we have been able to study sexual dependence in men, it has been shown to be the result of the overcoming of a psychical impotence by a particular woman, to whom the man in question has felt bound from that point onwards. This course of events seems to explain many unusual marriages and some tragic fates, even some of far-reaching importance.

We would not be properly describing the behaviour of primitive peoples if we said that they placed no emphasis on virginity, adducing as proof that they allow the defloration of girls outside of wedlock and before the first act of marital intercourse. It appears on the contrary that for these people, too, defloration is a significant act, but it has become the object of a taboo, a prohibition that could be called religious. Instead of making the accomplishment of the act the preserve of the girl's fiancé and later husband, custom requires that *he should avoid it*.[2]

It is not my intention to make a complete collection of all the literary testimonies for the existence of this moral prohibition, to pursue its geographic spread and list all the forms in which it is expressed. So I shall merely state that it is very widespread practice among primitive peoples living today to remove the hymen in this way, outside the marriage that will subsequently take place. Crawley puts it as follows: 'This marriage ceremony consists in perforation of the hymen by some appointed person other than the husband; it is common in the lowest stages of culture, especially in Australia.'[3]

But if defloration is not to occur as a result of the first act of marital intercourse, it must be undertaken – somehow, by someone – before this. I shall cite some passages from Crawley's book mentioned above, which are informative on these points, but which also justify us in making our own critical observations.

p. 191: 'Thus in the Dieri and neighbouring tribes (in Australia) it is the universal custom when a girl reaches puberty to rupture the hymen (*Journ. Anthrop. Inst.*, XXIV, 169). In the Portland and Glenelg tribes this is done to the bride by an old woman; and sometimes white men are asked for this reason to deflower maidens (Brough Smith, op. cit., II, 319).'

p. 307: 'The artificial rupture of the hymen sometimes takes place in infancy, but generally at puberty . . . It is often combined, as in Australia, with a ceremonial act of intercourse.'

p. 348: (On Australian tribes where the well-known exogamous restrictions on marriage prevail, from communications by Spencer and Gillen): 'The hymen is artificially perforated, and then the assisting men have access (ceremonial, be it observed) to the girl in a stated order . . . The act is in two parts, perforation and intercourse.'

p. 349. 'An important preliminary of marriage amongst the Masai (in Equatorial Africa) is the performance of this operation on the girl (J. Thompson, op. cit., 258). This defloration is performed by the father of the bride among the Sakais (Malay), Battas (Sumatra) and Alfoers of Celebes (Ploss and Bartels, op. cit., II, 490). In the Philippines there were certain men whose profession it was to deflower brides, in case the hymen had not been ruptured in childhood by an old woman who was sometimes employed for this (Featherman, op. cit., II, 474). The defloration of the bride was amongst some Eskimo tribes entrusted to the angekok, or priest (ibid., III, 406).'

The observations that I have reported refer to two points. First, it is regrettable that in these accounts no more careful distinction has been made between the rupture of the hymen without coitus and coitus for the purpose of such a rupture. Only at one point do we expressly hear that the process is divided into two parts, the (manual or instrumental) defloration and the subsequent sex act. The otherwise very rich material in Bartels and Ploss is almost unusable for our purposes because in this account the psychological significance of the act of defloration, as against its anatomical result, is completely absent. Secondly, one would like to be told in what respect 'ceremonial' (purely formal, solemn, official) coitus on these occasions differs from regular sexual intercourse. The authors to whom I have had access were either too ashamed to say anything about it, or underestimated the psychological significance of such sexual details. We may hope that the original reports of travellers and missionaries are more thorough and unambiguous, but given the current difficulty[4] of getting access to this generally foreign literature I can say nothing definite about it. Besides, we may dispel any doubts concerning this second point by observing that ceremonial, mock coitus represents only a substitute, perhaps a replacement, for an act that was performed in its entirety in former times.[5]

To explain this virginity taboo, various different elements might be introduced, of which I shall give a brief account. The defloration of girls generally involves the spilling of blood; the first attempt at explanation then refers to primitive man's fear of blood, with blood being seen as the seat of life. This blood taboo has been proven by numerous proscriptions that have nothing to do with sexuality. It clearly has something to do with the prohibition on killing and forms a protective defence against the primal thirst for blood, primeval man's lust for killing. In this view, the taboo of virginity is allied with the almost universal taboo on menstruation. Primitive man cannot separate the mysterious phenomenon of the monthly blood flow from sadistic ideas. He interprets menstruation, particularly the first time it occurs, as the bite of a spirit animal, perhaps as the sign of sexual intercourse with that spirit. According to some, he recognizes this spirit as that of an ancestor, and then we understand, borrowing on other insights, that the menstruating girl is taboo because she is a property of this ancestral spirit.[6]

On the other hand, however, we are warned not to overestimate the influence of a factor such as a horror of blood. After all, no such horror has succeeded in suppressing practices such as the circumcision of boys and the even crueller circumcision of girls (excision of the clitoris and the labia minor), which are practised to some extent among the same people, or in abolishing the validity of other ceremonies during which blood is spilt. So it could hardly come as a surprise if that fear had been overcome to the benefit of the husband on the occasion of the first cohabitation.

A second explanation also turns away from the sexual, but reaches much further into the universal. It suggests that primitive man is the prey to a persistent anxious disposition that constantly lies in wait, very like the one that we assert in the psychoanalytic theory of neuroses. This anxious disposition is most apparent on all occasions which depart in some way from the familiar, and which introduce something new and unexpected, something not understood or strange and sinister. This is also the source of the ceremonial that extends far into later religions, and which is connected to the start of any new task, to the beginning of any new period of time, to first fruits, whether they be human, animal or vegetable. The dangers by which the anxious person believes himself threatened never present themselves more vividly to him than on the threshold of the dangerous situation, and it is then only sensible to protect oneself against them. The first act of sexual intercourse can certainly claim, because of its importance, to be preceded by such cautionary measures. The two attempts at explanation, based on the fear of blood and the fear of first occasions, do not contradict, but rather reinforce one another. The first act of sexual intercourse in marriage is certainly a serious act, all the more so if it is to involve the flow of blood.

A third explanation – the one preferred by Crawley – points out that the virginity taboo belongs in a wider context, encompassing the whole of the sexual life. It is not only the first coitus with the woman that is taboo, but sexual intercourse in general; we might almost say that woman as a whole is taboo. Woman is not only taboo in particular situations deriving from her sexual life – menstruation, pregnancy, childbirth and confinement. Even outside of these situations, intercourse with a woman is subject to prohibitions so serious and so numerous that we have every reason to doubt the supposed sexual freedom of primitive people. It is correct that the sexuality of primitive peoples is on certain occasions free of inhibitions; usually, however, it seems to be more strongly bound by prohibitions than it is at higher levels of civilization. Whenever men undertake something special, an expedition, a hunt, a war campaign, they must stay far from women, particularly from sexual intercourse with them; otherwise it will paralyse their strength and bring failure. Even in the customs of daily life, efforts to keep the sexes apart are unmistakable. Women live with women, men with men; family life in our sense is thought barely to exist in many primitive tribes. The separation is sometimes taken so far that one sex is forbidden to pronounce the personal names of the other sex, and women develop a language with a special vocabulary. Sexual need may repeatedly break through these barriers of separation, but in some tribes even meetings between the spouses must take place outside the house and in secret.

Wherever primitive man has set a taboo, he fears a danger, and we should not dismiss the idea that all these prescriptions of avoidance manifest an essential fear of woman. Perhaps this fear is based on the fact that women appear different from men, eternally incomprehensible and mysterious, strange and therefore hostile. Men fear that women will weaken them, infecting them with their femininity, and that the men will consequently prove to be unfit. The sleep-inducing, relaxing effect of coitus may be the model for this fear, and along with the perception of the influence that women acquire through sexual intercourse with men, and the consideration that they compel, may justify the spread of that fear. There is nothing ancient about all this, nothing that does not live on among us.

Many observers of primitive people living today have judged that their tendencies towards love are relatively weak, and never reach the intensity that we are used to finding among civilized people.

Others have contradicted this assessment, but at any rate the taboo practices listed above reveal a power that contradicts love in rejecting the woman as strange and hostile.

In terms little different from the usual terminology of psychoanalysis, Crawley reveals that each individual is separated from the others through a 'taboo of personal isolation', and that it is precisely the small differences, all else being similar, that explain the feelings of strangeness and hostility between them. It would be tempting to pursue this idea and deduce from this 'narcissism of small differences' the hostility that we see successfully arguing against the feelings of solidarity and the commandment of universal human love. As to the basis for the narcissistic, highly contemptuous rejection of women by men, psychoanalysis believes it has guessed a chief cause in the castration complex and its influence on the judgement of women.

However, we note that these last observations have taken us far beyond our theme. The universal taboo on women sheds no light on the particular prescriptions set down for the first sexual act with the individual virgin. Here we are referred back to our initial explanations: the fear of blood and the fear of the first occasion, and even of these we would have to say that they do not get to the heart of the taboo precept. This is quite clearly based on the intention of *refusing or sparing the later husband* something inseparable from the first sexual act, although, according to the observation we made at the beginning, this relationship would require a particular bond between the woman and that particular man.

This is not the place to discuss the origin and the ultimate significance of the taboo prescriptions. I have done that in my book *Totem and Taboo*, where I acknowledged the condition of an original ambivalence for the taboo and argued that its origins lay in prehistoric processes that have led to the foundation of the human family. We can no longer discern such a primal significance in the taboo customs practised by primitives today. We forget all too easily that even the most primitive peoples live in a culture far removed from the primeval, one which is, in chronological terms, just as old as our own and which similarly corresponds to a later, albeit different, stage of development.

Today we find that taboos among primitives have already been spun into a deft system, much like the ones developed by our own neurotics in their phobias, in which ancient motives are replaced with more recent ones which harmoniously agree. Setting aside these genetic problems, then, we wish to return to the insight that primitive man applies a taboo where he fears a danger. This danger is, it is generally understood, a psychical one, because the primitive is not obliged to make two distinctions that strike us as unavoidable. He does not separate the material danger from the psychical, or the real from the imaginary. In his consistent animistic view of the world, all danger – both the danger that comes from a natural force and that from other people or animals – arises from the hostile intention of a creature which possesses a soul just as he does. On the other hand, however, he is accustomed to projecting his own inner impulses of hostility on to the outside world, and shifting them on to the objects which he feels to be unpleasant or even merely strange. Women are also now recognized as a source of such dangers, and the first sexual act with a woman is marked out as a particularly intense danger.

I believe that we will obtain some information about the nature of this intensified danger, and why it particularly threatens the future husband, if we examine the behaviour of contemporary women at our own stage of civilization more precisely in the same context. I can confirm as a result of this examination that such a danger really does exist, and this proves that with the virginity taboo, primitive man is defending himself against a danger that he is right to suspect, although it is a psychical danger.

We consider it a normal reaction if the woman, after coitus and at the peak of satisfaction, embraces the man and presses him to her. We see this as an expression of her gratitude and an affirmation of lasting dependence. But we know it is by no means the rule for a first act of intercourse to lead to such behaviour; in very many cases it is a disappointment for the woman, who remains cold and unsatisfied, and it usually takes more time and frequent repetition of the sexual act before it begins to lead to satisfaction for the woman. A whole series of such cases leads from an initial, fleeting frigidity to the regrettable result of long-term frigidity that cannot be overcome by any efforts of affection on the part of the man. I believe that this frigidity in women has not yet been satisfactorily understood, and apart from cases in which it can be attributed to the unsatisfactory potency of the man, it demands elucidation, possibly with reference to related phenomena.

I do not wish to refer here to those frequent attempts to avoid the first act of sexual intercourse, because they are ambiguous and should be understood primarily, if not wholly, as an expression of universal efforts on the part of women to defend themselves. I believe, on the other hand, that certain pathological cases shed light on the mystery of female frigidity. In these, after the first act, indeed, after every new act of intercourse, the woman manifests her unconcealed hostility towards the man by cursing him, raising her hand to him or actually striking him. In one eminent case of this kind, which I have been able to subject to a detailed analysis, this happened despite the fact that the woman loved the man very much, that it was she herself who tended to demand coitus, and that she clearly derived a high level of satisfaction from it. I think that this strange and contrary reaction is the result of the same impulses that are usually manifested only as frigidity, that is, they are capable of preventing the affectionate reaction without in the process being expressed themselves. In the pathological case, what in frigidity – which occurs far more frequently – is united into an inhibiting effect, is, so to speak, broken down into its two components; this is something we observed long ago in the so-called 'dual-phase' symptoms of compulsive neurosis. According to this theory, the danger thrown up by the defloration of the girl would consist in the fact that one would attract her hostility, and the future husband would have every reason to avoid such enmity.

Analysis easily allows us to guess which of the woman's impulses are involved in the establishment of this paradoxical behaviour, in which I expect to find the explanation of frigidity. The first act of coitus sets in motion a series of such impulses which have no place in the desired feminine attitude, and some of which will not reappear even in later instances of intercourse. We would immediately think of the pain suffered by the virgin during defloration, and we would perhaps be inclined to see that moment as decisive, and desist from looking for others. But we would be wrong in attributing such a meaning to that pain, and should put in its place a narcissistic insult that grows out of the destruction of an organ; this insult finds a rational representation in the knowledge of the diminished sexual value of the deflowered girl herself. The marriage practices of primitive people, however, contain a warning against such overvaluation. We have heard that in some cases the ceremonial occurs in two phases: the rupture of the hymen (with hand or instrument) is followed by an official coitus or a simulacrum of intercourse with the man's representative. This tells us that the significance of the taboo proscription is not fulfilled by the avoidance of anatomical defloration, that the husband should be spared something other than the woman's reaction to the painful injury.

A further reason for disappointment in the first coitus lies in the fact that, for civilized women at least, expectation and fulfilment cannot coincide. Until now, sexual intercourse has been most strongly associated with prohibition, and hence legal and permitted intercourse is not felt to be the same. How deep-seated this connection can be is revealed in an almost comical way by the efforts of so many fiancées to conceal their new amorous relations from all strangers, even from their parents, where there is no need to do so, and no opposition to be feared. The girls say openly that their love will lose value for them if other people know about it. Sometimes this motive can become overpowering, and prevents development of the capacity for love in marriage. The woman can only find her capacity for tender emotions in a forbidden relationship that must remain secret, the only one in which she is sure she will be able to act on the basis of her own will, uninfluenced by anyone else.

However, this motive does not go deep enough either; being linked to civilized conditions, it does not enable us to make a good comparison with the state of affairs among primitive people. More important is the next element, based on the evolution of the libido. The efforts of analysis have enabled us to learn how regular and how powerful the first allocations of the libido are. These concern sexual desires that are preserved from childhood; in women they generally involve fixation of the libido on the father or the brother who takes his place, desires that were often directed at something other than coitus, or included coitus only as a vaguely acknowledged goal. The husband is, so to speak, only ever a substitute, never the right man; someone else, in typical cases the father, has first claim on the woman's capacity for love, the husband has at best the second claim. It now depends how intense that fixation is, and how stubbornly it is maintained, as to whether the substitute-man will be rejected as incapable of giving satisfaction. Frigidity is thus subject to the genetic conditions of neurosis. The more powerful the psychical element in the woman's sexual life, the better the distribution of her libido will prove able to withstand the shock of the first sexual act, the less overwhelming physical possession of her will be. Frigidity may then become fixed as a neurotic inhibition, or act as a basis for the development of other neuroses, and even a moderate reduction of the man's potency can supply a great deal of assistance in this process.

The custom of primitive people in transferring the task of defloration to a high elder, a priest, a holy man, a father substitute (see above p. 264) seems to take account of an old sexual desire. From here it seems to me to be a simple step to the much-debated *Ius primae noctis* of the medieval lord. A. J. Storfer[7] has defended the same position, and also the widespread institution of 'Tobias nights' (the custom of chastity for the first three nights of marriage) as an acknowledgement of the rights of the patriarch, as C. G. Jung did before him.[8] It thus only confirms our expectations if we encounter the godhead among the father surrogates to whom the task of defloration is entrusted. In some areas of India the newly-wed woman had to sacrifice her hymen to the wooden lingam, and according to St Augustine's account, in the Roman marriage ceremony (of his own time?) the same custom was followed, mitigated by the fact that the young woman had only to sit down on the huge stone phallus of Priapus.[9]

Another motive returns to yet deeper layers, one which demonstrably bears the chief responsibility for the paradoxical reaction against men, and whose influence in my opinion is manifested in the frigidity of women. In women, the first coitus activates yet other impulses than those already described, impulses which resist the feminine function and the feminine role in general.

The analysis of many neurotic women tells us that they pass through an early stage in which they envy their brother the sign of masculinity and, because they lack that sign (although in fact it is only reduced in size), they feel disadvantaged and handicapped. We place this 'penis-envy' under the heading of the 'castration complex'. If we allow 'masculine' to include 'wanting to be masculine', we might apply to such behaviour the term 'masculine protest', coined by Alfred Adler, to proclaim this factor the bearer of neurosis in general. During this phase, girls often make no secret of their envy of their brother, and the enmity towards him that follows on from it; they even try to urinate standing up like their brother, as a way of representing their supposed equality. In the case, mentioned above, of unrestrained post-coital aggression against an otherwise beloved husband, I was able to establish that this phase had existed before the object-choice. Only later on did the little girl's libido turn towards the father, and then, rather than wishing for a penis, she wished for – a child.[10]

I should not be surprised if, in other cases too, the chronological sequence of these impulses were reversed and this part of the castration complex only came into effect after the successful object-choice. But the woman's masculine phase, in which she envies the boy his penis, is also earlier in terms of the history of development, and closer to original narcissism than to object love.

Some time ago I happened to have the opportunity to study the dream of a newly married woman, which was recognizable as a reaction to the loss of her virginity. It betrayed without constraint the woman's desire to castrate the young husband and keep his penis for herself. Of course there was also room for the more innocuous interpretation, that she had desired the act to be prolonged and repeated, only some details of the dream passed beyond that meaning, and both the character and the subsequent behaviour of the dreamer bore out the former interpretation. Behind this penis-envy there is now revealed the hostile bitterness of the woman towards her husband, which can never quite be ignored in relations between the sexes, and the clearest signs of which are present in the aspirations and literary productions of 'emancipated' women. This hostility on the part of the woman leads Ferenczi – I do not know if he was the first to do this – to engage in palaeobiological speculation about the time when the differentiation of the sexes occurred. At first, he says, copulation took place between two individuals of the same species, one of whom, however, developed into the stronger partner and forced the weaker to endure sexual union. Bitterness over this subjection has survived in the contemporary situation of woman. I do not believe that anyone can be reproached for making use of such speculations, as long as they are careful not to place too much value upon them.

After giving this list of motives for the woman's paradoxical reaction to defloration, traces of which persist in frigidity, we may sum up by saying that the woman's *immature sexuality* is discharged upon the man who first teaches her the sexual act. If that is the case, the virginity taboo is reasonable enough, and we can understand the prescription that the man who is to join in a lasting cohabitation with the woman should avoid such dangers. At higher levels of civilization the appreciation of this danger makes way for the promise of dependence and no doubt for other motives and temptations as well; virginity is held to be a good that the man must not renounce. But the analysis of marital disorders teaches us that those motives which seek to force the woman to avenge herself for her defloration are never entirely extinguished, even from the mental life of the civilized woman. I think it must strike the observer in what seems to be a large number of cases that the woman remains frigid and feels unhappy in a first marriage, while after the dissolution of that marriage she becomes a tender and gratifying wife to her second husband. The archaic reaction has exhausted itself, so to speak, on the first object.

In some other respects, however, the virginity taboo has not completely disappeared from our civilized life. The popular mind is aware of it, and poets have sometimes made use of it. Anzengruber, in a comedy, shows how a simple farmer's boy is held back from marrying the bride meant for him because she is 'a whore that'll cost him 'is life'. For that reason he agrees that someone else should marry her, and he will then take her as a widow, by which time she will have ceased to be dangerous. The title of the play, *Das Jungferngift* [*Virgin's Venom*], recalls the fact that snake-tamers first induce poisonous snakes to bite upon cloths so that they can then handle them unharmed.[11]

The virginity taboo and part of its motivation has its most powerful depiction in Hebbel's tragedy *Judith and Holofernes*. Judith is one of those women whose virginity is protected by a taboo. Her first husband was paralysed by a mysterious anxiety on their wedding night, and did not dare touch her again. 'My beauty is the beauty of deadly nightshade,' she says. 'Enjoyment of it brings madness and death.' When the Assyrian general besieges her city, she devises the plan of seducing and corrupting him with her beauty, employing a patriotic motive to disguise a sexual one. After her defloration by the powerful man, who boasts of his strength and fearlessness, she finds in her rage the strength to cut off his head, and thus becomes the liberator of her people. Decapitation is well known to us as a symbolic substitute for castration; accordingly, Judith is the woman who castrates the man by whom she has been deflowered, as in the dream told to me by the newly married woman. Hebbel has sexualized the patriotic tale from the Apocrypha of the Old Testament with clear intent, because in the biblical account Judith is able, after her return, to boast that she remains unsullied, and the biblical text makes no mention of her sinister wedding night. With the poet's sensitivity, though, he has probably perceived the ancient motif underlying that tendentious story, and only restored the material's older content.

In an excellent analysis, I. Sadger has demonstrated how Hebbel's choice of material was determined by his own parental complex, and how he came so regularly to take the side of woman in the battle of the sexes, empathizing with the hidden impulses of her soul.[12] He also quotes the motivation that the poet himself gave for the changes he had introduced into the material, and rightly finds it specious, seemingly designed outwardly to justify and fundamentally to conceal something of which the poet himself was unconscious. I shall not touch upon Sadger's explanation of why it was necessary for Judith, widowed in the biblical tale, to become a virgin widow. He refers to the intention of the childhood fantasy, disavowing parental sexual intercourse and turning the mother into an intact virgin. But to continue: after the poet had established his heroine's virginity, his sympathetic fantasy persisted in the hostile reaction set off by the violation of her virginity.

In conclusion we may say: defloration does not just have one civilized consequence of binding the woman to the man in a lasting fashion; it also unleashes an archaic reaction of hostility against the man, which can assume pathological forms that are expressed often enough in phenomena of inhibition in marital love-life, and to which we can attribute the fact that second marriages are so often more successful than first ones. The surprising taboo of virginity, and the fear with which, among primitive people, the husband avoids the defloration, find their complete justification in this hostile reaction.

It is interesting, then, that as an analyst one can encounter women in whom the opposite reactions of bondage and enmity are both manifest, and have remained profoundly linked to one another. There are women who seem to have fallen out completely with their husbands, and yet can make only vain attempts to leave them. As soon as they try to turn their love to another man, the image of the first, unloved though he now is, appears as an inhibiting factor between them. Analysis then teaches us that these women are still in a state of bondage with their first husbands, but no longer out of affection. They cannot free themselves from their husbands because they have not yet completed their revenge; in pronounced cases, the vengeful impulse has not even reached consciousness.

(1918)

Notes

1. V. Krafft-Ebing, 'Bemerkungen, über geschlechtliche Hörigkeit und Masochismus' ['Remarks on Sexual Bondage and Masochism'], *Jahrbücher fur Psychiatrie*, 10, 1892.

2. E. Crawley, *The Mystic Rose, a Study of Primitive Marriage*, London, 1902; Bartels and Ploss, *Das Weib in der Natur- und Völkerkunde* [*Women in Biology and Anthropology*], Leipzig, 1891; various passages in Frazer, *Taboo and the Perils of the Soul* [London, 1911], and Havelock Ellis, *Studies in the Psychology of Sex* [Philadelphia, 1915].

3. Crawley, op. cit., p. 347.

4. [Caused by the First World War.]

5. Where many other cases of marriage ceremonial are concerned, there is no doubt that people other than the bridegroom, such as his helpers and colleagues (the 'groomsmen' of our own traditions), are given complete sexual access to the bride.

6. Cf. *Totem und Tabu* [*Totem and Taboo*, Vienna], 1913.

7. 'Zur Sonderstellung des Vatermordes' ['On the Special Status of Patricide'], *Schriften zur angewandten Seelenkunde*, XII, 1911.

8. 'Die Bedeutung des Vaters für das Schicksal des Einzelnen' ['The Significance of the Father for the Fate of the Individual'], *Jahrbuch für psychoanalytische und psychopathologische Forschungen*, I, 1909.

9. H. H. Ploss and M. Bartels, *Das Weib in der Natur- und VölkerKunde* [*Women in Nature and Ethnography*], I, XII [Leipzig, 1891] and [J. A.] Dulaure, *Des Divinités géneratrices* [*The Generative Divinities*], Paris, 1885, reprinted from the 1825 edition, p. 142ff.

10. See 'Über Triebumsetzungen, insbesondere der Analerotik' ['On Transformations of Instinct as Exemplified in Anal Eroticism'], *Internationale Zeitschrift für Psychoanalyse*, IV, 1916/18.

11. A masterfully concise short story by Arthur Schnitzler ('Das Schicksal des Freiherrn v. Leisenbogh' [The Fate of Baron von Leisenbogh] deserves inclusion here, despite the disparity of the situation. The lover of a sexually experienced actress, injured in an accident, has, so to speak, created a new virginity for her by uttering a fatal curse upon the first man to possess her after him. The woman placed under this taboo does not dare to engage in sexual intercourse for a while. But after falling in love with a singer, out of curiosity she first decides to grant a night to Baron von Leisenbogh, who has been wooing her unsuccessfully for years. He falls victim to his own curse; he suffers a heart-attack the moment he learns the motive for his unexpected luck in love.

12. 'Von der Pathographie zur Psychographie' ['From Pathography to Psychography'], *Imago*, I, 1912.

'A Child is Being Beaten'

Contribution to the Understanding of the Origin of Sexual Perversions

I

The fantasy 'a child is being beaten' is one confessed with surprising frequency by those who have sought psychoanalytic help for hysteria or compulsive neurosis. It is very likely that it occurs even more frequently among others who have not been driven to this decision by any manifest illness.

The fantasy is connected with feelings of pleasure, and for that reason it has been reproduced countless times in the past, or is still being reproduced. At the climax of the imagined situation an onanistic satisfaction (that is to say, in the genitals) is achieved in almost every case, at first deliberately, but also, later on, with a compulsive character counter to the person's resistance.

The fantasy is only confessed hesitantly, the memory of its first appearance is uncertain, analytic treatment of the object meets with unambiguous resistance, and shame and a sense of guilt may emerge more powerfully here than they do in the case of similar communications about the remembered beginnings of sexual life.

Finally, we are able to establish that the first fantasies of this kind are fostered very early, certainly before the individual attends school, as early as the age of four or five. If, at school, the child has watched as other children were being beaten by the teacher, this experience will have conjured up the fantasies once more when the child has gone to sleep, intensifying them if they still existed and perceptibly modifying their content. From that point onwards 'an indeterminately large number' of children have been beaten. The influence of school is so clear that the patients in question were at first tempted to trace back their beating fantasies exclusively to the impressions gleaned during their time at school, after the age of five. But this never lasted; the fantasies had already been present before that time.

If the beating of children stops in higher school classes, its influence is more than merely replaced by the effect of the reading matter that soon assumes importance. In my patients' milieu it was almost always the same books to which young people had access that gave fresh stimulus to the beating fantasies: the so-called *Bibliothèque rose*, *Uncle Tom's Cabin* and the like. In competition with these writings, the child's own imagination began to invent a wealth of situations and institutions in which children were beaten or otherwise punished and disciplined because of their naughtiness and bad habits.

As the fantasy of the beaten child was regularly invested with a high degree of pleasure, and culminated in an act of pleasurable auto-erotic satisfaction, it might be expected that watching another child being beaten in school had become a source of similar pleasure. But this was never the case. Being present at real scenes of beating in school provoked a curiously excited, probably mixed feeling in which opposition probably played a large part. In some cases the real experience of beating scenes was felt to be unbearable. Incidentally, even in the refined fantasies of later years the patients insisted on the condition that no serious harm came to the punished children.

One was obliged to raise the issue of what relationship might exist between the significance of beating fantasies and the role that real physical punishments played in the child's upbringing at home. The most obvious assumption, that an inverse relationship would be produced, was not proven because of the one-sidedness of the material. The people who supplied material for these analyses were very rarely beaten in their childhood, or at least beatings did not form a part of their education. Each of these children, of course, had felt the superior physical strength of its parents or teachers; we do not need to place particular stress on the fact that no nursery is free of fights between children themselves.

Our research was eager to know more about those early, simple fantasies, which did not obviously refer to the influence of school impressions or scenes taken from reading-matter. Who was the child being beaten? The fantasist herself or a third party? Was it always the same child, or a different one, at the patient's whim? Who was beating the child? An adult? In that case, who? Or was the child fantasizing that it was itself beating another child? No enlightening information came to any of these questions, only ever the timid answer: 'That is all I know; a child is being beaten.'

Inquiries about the sex of the beaten child were more successful, but they too supplied no illumination. Sometimes one received the answer: 'Only ever boys', or 'Only children'. More often the patients said: 'I don't know', or 'It doesn't matter'. No information was ever produced about an issue that greatly concerned the questioner: a constant relationship between the sex of the fantasist and that of the beaten child. Sometimes another characteristic detail became apparent from the content of the fantasy: the little child was being beaten on its naked bottom.

In these circumstances it was not even possible at first to decide whether the pleasure attached to the beating fantasy would better be described as sadistic or as masochistic.

II

On the basis of our insights so far, the only possible view of such a fantasy, which appears in early childhood, perhaps for arbitrary reasons, and which is preserved for auto-erotic satisfaction, is that it is a primary trait of perversion. One of the components of the sexual function has rushed on ahead of the others in its development, and has made itself prematurely autonomous, become fixated and thus excluded from later developmental processes, but at the same time it has borne witness to a particular, abnormal constitution in the individual. We know that such an infantile perversion does not necessarily last a lifetime: it may succumb to repression later on, it may be replaced by a reaction formation or transformed by a sublimation. (Although it may be that this sublimation arises out of a particular process that is delayed by repression.) But if these processes are absent, the perversion is preserved into maturity, and where we encounter a sexual deviation in the adult – perversion, fetishism, inversion – we rightly expect to reveal such a fixating event from childhood as the result of anamnestic investigation. Indeed, long before the age of psychoanalysis, observers such as Binet were able to trace the strange sexual deviations of maturity back to such impressions, to precisely the same years of childhood, between the fifth and sixth years. Here, however, we had reached the limit of our understanding, because the fixating impressions lacked any traumatic force, they were generally banal, and they were not exciting to other individuals. It would have been impossible to say why sexual strivings had become fixated on precisely those impressions. But their significance could be sought in the fact that they had given the sexual component, impetuous and ready to pounce, the opportunity, however arbitrary, for attachment, and we had to be prepared to see the chain of causality reaching a provisional end somewhere. It was the innate constitution that appeared to correspond to all demands for a stopping-point of that kind.

If the sexual component that has broken away prematurely is the sadistic one, on the basis of insights gained elsewhere we might expect that its later repression will create a predisposition for compulsive neurosis. We cannot say that this expectation is contradicted by the result of the investigation. The six cases, intense study of which has been the basis of this little communication (four women, two men), included cases of compulsive neurosis, one of which was highly serious and life-destroying, one that was moderately serious but amenable to influence, and a third that showed at least distinct individual traits of compulsive neurosis. A fourth case, admittedly, was straightforward hysteria, involving pains and inhibitions, and a fifth, in which the patient was only seeking analysis in order to resolve some indecisions in life, would not have been classified at all by broad clinical diagnosis, or else would have been dismissed as 'psychaesthenia'. We should not be disappointed by this statistic, because first of all we know that not every predisposition is bound to develop into an illness, and secondly we should content ourselves with explaining what actually exists, and we may in general shirk the task of explaining why something has not occurred.

It is up to this point and no further that our present insights can be said to grant us an understanding of beating fantasies. Naturally, however, the analysing doctor has come to sense that the problem is not fully resolved by this, when he is forced to admit that these fantasies generally remain apart from the rest of the content of the neurosis and do not assume a real place within its fabric; but, as I know from my own experience, we prefer to move beyond such impressions.

III

Strictly speaking – and why should we not take this as strictly as possible? – in order for something to merit acknowledgement as correct psychoanalysis, all that is needed is the analytic effort that has successfully removed the amnesia which hides from the adult the knowledge of his childhood from its very beginning (more or less from the second to the fifth year). This cannot be said forcefully enough among analysts, or repeated frequently enough. However, the motives for ignoring this admonition are understandable. One would prefer to achieve usable successes in a shorter time and with less effort. But at present, theoretical knowledge is a great deal more important for each one of us than therapeutic success, and anyone who neglects the analysis of childhood will inevitably succumb to the most grievous errors. This emphasis on the importance of the earliest experiences does not lead to the underestimation of the influence of later experiences; but the later impressions left by life speak clearly enough in analysis through the mouth of the patient. For the rights of childhood to be heard, the doctor must first raise his voice.

The period of childhood between the ages of two and four or five is the period in which innate libidinous factors are first awakened by experiences and linked to certain complexes. The beating fantasies dealt with here reveal themselves only at the end of this period or once it is over. Hence it might be that they have a prehistory, that they undergo a development and amount to a conclusion rather than an initial expression.

This hypothesis is confirmed by analysis. Consistent application of the analytic method teaches us that beating fantasies have a developmental history that is far from simple, in the course of which most of its aspects alter more than once: their relationship with the fantasizing person, their object and content, and their significance.

In order more easily to pursue these transformations in the beating fantasies, I shall now take the liberty of restricting my account to female individuals, who in any case (four against two) constitute the majority of my material. Furthermore, there is another theme, which I should like to exclude from this communication, connected with the men's beating fantasies. At the same time I shall try to avoid schematizing any more than is unavoidable if one wishes to depict an average state of affairs. Then, if further observation also produces a greater diversity of relations, I shall be sure that I have grasped a typical event, and not one that is rare in nature.

The first phase of beating fantasies in girls, then, must belong to very early childhood. Some aspects of these fantasies remain curiously indefinable, as though they were of no account. The sparse information that we have received from the patients on the first communication – a child is being beaten – appears to be justified where this fantasy is concerned. Except that something else is certainly definable, and always in entirely the same sense. In fact, the beaten child is never the fantasizing child, but regularly another child, generally a little brother or sister if there is one. Since this child can be either a brother or a sister, here too no constant relationship can be established between the sex of the fantasizing child and the child being beaten. So the fantasy is certainly not masochistic; we might call it sadistic, but we should never ignore the fact that the fantasizing child is also never itself the person doing the beating. The actual identity of that person remains at first unclear. We can establish only that it is not another child, but an adult. This indeterminate adult then later becomes clearly and unambiguously recognizable as the *father* (of the girl).

This first phase of the beating fantasy, then, is fully captured in the sentence: *'The father is beating the child.'* I will be betraying much of the content that I would prefer to reveal later on if I say instead: the father is beating the child *that I hate*. One might also vacillate about whether this preliminary stage towards the later beating fantasy should be characterized as a 'fantasy'. It might be more accurate to say that these are memories of events of which the child has been a co-spectator, of desires which have appeared for various reasons; but doubts such as these are unimportant.

Major transformations have taken place between this phase and the next. The person doing the beating has remained the same – the father – but the beaten child has become a different one, regularly the fantasizing child itself. To a large extent the fantasy is tinged with pleasure, and has been filled with a significant content the source of which will be of interest to us below. Its wording is now: '*I am being beaten by my father*.' Beyond a doubt, it has a masochistic character.

This second phase is the most important, and of them all the one with the most severe consequences. But in a sense we might say that it has never in fact had a real existence. In no instance is it remembered, it has never reached consciousness. It is a construction of analysis, but no less necessary for that.

The third phase in turn resembles the first. It has the wording familiar from the patient's communication. The beating person is never the father, it is either an indeterminate character, as in the first phase, or it is, typically, a father substitute (a teacher). The person of the fantasizing child no longer appears in the beating fantasy. On intensive questioning, patients only reply: I am probably watching. Instead of a single beaten child, many children are generally present. Predominantly (in the fantasies of girls) it is boys who are being beaten, but not boys individually known to them. The original simple and monotonous situation of being beaten can experience the most diverse changes and embellishments, and beating itself can be replaced by other kinds of punishment and humiliation. The essential characteristic, however, which also distinguishes the simplest fantasies of this phase from those of the first, and which generates the relationship in its middle phase, is the following: the fantasy is now the vehicle for a strong, unambiguously sexual excitement, and as such it conveys masturbatory satisfaction. But that is exactly what is puzzling about it: along what paths did this by now sadistic fantasy, of strange and unknown boys being beaten, enter the lasting possession of the little girl's libidinous strivings?

Neither can we deny that the connection between the three phases of the beating fantasy and the sequence in which they occur, like all their other characteristics, have so far remained quite incomprehensible.

IV

If we guide the analysis through those early periods to which the beating fantasy has been transferred and from which it is recalled, the child is shown to be involved in the excitements of its parent complex.

The little girl is affectionately fixated on the father, who has probably done everything to win her love, and who is thus sowing the seeds of an attitude of hatred and competition towards the mother, which co-exists with a current of affectionate devotion, and which may have the option of becoming increasingly strong and more clearly conscious, or else provide the impetus for an immoderate and reactive bond of love with her. But the beating fantasy is not linked to the relationship with the mother. In the nursery there are other children, a very few years older or younger, whom one dislikes for all sorts of reasons, but principally because one is supposed to share the parents' love with them, and whom one therefore repudiates with all the wild energy that belongs to the emotional life of those years. If this child is a younger brother or sister (as it is in three of my four cases), one despises it as well as hating it, and must none the less watch it attracting that share of affection that the dazzled parents always reserve for the youngest. One soon comes to understand that being beaten, even if it is not very painful, signifies a withdrawal of love and a humiliation. Thus many a child, having imagined itself securely enthroned in the unshakeable love of its parents, has been toppled by a single devastating blow from its imagined omnipotence. So it is a calming idea that the father should be beating that same hated child, quite regardless of whether one has seen him doing the beating. That is to say: father does not love that other child, *he only loves me*.

So that is the content and meaning of the beating fantasy in its first phase. The fantasy clearly satisfies the child's jealousy and is dependent upon its love-life, but it is also powerfully supported by its egoistic interests. So some doubt remains as to whether the fantasy may be described as purely 'sexual', and we would not dare to call it 'sadistic'. We know that all the features on which we are used to building our distinctions tend to blur the closer we get to the source. Perhaps this is not, then, dissimilar to the curse that the three weird sisters put on Banquo: not definitely sexual, not even sadistic, but providing the material from which these qualities will later emerge. Yet there is reason to suppose that even this first phase of the fantasy serves an excitement which, by involving the genitals, learns to achieve discharge in a masturbatory act.

In this premature object-choice of incestuous love, the child's sexual life clearly reaches the stage of genital organization. This is easier to demonstrate in the boy, but there can be no doubt about it in the girl. Something like a sense of its later definitive and normal sexual goals dominates the child's libidinous striving; we might be justified in wondering where this comes from, but we can take it as proof that the genitals have already begun their role in the process of excitement. The desire to have a child with his mother is never absent from the boy, the desire to have a child with her father is constant in the girl, and this coincides with an absolute inability to understand the path that might lead to the fulfilment of those desires. As far as the child is concerned, it seems certain that the genitals have something to do with it, although its brooding activity may seek the essence of the intimacy that it assumes between the parents in relations of a different kind, such as sleeping together, communal urination and the like, and this content can be grasped more easily through verbal ideas than the obscurity relating to the genitals.

But the time comes when this early blossom suffers frost-damage; none of these passionate incestuous loves can escape the fate of repression. They succumb to repression either as the result of demonstrable external occasions provoking disappointment, unexpected emotional injuries, the undesirable birth of a new little brother or sister, which is felt to be an act of infidelity, etc., or else they do so without any such occasions, from within, perhaps only because the fulfilment that the child has too long craved remains absent. It is unmistakable that these occasions are not the effective causes, but that these amorous relations are fated to come to an end at some point, and that we cannot say why that will be. In all likelihood they pass because their time is over, because the children are entering a new phase of development in which they are required to repeat the repression of the incestuous object-choice throughout human history, just as they were previously compelled to make such an object-choice (see destiny in the Oedipus myth). That which is present in the unconscious as a psychical product of the impulses of incestuous love is not accepted by consciousness in the new phase, and that which had already become conscious is driven back out again. Simultaneously with this process of repression there appears a conscious sense of guilt, also of unknown origin, but linked beyond a doubt to those incestuous desires and justified by their continuing existence in the unconscious.[1]

The fantasy of the period of incestuous love had been as follows: he (the father) loves only me, not the other child, because he beats that one. The sense of guilt can find no more severe punishment than the reversal of that triumph: 'No, he doesn't love you, because he beats you.' In this way the fantasy of the second phase, that one is being beaten by the father oneself, becomes the direct expression of the sense of guilt, based on love of the father. Consequently it has become masochistic; as far as I know it is always that way, in every case the sense of guilt is the element that transforms sadism into masochism. But this is certainly not the whole content of masochism. The sense of guilt cannot have claimed the field all by itself; the impulse of love must have its share too. Let us remember that these are children in whom the sadistic component was able to emerge, for constitutional reasons, prematurely and in an isolated fashion. There is no need for us to relinquish this point of view. In precisely these children a regression to the pre-genital, sadistic-anal organization of the sex life is made particularly easy. If the barely accomplished genital organization is affected by repression, the consequence is not only that all psychical representation of incestuous love becomes or remains unconscious, but that the genital organization itself experiences a regressive humiliation. This: father loves me, was meant in a genital sense; as a result of regression it is transformed into: father beats me (I am beaten by father). This being-beaten is only a coincidence of a sense of guilt and eroticism; *it is not only punishment for the abhorred genital relationship, but also a regressive substitute for it*, and from this latter source it draws the libidinous excitement that will henceforward be attached to it, and find an outcome in masturbatory acts. But this is only the essence of masochism.

The fantasy of the second phase, of oneself being beaten by the father, generally remains unconscious, probably because of the intensity of the repression. I cannot say why it was consciously remembered in one of my six cases (a male). This man, now adult, had clearly remembered that he used the idea of being beaten by his mother for masturbatory purposes; however, he soon replaced his own mother with the mothers of schoolmates or other women who were in some way similar. We should not forget that in the transformation of the boy's incestuous fantasy into the corresponding masochistic fantasy more of a reversal takes place than it does in the case of the girl, namely the substitution of passivity for activity, and this greater degree of displacement may protect the fantasy against remaining unconscious as a consequence of repression. Thus regression rather than repression would have been enough for the sense of guilt; in female cases the sense of guilt, perhaps because it is inherently more demanding, would only be pacified by a collaboration between the two.

In two of my four female cases, a superstructure of day-dreams, elaborate and highly significant for the life of those affected, had formed over the masochistic beating fantasy, whose function was to provide the possibility of a feeling of satisfied excitement without the necessity of the masturbatory act. In one of these cases the content, being beaten by the father, was allowed to venture back into consciousness, as long as the patient herself was rendered unrecognizable by a slight disguise. The hero of these stories was regularly beaten by his father, and later only punished, humiliated and so on.

But I repeat: in general the fantasy remains unconscious and can only be reconstructed in analysis. This may mean that those patients are right who claim to remember that masturbation made its appearance in them earlier than the third-phase beating fantasy which we shall shortly discuss; the fantasy, they said, was only a later addition, perhaps under the influence of classroom scenes. While we had often believed these assertions, we were always inclined to assume that masturbation had initially fallen under the dominion of unconscious fantasies, later replaced by conscious ones.

So it is as this kind of surrogate that we understand the familiar beating fantasy of the third phase, its definitive formation, in which the fantasizing child occurs only – if at all – as a spectator, while the father is preserved in the form of a teacher or some other authority figure. The fantasy, which is now similar to that of the first phase, seems to have reverted towards sadism. One has the impression that, in the sentence: 'father is beating the other child, he loves only me', the emphasis has shifted back to the first part, once the second has been subjected to repression. But only the form of this fantasy is sadistic; the satisfaction gained from it is masochistic, and its significance lies in the fact that it has absorbed the libidinous investment of the repressed part, and along with it the sense of guilt. All the many indeterminate children being beaten by the teacher are merely substitutes for the patient's own person.

Here, too, we encounter for the first time something like a constancy of sex in the people serving the fantasy. Almost all the children being beaten are boys, in the fantasies of boys as well as girls. Palpably, this trait is not explained by some kind of competition between the sexes, which would mean girls being beaten in the boys' fantasies; and neither has it anything to do with the sex of the hated child of the first phase, but refers rather to a complicated process at work in the girls. If they turn away from incestuous love of the father, with its genital intention, they can easily break away from their female role, animate their 'masculinity complex' (van Ophuijsen) and from that point onwards want only to be boys. Consequently the whipping-boys who stand in for them are boys as well. In both the cases that feature day-dreams – one was elevated to an almost poetic level – the heroes were only ever young men. Indeed, in these creations women did not occur at all, and only appeared in subsidiary roles after many years.

V

I hope I have presented what I have learned from my analysis in a sufficiently detailed manner, and only ask the reader to bear in mind that the six cases mentioned do not exhaust my material, but that I, like other analysts, have a much larger number of less well-examined cases. These observations can be evaluated in various ways, in order to explain the genesis of perversions in general, in particular of masochism, and in order to assess the role played by sexual difference in the dynamic of the neurosis.

The most striking result of such a discussion concerns the origin of perversions. The view that the constitutional intensity or impetuosity of a sexual component is prominent in the perversions may not be called into question, but it is not the whole story. The perversion is no longer isolated within the child's sexual life, but is incorporated into the context of the typical – not to say normal – development processes with which we are familiar. It is connected with the child's incestuous object-love, its Oedipus complex, and first emerges against the background of that complex. Once the complex has collapsed the perversion is all that remains of it, often alone, as a legacy of its libidinous charge, and freighted with the sense of guilt that attaches to it. The abnormal sexual constitution has finally demonstrated its strength by impelling the Oedipus complex in a particular direction and forcing it to become an unusual residual phenomenon.

As we know, childhood perversion can either become the basis of the formation of a similar perversion, that persists throughout the person's life, consuming his or her entire sexual life, or else it can be interrupted and kept in the background of a normal sexual development, from which it will always discharge a certain amount of energy. The former of these cases was already recognized in the days before analysis, but the gap between the two is effectively filled by the analytical examination of such full-blown perversions. We discover fairly often, in fact, among these perverts that they too have shown signs of normal sexual activity, usually during puberty. But it has never been strong enough, and has been abandoned at the first inevitable obstacles, before the person reverted to the infantile fixation once and for all.

Of course it would be important to know whether we might, as a universal principle, claim that the origin of the infantile perversions lies in the Oedipus complex. This question cannot be resolved without further examination, but it does not seem impossible. If we bear in mind the anamneses that are gained from the perversions of adults, we become aware that the definitive impression, the 'first experience' of all these perverts, fetishists and the like, is hardly ever located earlier than the sixth year. Around this time, however, the dominance of the Oedipus complex has already expired; the remembered experience, so mysteriously effective, might very easily have represented its legacy. The relationship between the experience and the complex, now repressed, must remain obscure, if analysis has cast no light upon the first, 'pathogenic' impression. Consider how little value, for example, there is in the assertion of innate homosexuality if it is supported by the statement that the person in question has felt attraction only for the same sex from his eighth or his sixth year.

But if the source of perversions is universally traceable to the Oedipus complex, our valuation of the complex is given fresh reinforcement. We believe that the Oedipus complex is the actual core of the neurosis, the infantile sexuality that peaks in it is the true cause of neurosis, and its residue in the unconscious represents a predisposition to later neurotic illness in the adult. If that is so, the beating fantasy and other similar perverse fixations are only expressions of the Oedipus complex; they are, so to speak, the scars that remain once the process is completed, like the notorious 'inferiority' that corresponds to just such a narcissistic scar. In this conception I must agree wholeheartedly with Marcinowski, who recently gave a fine account of this ('Erotic Sources of Feelings of Inferiority', *Zeitschrift für Sexualwissenschaft*, IV, 1918). This inferiority complex among neurotics is, as is well known, only partial, and entirely compatible with excessive self-esteem from other sources. I have written elsewhere about the origin of the Oedipus complex itself, and the fate reserved for human beings, probably alone among all animals, of having to begin their sexual lives twice – first, like all other creatures, from early childhood and then, after a long break, again during puberty – and about everything related to the 'archaic inheritance' of the complex, and I shall not go into it here.

The discussion of our beating fantasies makes only a minimal contribution to our understanding of the genesis of masochism. First of all, it appears to confirm the idea that masochism is not a primary manifestation of a drive, but arises out of sadism being turned back against the self, through regression from the object to the ego. (Cf. 'Triebe und Triebschicksale' ['Drives and their Vicissitudes'] in the collection of minor writings.)[2] The existence of drives with a passive goal should be taken for granted, particularly in women, but passivity is not the whole of masochism; there is also the characteristic of displeasure that is so startling in a drive fulfilment. The transformation of sadism into masochism seems to be influenced by the sense of guilt involved in the act of repression. Here, repression is manifested in three kinds of effect: it renders the consequences of genital organization unconscious; it forces the genital organization to regress to the earlier sadistic-anal stage; and it transforms it from sadism into passive masochism, which is in turn, so to speak, narcissistic. The second of these three consequences is made possible by what we may, in these cases, take to be weakness of the genital organization; the third becomes necessary because the sense of guilt draws a similar impulse from sadism to that which it does from the genitally understood incestuous object-choice. Where the sense of guilt itself comes from, the analyses do not relate. It appears to be inherent in the new phase that the child is entering, and, if it persists from that point onwards, to correspond to a scar-formation similar to the sense of inferiority. In terms of our still uncertain bearings within the structure of the ego, we would attribute it to that agency which, as a critical conscience, resists the rest of the ego, produces Silberer's functional phenomenon in dreams, and breaks with the ego in delusions of observation.

In passing we should also recall that the analysis of the childhood perversions treated here also helps to solve an old mystery which has in the past tormented those outside analysis more than it has the analyst himself. But recently even Bleuler has acknowledged it as a curious and inexplicable fact that in neurotics masturbation becomes the focus of their sense of guilt. We have always assumed that this sense of guilt referred to masturbation in early childhood rather than in puberty, and that for the most part it refers not to the act of masturbation but to the fantasy underlying it, even if it is unconscious and thus a product of the Oedipus complex.

I have already written about the importance that the third, apparently sadistic phase of the beating fantasy tends to acquire as a vehicle for the excitement that compels the patient to masturbate, and the fantasy activity – partly a continuation in the same vein and partly a compensatory abolition – that it tends to stimulate. But the second, unconscious and masochistic phase, the fantasy that one is oneself being beaten by one's father, is disproportionately more important. It not only goes on working through the mediation of that which is substituted for it; it can also be shown to have effects on the character which derive directly from its unconscious version. People who carry such a fantasy with them develop a special sensitivity and irritability towards people whom they can locate within the paternal series. They are easily hurt by these people, and thus bring about the fantasized situation of being beaten by their father, incurring suffering and harm in the process. I should not be surprised if the same fantasy were some day proven to be the basis of querulous paranoia.

VI

The account of infantile beating fantasies would have grown beyond all bounds had it not, a few connections aside, restricted itself to conditions among females. I shall briefly repeat the results: the beating fantasy among little girls passes through three phases, of which the first and last are remembered consciously, while the middle one remains unconscious. The two conscious fantasies appear sadistic, while the middle, unconscious fantasy is beyond any doubt masochistic in nature. Its content consists of being beaten by the father, and the libidinous charge and the sense of guilt both depend upon it. In the two first fantasies the child being beaten is always someone else, in the middle phase it is only ever the patient, in the third, conscious phase in by far the predominant number of cases it is only boys who are beaten. From the start, the beating person is the father, and later a substitute from the paternal series. The unconscious fantasy of the middle phase originally had a genital significance, and arose, through repression and regression, out of the incestuous desire to be loved by the father. In an apparently loose context there is the additional fact that girls change sex between the second and third phase, fantasizing themselves into boys.

I have made less progress, perhaps only because of the disadvantageous nature of the material, in my understanding of beating fantasies in boys. Understandably, I expected a complete analogy in relations between boys and girls, with the mother occupying the father's place in the fantasy. And this expectation seemed to be confirmed because the content of what we took to be the boy's corresponding fantasy consisted in being beaten by his mother (and later by a substitute figure). This fantasy on its own, in which the patient's own person was preserved as the object, differed from the second phase in girls in that it was capable of reaching consciousness. But if we therefore sought to equate it with the third phase in the girl, one new difference remained in that the boy's own person was not replaced by many indeterminate, strange girls, or at the very least by many girls. So the expectation of a complete parallel was mistaken.

My masculine material comprised only a few cases involving an infantile beating fantasy without any other serious harm to sexual activity, while on the other hand it involved many people who would have been described as actual masochists in the sense of the sexual perversion. They were either those who found their sexual satisfaction exclusively in masturbation with masochistic fantasies, or those who had managed to couple masochism and genital activity in such a way that they achieved erection and ejaculation during masochistic activities and under those precise conditions, or those who were capable of normal coitus. Along with this there was the rare case of a masochist's perverse behaviour being disturbed by the appearance of unbearably powerful compulsive ideas. Satisfied perverts seldom have cause to seek analysis. For the three groups of masochist mentioned above, however, there may have been powerful reasons that brought them to the analyst. The masochistic masturbator finds himself absolutely impotent if he finally attempts coitus with a woman, and someone who has previously managed to accomplish coitus with the help of a masochistic idea or event may suddenly discover that this association, with which he has been comfortable, has failed, when the genitals no longer react to the masochistic stimulus. We are accustomed to giving confident promises of cure to those psychically impotent patients who come to us for treatment, but even when that prognosis is made, we should be more cautious while the dynamic of the disorder remains unknown to us. It comes as an unpleasant surprise if the analysis reveals as the cause of 'merely psychical' impotence an exquisite masochistic attitude that may have taken root a long time previously.

Among these masochistic men we now make a discovery which

warns us not to pursue the analogy with the situation of women any further for now, but to judge this state of affairs in its own right. It turns out, in fact, that these men regularly place themselves in the role of women in their masochistic fantasies, as well as in activities leading to the realization of those fantasies, and that their masochism thus coincides with a *feminine* attitude. This can be easily demonstrated in reference to the details of the fantasies; but many patients know it too, and express it as a subjective certainty. Nothing changes in this respect if the playful attire of the masochistic scene is maintained in the fiction of a naughty boy, page or apprentice who needs to be punished. In both fantasies and activities, however, the figures doing the punishing are always women. That is confusing enough; one would also like to know whether the masochism of the infantile beating fantasy is also based on a similarly feminine attitude.[3]

So let us leave to one side the thorny question of the conditions of masochism among adults, and turn instead to the infantile beating fantasies we find in the male sex. Here the analysis of earliest childhood in turn allows us to make a surprising discovery: the conscious fantasy, or the fantasy that is capable of becoming conscious, with the content of being beaten by the mother, is not primary. It has a preliminary stage that is generally unconscious and has the content: *I am being beaten by my father*. So this preliminary stage really corresponds to the second phase of the fantasy in the girl. The familiar, conscious fantasy: I am being beaten by my mother, corresponds to the third phase in the girl in which, as I have mentioned, the objects are unknown boys. I was unable to demonstrate a preliminary, sadistic stage, comparable to the girl's first phase in the boy, but I do not wish to express a definitive rejection here, because I can easily see the possible existence of complicated types.

Being beaten in the male fantasy – as I shall briefly refer to that fantasy, hopefully without the risk of misunderstanding – is also being loved in the genital sense, degraded by regression. The unconscious male fantasy, then, was not originally: I am being beaten by my father, as we previously put it provisionally, but rather: *I am loved by my father*. The familiar processes have inverted it into the conscious fantasy: *I am being beaten by my mother*. So from the outset the boy's beating fantasy is a passive one, which has probably arisen from the feminine attitude towards the father. Just as much as the female fantasy (the girl's) it corresponds to the Oedipus complex, except the parallelism that we would expect between the two needs to be abandoned for a shared characteristic: *In both cases the beating fantasy is derived from the incestuous connection to the father*.

It will help our overall understanding if at this point I add the other points of agreement and differences between the beating fantasies of the two sexes. In the girl, the unconscious masochistic fantasy arises out of the normal Oedipal attitude; in the boy, from the inverted attitude, taking the father as its love object. In the girl, the fantasy has a preliminary stage (the first phase) in which the beating appears in its indifferent meaning and is applied to a jealously hated person; both of these are absent in the case of the boy, but that very difference could be removed by more successful observation. In the transition towards the substitute conscious fantasy the girl clings to the person of the father and thus to the sex of the beating person; but the sex of both the person being beaten and the person beating changes, so that in the end a man is beating male children; the boy, on the other hand, changes the person and the sex of the beater, by substituting mother for father, and maintains his own person so that at the end the beating and the beaten person are of different sexes. In the girl, the originally masochistic (passive) situation is transformed by repression into a sadistic situation whose sexual character is very vague. In the boy's case it remains masochistic, and as a result of the sexual difference between the beating and the beaten person maintains a greater similarity with the original, genitally determined fantasy. The boy escapes his homosexuality through the repression and reworking of the unconscious fantasy; the curious thing about his later conscious fantasy is that its content is a feminine attitude without a homosexual object-choice. In the same process the girl, on the other hand, escapes the demands of love-life in general, fantasizes herself into the figure of a man, without herself being active in a male way, and is only present at the act, which substitutes a sexual one, as a spectator.

We would be justified in suggesting that not a great deal is changed by the repression of the original unconscious fantasy. Everything that is repressed and substituted as far as the consciousness is concerned is preserved in the unconscious and capable of causing effects. Matters are different as regards the effect of regression to an earlier stage of sexual organization. Where this is concerned, we are right to believe that it alters circumstances in the unconscious, so that after repression what remains in the unconscious in both sexes is not the (passive) fantasy of being loved by the father, but the masochistic one of being beaten by him. Neither is there any shortage of signs that repression has only achieved its intention very imperfectly. The boy who wanted to escape the homosexual object-choice and has not changed his sex none the less feels like a woman in his conscious fantasies, and equips the beating women with male attributes and properties. The girl, who has herself abandoned her sex and generally achieved more fundamental repression-work, does not rid herself of her father, does not dare do the beating herself, and because she herself has become a boy she chiefly allows boys to be beaten.

I know that the differences in attitude towards the beating fantasy described here in the two sexes have not been satisfactorily explained, but I shall not attempt to disentangle these complications by pursuing their dependence upon other elements, because I myself do not consider the observed material to be exhaustive. But in so far as it exists I should like to use it to test two theories which, placed in opposition, both deal with the relationship of repression towards sexual characteristics, and present that relationship, each in its own way, as being very profound. I should say in advance that I have always considered both to be inaccurate and misleading.

The first of these theories is anonymous; it was brought to my attention many years ago by a colleague who was a friend at the time. Its generous simplicity is so seductive that one must wonder in amazement that only a few scattered references have ever been made to it in the literature. It is based on the bisexual constitution of human individuals and asserts that in each individual the battle between the sexual characteristics is the reason for repression. The more intensely formed, dominant sex in the person has repressed the mental representation of the inferior sex. Hence the core of the unconscious, the repressed, deals with those aspects of the opposite sex that exist in all people. That can only have a tangible meaning if we accept that a person's sex is determined by the formation of his or her genitals, otherwise the sex that is stronger in a person becomes uncertain, and we risk deducing what should be the starting point of our examination from its result. In brief: in men, the unconscious repressed should be traced back to impulses of the female drive; and the reverse is true in women.

The second theory is newer in origin; it coincides with the first in that it once again posits the battle between the two sexes as being defining of repression. It must also enter into a contradiction with the first; it too is based not on biological but on sociological supports. The content of this theory of 'masculine protest', as set out by Alfred Adler, is that each individual resists the idea of remaining on the inferior 'female line' and strives towards the only satisfying line, the male. Adler takes this masculine protest as a universal explanation both of character and of neuroses. Unfortunately the two processes, although they are certainly to be kept separate, are so little differentiated in Adler, and he pays the fact of repression so little attention, that we will risk a misunderstanding if we attempt to apply the theory of masculine protest to repression. In my opinion this attempt would inevitably lead to the conclusion that masculine protest, the wish to distance oneself from the female line, is the motive for repression in every case. The agent of repression, then, would always be the impulse of a masculine, and the repressed of a feminine drive. But the symptom would in that case also be the result of a feminine impulse, for we cannot abandon the characteristic of the symptom being a substitute for that which is repressed, which has asserted itself in the face of repression.

Let us now test out the two theories, which, we might say, have in common the sexualization of the process of repression, on the beating fantasy under examination. The original fantasy: 'I am being beaten by my father', corresponds to a feminine attitude in the boy, and is thus the manifestation of that part of his predisposition that belongs to the opposite sex. If it is subjected to repression, the first theory seems to be correct, establishing the rule that that which pertains to the opposite sex coincides with the repressed. Of course it is not fully in line with our expectations if what appears after successful repression, the conscious fantasy, once again reveals the feminine attitude, this time as regards the mother. But let us not voice doubts when we are so close to a decision. The original fantasy in girls: 'I am being beaten (that is: loved) by my father', certainly corresponds, as a feminine attitude, to the predominant sex. According to the theory, then, it should escape repression, and does not even need to be unconscious. In fact it is unconscious, however, and it is replaced by a conscious fantasy which denies the manifest sexual characteristic. This theory, then, is useless for an understanding of the beating fantasy, and is contradicted by it. One might object that these fantasies occur among womanly boys and mannish girls, and they are the ones who experience these fates, or that a trait of femininity in the boy and masculinity in the girl should be held responsible, in the boy for the emergence of the passive fantasy, and in the girl for its repression. We would probably agree with this view, but the asserted relationship between manifest sexual characteristics and the selection of what is destined for repression would be no less untenable for that. Fundamentally, we see only that in male and female individuals impulses of both the masculine and feminine drives co-exist, and can be rendered equally unconscious by repression.

The theory of masculine protest seems to stand up much more effectively to the beating fantasies. In both boys and girls the beating fantasy corresponds to a feminine attitude, a persistence on the female line, and both sexes hurry to rid themselves of this attitude by means of the repression of the fantasy. However, masculine protest seems to achieve full success only in girls, and in this case an almost ideal example for the effectiveness of masculine protest is produced. In boys, success is not completely satisfying; the female line is not abandoned, and the boy is certainly not 'on top' in a conscious masochistic fantasy. Hence it accords with expectations derived from the theory if we recognize this fantasy as a symptom that has arisen out of the failure of masculine protest. It is disturbing, certainly, that the girl's fantasy, which has arisen out of repression, also has the value and meaning of a symptom. Here, where masculine protest has achieved its object completely, the precondition for symptom formation must be absent.

Before this difficulty leads us to assume that the whole observational method of masculine protest is inadequate to the problems of neuroses and perversions, and consequently that its application towards them is fruitless, we will direct our attention away from passive beating fantasies to other drive manifestations of the sexual lives of children, which are also subjected to repression. But no one can doubt that there are also desires and fantasies which, from the outset, follow the male line and are the manifestation of impulses of the male drive, such as sadistic impulses or the boy's lust for his mother, which arises out of the normal Oedipus complex. It is equally doubtful that these too are touched by repression; if masculine protest has subsequently explained masochistic fantasies, by the same token it becomes completely unusable for the contrary case of active fantasies. In other words, the theory of masculine protest is irreconcilable with the fact of repression. Only someone prepared to discard all the psychological acquisitions made since Breuer's first cathartic cure, and as a result of it, can expect the principle of masculine protest to assume significance in the explanation of the neuroses and perversions.

Psychoanalytical theory, based on observation, firmly maintains that the motives for repression must not be sexualized. The core of the psychical unconscious is man's archaic legacy, and what succumbs to the process of repression is the part of that legacy that must always be left behind in the case of progress towards later phases of development, because it is unusable and incompatible with innovation, and could be harmful to it. This choice occurs more successfully in one group of drives than in the other. The latter, the sexual drives, because of particular circumstances that have already been demonstrated on several occasions, are able to thwart the efforts of repression and compel their own representation by means of troubling substitute formations. Consequently infantile sexuality, subjected to repression, is the main drive force of symptom formation, and the essential part of its content, the Oedipus complex, is the core complex of neurosis. I hope that this communication will have prompted the reader to expect that the sexual deviations of childhood and those of adults are ramifications of the same complex.

(1919)

Notes

1. [*Addition 1924*:] See the continuation of this argument in 'Der Untergang des Ödipuskomplexes' ['The Decline of the Oedipus Complex'], p. 393, vol. XIII of the *Gesammelte Werke*.
2. [*Zur Neurosenlehre*, 5 volumes, Vienna, 1906–22, vol. IV, 1918: vol. X of the *Gesammelte Werke*.]
3. [*Addition 1924*:] There is more on this subject in 'Das ökonomische Problem des Masochismus' ['The Economic Problem of Masochism'], 1924 (vol. XIII of the *Gesammelte Werke*).

On Female Sexuality

I

During the phase of the normal Oedipus complex, the child is seen as being affectionately attached to the parent of the opposite sex, while hostility predominates in his relations with the parent of the same sex. We have no difficulty in extrapolating from this result where boys are concerned. His mother was the first love object; she remains so, and as his passionate strivings are reinforced and he comes to a deeper understanding of the relationship between father and mother, the father inevitably becomes a rival. Not so where the little girl is concerned. Her first object was also her mother; how can she find her way to her father? How, when and why does she break away from her mother? We have long understood that the development of female sexuality is complicated by the task of relinquishing the originally dominant genital zone, the clitoris, for a new one, the vagina. Now a second such transformation, the exchange of the original object, the mother, for the father, is no less characteristic and significant for woman's development. How the two tasks are connected to one another we cannot yet tell.

As we know, one frequently encounters women who have strong attachments to their fathers; they are by no means necessarily neurotic. It is among women such as these that I have made the observations that I am reporting here, and which have led me to a particular view of female sexuality. Two facts in particular have struck me about this. The first was: where there was a particularly intense attachment to the father, according to the testimony of the analysis there had previously been a phase of exclusive attachment to the mother, of equal intensity and passion. The second phase had barely added any new features to the patient's love-life apart from a change in object. The primary relationship with the mother had been built up in a very rich and varied way.

The second fact taught us that the duration of this maternal attachment had been greatly underestimated. In several cases it lasted up until the fourth year, in one case until the fifth, and hence it occupied a much longer part of the early blossoming of sexuality than had previously been imagined. Indeed, we had to accept the possibility that a number of females remain frozen in this original maternal attachment, and never really apply it to a man.

The pre-Oedipal phase in women thus attains an importance which we have never previously attributed to it.

Since this phase is able to accommodate all the fixations and repressions to which we trace the origin of the neuroses, it seems necessary to revoke the universality of the thesis that the Oedipus complex is the core of neuroses. But anyone who balks at this correction is not obliged to make it. On the one hand, the Oedipus complex may be extended to encompass all relations between the child and both parents, while on the other, new discoveries may also be taken into account if we say that the woman enters the normal positive Oedipus situation only after overcoming a previous phase governed by the negative complex. During this phase the father is not really much to the girl apart from an annoying rival, although hostility towards him never reaches the characteristic pitch that it does for the boy. We long ago abandoned any expectations of close parallelism between male and female sexual development.

Our insight into the pre-Oedipal early history of the girl comes as a surprise, similar to the revelation, in another field, of the Minoan-Mycenaean culture behind the Greek.

Everything that touches upon this first attachment to the mother seemed to me to be as difficult to grasp analytically, as hoary, shadowy, nearly impossible to revive, as though it had undergone a particularly remorseless repression. Perhaps, though, this impression was due to the fact that women in analysis with me were able to preserve the same attachment to the father, in which they had sought refuge from this earlier phase. In fact, it appears that female analysts like Jeanne Lampl-de Groot and Helene Deutsch have been able to perceive these states of affairs with greater ease and clarity because in their patients the transference to an appropriate mother-substitute was able to take place. Neither have I yet been able to see a case through to its conclusion, so I shall limit myself to communicating results of the most general kind, and give only a few examples of the new insights I have gained. These include the idea that this phase of attachment to the mother is particularly closely connected to the aetiology of hysteria, which can hardly surprise us if we bear in mind that both the phase and the neurosis are among the particular characteristics of femininity, and also that the germ of woman's later paranoia dwells in this dependence on the mother; this seems to be the fear, surprising but regularly encountered, of being killed (devoured?) by the mother.[1] It is natural to assume that this fear corresponds to a hostility towards the mother which develops in the child as a result of the various restrictions of up-bringing and physical care, and that the mechanism of projection is encouraged by the fact that psychical organization is in its early stages.

II

I have presented in advance the two facts which have struck me as new: that the woman's strong dependence upon her father only represents the legacy of an equally strong maternal attachment, and that this earlier phase has persisted over an unexpectedly long period of time. Now I should like to go back, to insert these results into the picture of female sexual development with which we are familiar. I will be unable to avoid repeating myself. Our account can only benefit from continuous comparison with the male situation.

First of all, it is unmistakable that the bisexuality claimed for the human constitution is much more clearly present in women than in men. Men, after all, have only one leading sex zone, one sexual organ, while women have two: the actual female vagina and the clitoris, analogous to the male member. We consider ourselves justified in assuming that the vagina is as good as non-existent for many years, and may only supply sensations during puberty. Recently, however, observers have increasingly been suggesting that vaginal impulses also date back to those early years. In girls, therefore, the essential occurrences relating to the genitalia in childhood must take place in the clitoris. The sexual life of women generally divides into two phases, the first of which is male in character; only with the second does it become specifically female. In female development there is thus a process of transport from one phase to the other, and there is nothing analogous to this in men. A further complication arises from the fact that the function of the virile clitoris continues into the later sex life of women, in highly variable ways that we have not satisfactorily understood. Of course we do not know the psychological foundations of these particular qualities in women; even less can we explain their teleological purpose.

Parallel to this first great difference is the difference in the finding of the object. Where the man is concerned, his first love object is his mother, by virtue of the fact that she feeds him and attends to his bodily needs, and she remains so until she is replaced by someone whose nature is similar to her, or derived from her. As to the female concerned, the mother must be her first object too. The primal conditions of object-choice are identical for all children. But by the end of the woman's development the man-father should have become the new love object; that is, the woman's sexual change requires a corresponding change in the sex of the object. New tasks for research arise here, concerning the ways in which this transformation takes place, how thoroughly or incompletely it is accomplished, and what different possibilities arise in this development.

We have already observed that a further difference between the sexes refers to the relationship with the Oedipus complex. It is our impression here that our statement about the Oedipus complex only applies, strictly speaking, to the male child, and that we are right in rejecting the name Electra complex, which seeks to stress the analogy in the behaviour of the two sexes. The fateful relationship of simultaneous love for one parent and a rivalrous hatred for the other only arises in the male child. In him it is then the discovery of the possibility of castration, as proven by the sight of the female genitals, that compels him to transform his Oedipus complex, leads at the same time to the creation of the super-ego, and thus sets in motion all those processes which aim to incorporate the individual within civilized society. Once paternal authority has been internalized into the super-ego, there is a further task which needs to be resolved: the liberation of that authority from the people of whom it was originally a psychical representation. Along this curious path of development it is precisely the narcissistic genital interest, the one concerned with the preservation of the penis, that has been turned towards the restriction of infantile sexuality.

In the man, another remnant of the influence of the castration complex is a degree of disdain for the woman, who is recognized as having been castrated. From this, *in extremis*, an inhibition in object-choice develops, and with support from organic factors this can lead to exclusive homosexuality. The effects of the castration complex are quite different in the woman. She acknowledges the fact of her castration, and thus the superiority of the man and her own inferiority, but she also resists this irksome state of affairs. Three developmental directions lead off from this contradictory attitude. The first leads to the woman generally turning away from sexuality. The little girl, alarmed by comparison with the boy, becomes dissatisfied with her clitoris, relinquishes her phallic activity and thus sexuality in general, as well as a good proportion of her masculinity in other areas. The second direction clings with defiant self-assertion to her threatened masculinity; the hope of getting another penis is maintained until an unbelievably late age, it is elevated to a purpose in life, and the fantasy of being a man in spite of everything often remains a defining characteristic for long periods of life. This 'masculinity complex' in the woman can also issue in a manifestly homosexual choice of object. It is only the third, very tortuous path of development that ends up in the final normal feminine attitude, which chooses the father as its object and thus arrives at the female form of the Oedipus complex. In women, then, the Oedipus complex is the end result of a longer development, it is not destroyed by the influence of castration, but rather created by it, and it escapes the strong hostile influences that have a destructive effect upon the man; all too often, indeed, the female does not overcome it at all. For this reason the cultural results of its dissolution are also minor and less important. One would probably not be mistaken in saying that it is this difference in the reciprocal relationship between the Oedipus complex and the castration complex that shapes the woman as a social being.[2]

The phase of exclusive attachment to the mother, which may be called *pre-Oedipal*, can thus claim far greater significance in women than it does in men. Many phenomena in female sexual life, which were previously far from accessible to understanding, are completely explained by being traced back to this phase. We have for a long time observed, for example, that many women who have chosen their husband on the model of their father, or put him in the father's place, then repeat in their marriage to him their bad relationship with their mother. The husband is supposed to inherit the relationship with the father, but in fact he inherits the relationship with the mother. That is easily understood as a clear case of regression. The relationship with the mother was the original one, and the attachment to the father was constructed upon it; and now, in marriage, the original relationship emerges out of repression. The transfer of emotional connections from the mother- to the father-object form the chief content of the development leading to womanhood.

If so many women give us the impression that their maturity is filled with quarrels with their husband, just as their youth was spent quarrelling with their mother, in the light of the above observations we will conclude that their hostile attitude towards their mother is not a consequence of the rivalry of the Oedipus complex, but arises from the foregoing phase, and has only been intensified and applied in the Oedipal situation. This is also confirmed by direct analytical examination. We must turn our attention to those mechanisms which have worked to turn the subject away from the maternal object, which was loved so intensely and so exclusively. We are prepared to find not one such element but a whole series of elements, working together towards the same final goal.

Among these some emerge which arise from the conditions of infantile sexuality in general, and which thus apply equally well to the erotic life of boys. First among these we should mention jealousy of other people, of brothers and sisters, rivals, also allowing room for the father. Children's love is boundless, it demands exclusivity, it is not satisfied with scraps. But a second characteristic of this love is that in reality it also has no goal, it is incapable of complete satisfaction, and for that reason it is to a large extent condemned to end in disappointment and make way for an attitude of hostility. In later life the absence of final satisfaction may favour a different outcome. As in erotic relationships in which the goal is inhibited, this element may ensure the undisturbed continuation of libidinal investment, but under the compulsion of developmental processes the libido regularly abandons the unsatisfying position in order to seek a new one.

Another much more specific motive for turning away from the mother emerges from the effect of the castration complex upon the creature without a penis. At some point the little girl discovers her organic inferiority, and she naturally does this earlier and more easily if she has brothers or if there are other boys near by. We have already heard of the three paths that part in that case: *a)* one leads towards the cessation of the whole of the sexual life; *b)* one leads towards the defiant over-emphasis of masculinity; *c)* one leads towards the beginnings of a final femininity. It is not easy to make more precise statements concerning time, or to establish typical modes of evolution. The moment of the discovery of castration is itself variable, and other elements appear to be inconstant and dependent on chance. The condition of the girl's own phallic activity also comes into consideration, along with the question of whether or not it has been discovered, and, if it has been, what level of prohibition has been imposed upon it.

In most cases the little girl spontaneously finds her own phallic activity, clitoral masturbation, and it is at first practised without a fantasy. The frequently occurring fantasy that turns the mother, nurse or nanny into a seducer is due to the influence of bodily care upon the first awakening of this activity. Whether masturbation among girls is rarer and, from the start, less energetic than among boys is an open question; it is certainly possible. Real seduction, too, is frequently enough, whether by other children or carers who wish to calm the child down, send her to sleep or make her dependent upon them. Where seduction is involved, it generally disturbs the natural course of developmental processes; it often has far-reaching and lasting consequences.

As we have heard, the prohibition on masturbation becomes a reason for abandoning the practice, but it is also a reason to rebel against the person imposing the prohibition, the mother, or the mother-substitute, who generally merges with the mother later on. The defiant assertion of masturbation seems to open the way to masculinity. Even where the child has not succeeded in suppressing masturbation, the outcome of the seemingly ineffectual prohibition becomes apparent in her later efforts to free herself, at the cost of greater sacrifices, from the satisfaction that has been spoiled for her. Even the object-choice of the adolescent girl can be influenced by the persistence of this intention. Rancour over the prevention of free sexual activity plays a major part in separation from the mother. The same motive will once again come into effect after puberty, when the mother recognizes her duty to protect her daughter's modesty. We will not, of course, forget that the mother takes similar steps against her son's masturbation, and thus gives him, too, a strong motive for rebellion.

If the little girl experiences her own deficiency as the result of seeing the male genitals, she does not accept this undesirable information without hesitation or resistance. As we have heard, she stubbornly clings to the expectation that she will herself at some point acquire such a set of genitals, and the desire for this to happen survives the hope for a long time. In all cases the child initially sees castration as an individual misfortune, and only later does it extend that misfortune to individual children, and finally to individual adults. When the child comes to understand the universality of this negative characteristic, the result is a great devaluation of femininity, and hence of the mother.

It is entirely possible that the above description of the little girl's response to the impression of castration and the prohibition on masturbation will make a confused and contradictory impression on the reader. That is not entirely the fault of the author. In fact, it is barely possible to produce an account that is universally applicable. We encounter the most diverse reactions, and contradictory attitudes can exist side by side in a single individual. The first imposition of the prohibition creates a conflict which will henceforward accompany the development of the sexual function. Comprehension of this idea is made even harder by the efforts involved in distinguishing the mental processes of this first phase from later phases, which cover it over and distort it in the memory. Thus, for example, the fact of castration is understood as a punishment for masturbatory activity, but its execution is transferred to the father; two things that must certainly not be original. The boy, too, generally fears castration by his father, although the threat is usually expressed by his mother.

Be that as it may, it is at the end of this first phase of attachment to the mother that the strongest motive for turning away from her appears, in the notion that she has not given the child proper genitals; which is to say that she has given birth to the child as a female. One is not surprised to hear another accusation with a rather shorter history: the mother has given the child too little milk, and not nursed it for long enough. In our cultural conditions that may often be the case; but it is certainly not true as often as is claimed in analysis. It seems rather that this accusation is an expression of universal dissatisfaction among children, who are, under the cultural conditions of monogamy, weaned off the breast after six to nine months – whereas primitive mothers devote themselves exclusively to their child for two to three years – as though our children were to remain unsatisfied for ever, as though they had never sucked long enough on their mother's breast. But I am not sure whether one would encounter the same complaint in the analysis of children who were nursed for as long as the children of primitive people. So great is the appetite of the child's libido! If we consider the whole series of motivations uncovered by analysis for turning away from the mother: that she neglected to equip the girl with the only correct form of genitals, that she fed her inadequately and forced her to share maternal love with others, that she never fulfilled all the expectations of love, and finally that she first stimulated and then prohibited the girl's sexual activity – none of these motivations seems adequately to justify the final hostility. Some are inevitable consequences of the nature of infantile sexuality, others are distinguished as later rationalizations of an emotional change that has not been understood. Perhaps it is truer to say that the attachment to the mother is doomed to collapse precisely because it is the first and because it is so intense, as we can often observe in the first marriages of young women which occurred when they were very much in love. I would suggest that in both cases the attitude of love can be seen to fail because of the inevitable disappointments and the accumulation of causes for aggression. Second marriages are generally more successful.

We cannot go so far as to claim that the ambivalence of emotional investments is a universally valid psychological law, that it is in general impossible to feel great love for a person without the addition of a hatred that may be equally great, or vice versa. There is no doubt that the normal person, the adult, manages to keep the two attitudes separate, not hating the object of his love or loving his enemy. But that seems to be the result of later developments. During the first phase of erotic life ambivalence is clearly the rule. In many people this archaic trait is preserved throughout the whole of life, and it is characteristic of compulsive neurotics that love and hatred are kept in balance in their object relations. We may assert the predominance of ambivalence among primitive people, too. The little girl's intense attachment to her mother must therefore also be highly ambivalent, and, with the help of other elements, it must, because of this very ambivalence, be forced away from the mother; once again, then, this is down to a universal characteristic of infantile sexuality.

Against this attempt at explanation a question immediately arises: how is it possible for boys to hold on to their attachment to their mother, which is certainly no less intense? We also have a ready answer to that question: it is because they have been enabled to deal with their ambivalence towards their mother by placing all their hostile emotions upon their father. First, though, we should not give this answer without having thoroughly studied the pre-Oedipal phase in boys; and secondly it would probably be more prudent to admit to ourselves that we have not gained a complete understanding of these processes, of which we have just become aware.

III

One further question is: What does the little girl demand from her mother? Of what nature are her sexual goals during the period of the exclusive attachment to the mother? The answer that we draw from the analytical material accords completely with our expectations. The girl's sexual goals as regards her mother are both active and passive in nature, and they are defined by the phases of the libido through which the child passes. In this context the relationship between activity and passivity deserves our particular interest. We may easily observe that in every area of mental experience, and not only that of sexuality, a passively received impression in the child provokes an active reaction. The child itself tries to do what has in the past been done to it. This is a task involving the mastery of the external world that has been imposed upon the child, and it can even lead to the child attempting to repeat impressions that it would have cause to avoid because of their painful content. Children's play serves this intention of complementing a passive experience with an active action, as a way, we might say, of abolishing it. If the doctor has opened the mouth of the resisting child to look into its throat, after the doctor has left the child will act out his role, repeating the violent procedure with its little sister, who is just as helpless towards the child as the child was to the doctor. It is impossible not to see this as a rejection of passivity and a preference of the active role. This swing from passivity to activity does not occur equally regularly and energetically in all children, and in some it may not happen at all. From this behaviour in the child we may draw conclusions about the relative strength of masculinity and femininity that it will manifest in its sexuality.

The child's first sexual, or sexually tinged, experiences with its mother are naturally passive in nature. It is by the mother that the child is suckled, fed, cleaned, dressed and guided in everything it does. Part of the child's libido persists in these experiences and enjoys the satisfactions connected with them, while another part tries to convert them into activity. Being nursed at the mother's breast is replaced by active sucking of the breast. In other respects the child contents itself either with autonomy, that is, by accomplishing on its own something that was previously done to it, or by actively repeating its passive experiences in play; or else it will actually make the mother its object, behaving towards her as an active subject. This last kind of behaviour, which occurs in the field of actual activity, seemed incredible to me for a long time until experience refuted my doubts.

We seldom hear of a little girl wanting to wash or dress her mother, or instructing her to perform her excretory functions. Certainly, the girl will sometimes say: 'Now let's play me being the mother and you being the child' – but more usually she fulfils these active desires indirectly, in play with her doll, with herself representing the mother as the doll represents the child. The fact that girls, unlike boys, prefer to play with dolls, is usually taken as a sign that femininity has awoken early. And that would not be a mistake, but we should not ignore the fact that it is the active side of femininity that is being manifested here, and that this preference on the part of the girl probably testifies to the passivity of the attachment to the mother, to the complete neglect of the father-object.

The highly surprising sexual activity of the girl towards the mother is expressed chronologically in oral, sadistic and finally even in phallic efforts directed at her. It is difficult to give an account of the details, because they are often obscure drive impulses which the child was unable to grasp psychically when they occurred, which have therefore been interpreted only retrospectively, and which then appear in analysis in modes of expression that they would certainly not originally have possessed. Sometimes we encounter these as transferences to the later father-object, where they should not be and where they severely obstruct understanding. We encounter aggressive oral and sadistic desires in the form into which they were compelled by early repression, as a fear of being killed by the mother which in turn justifies a desire for the mother's death if the desire becomes conscious. We cannot tell how often this fear of the mother is supported by unconscious hostility on the mother's part, and guessed by the child. (Hitherto I have only ever encountered the fear of being eaten among men; it is linked to the father, but it probably results from the transformation of oral aggression directed at the mother. One wants to devour the mother from whom one has been fed; in the case of the father the immediate cause for this desire is absent.)

People of the female sex who have a strong attachment to their mother, and whose pre-Oedipal phase I have been able to study, are agreed in stating that they showed the greatest resistance to the enemas that their mother performed upon them, reacting with fear and cries of rage. This may be a very common or even a universal form of behaviour among children. I acquired my understanding of the explanation of this particularly violent resistance from an observation by Ruth Mack Brunswick, who was dealing with the same problems at the same time, in which she sought to compare the outbreak of fury after an enema to orgasm after genital stimulation. The anxiety aroused in this context would then be understood as a translation of the pleasure in aggression stimulated by these injections. I believe that this is in fact the case, and that during the sadistic/anal stage the response to the intense passive stimulation of the colonic zone is an outbreak of aggression, which presents itself directly as rage or, when suppressed, as anxiety. This reaction seems to cease in later years.

Among the passive impulses of the phallic phase, one stands out: the girl regularly accuses the mother of being a seducer because she has felt her first or strongest genital sensations when her mother (or her substitute, a carer) was cleaning her and tending to her bodily functions. Mothers, from observation of their two- to three-year-old daughters, have often told me that the child enjoys these sensations and requires the mother to intensify them with repeated contact and rubbing. It is, I believe, because the mother so inevitably inaugurates the child's phallic phase that in the fantasies of later years it is the father who so regularly appears as the sexual seducer. In the act of turning away from the mother the introduction into sexual life has been transferred to the father.

Finally, during the phallic phase, there arise intense active impulses of desire directed towards the mother. Sexual activity during this period culminates in masturbation with the clitoris, probably while the mother is being imagined, but my experience would not enable me to guess whether the child is imagining a sexual goal, or what that goal might be. Such a goal can be clearly discerned only when the interests of the child have been given fresh impetus by the arrival of a little brother or sister. The little girl claims to have given the mother this new child, just as the boy does, and her reaction to this event and her behaviour towards the child are identical. That sounds fairly absurd, but perhaps only because it sounds so unfamiliar to us.

The fact that the girl turns away from the mother is an extremely significant step along her path of development, and it is more than a mere change of object. We have already described its source and its many supposed motivations; we shall now add that hand in hand with it we may observe a pronounced decline in active, and a rise in passive sexual impulses. Certainly, active strivings are more strongly affected by frustration, they have proved entirely incapable of accomplishment, and for that reason they are also more easily abandoned by the libido, but at the same time there has been no shortage of disappointments on the passive side. Clitoral masturbation often begins as the girl turns away from her mother, and in many cases, when the little girl's earlier masculinity is repressed, lasting damage is done to a great proportion of her sexual striving. The transition to the father-object is completed with the help of passive strivings, where these have escaped disaster. The path towards the development of femininity is now opened to the girl, in so far as it is not obstructed by the residues of the pre-Oedipal attachment to the mother, now overcome.

If we now survey the phase of female sexual development described above, we cannot avoid making a certain judgement about femininity as a whole. We have found the same libidinal forces at work here as in the male child, and have been able to convince ourselves that for a while they both take the same paths and attain the same results.

Then it is biological factors that distract them from their original goals, and guide even active strivings, masculine in every sense, on to the tracks of femininity. As we cannot help attributing sexual excitement to the effect of certain chemical substances, we may expect that biochemistry will one day offer us a substance whose presence provokes masculine sexual excitement, and one that provokes female sexual excitement. But this hope seems no less naïve than the hope, fortunately now a thing of the past, that one might discover stimuli for hysteria, compulsive neurosis, melancholy and so on individually under the microscope.

More complicated factors must also be at work in sexual chemistry. For psychology, however, it is irrelevant whether the body contains a single sexually stimulating substance, or two, or a huge number. Psychoanalysis teaches us to get by with a single libido, albeit one which has active and passive goals or types of satisfaction. It is in this opposition, and above all in the existence of libidinous strivings with passive goals, that the rest of the problem is contained.

IV

If we study the analytic literature about our subject, we will be convinced that everything I have presented here is already contained within it. There would have been no need to publish this work if, in an area so difficult of access, it was not always valuable to give an account of one's own experiences and personal conceptions. I myself have attained a keener understanding of things, and have isolated them more carefully. In some other studies, the exposition cannot be grasped all at once because of the simultaneous discussion of the problems of guilt and the super-ego. I have avoided that, and in the description of the various outcomes of this phase of development I have not examined the complications that result if the child, following the disappointment with her father, returns to the abandoned attachment to her mother, or throughout the course of her life switches repeatedly between one attitude and the other. But precisely because my work is only one contribution among others, I may spare myself an in-depth appraisal of the literature, and can limit myself to stressing significant agreements with some of these works and important deviations from others.

In Abraham's currently unsurpassed description of the 'Äusserungsformen des weiblichen Kastrationskomplexes' ['Manifestations of the Female Castration Complex'], (*Internatationale Zeitschrift für Psychoanalyse*, VII, 1921), one would like the element of the initially exclusive attachment to the mother to have been included. I must agree with the essential points in the important work of Jeanne[3] Lampl-de Groot.[4] This author acknowledges the complete identity of the pre-Oedipal phase in boys and girls, asserts the sexual (phallic) activity of the girl in regard to her mother, and proves it through observations. She traces the turning-away from the mother back to the influence of the knowledge of castration, which forces the child to renounce its sexual object and thus, in many cases, masturbation as well; she has expressed the overall development in the formula that the girl passes through a phase of 'negative' Oedipus complex, before she can enter the positive one. I see one shortcoming of this work in that it portrays turning away from the mother as a mere change of object, and does not take into account the fact that it is accomplished amid clear indications of hostility. This hostility is fully appreciated in the final work of Helene Deutsch ('Der feminine Masochismus und seine Beziehung zur Frigidität' ['Feminine Masochism and its Relation to Frigidity'], *Internationale Zeitschrift für Psychoanalyse*, XVI, 1930), which acknowledges the girl's phallic activity and the intensity of her attachment to her mother. Helene Deutsch also states that the act of turning towards the father also occurs via passive strivings (which have already been aroused in relation to the mother). In her earlier (1925) published book *Psychoanalyse der weiblichen Sexualfunktionen* [*Psychoanalysis of Female Sexual Functions*] she had not yet dispensed with application of the Oedipal scheme, and therefore interpreted the girl's phallic activity as identification with the father.

Fenichel ('Zur prägenitalen Vorgeschichte des Ödipuskomplexes' ['On the Pre-genital History of the Oedipus Complex'], *Internationale Zeitschrift für Psychoanalyse*, XVI, 1930) correctly stresses the difficulty of identifying, from the material thrown up by analysis, the content from the pre-Oedipal phase that persists unaltered in it, and which has been regressively (or otherwise) distorted. He does not acknowledge the girl's phallic activity as identified by Jeanne Lampl-de Groot, and also protests against the 'precipitation' of the Oedipus complex undertaken by Melanie Klein ('Frühstadien des Ödipuskonfliktes' ['Early Stages of the Oedipus Conflict'], *Internationale Zeitschrift für Psychoanalyse* XIV, 1928 and elsewhere), which she shifts back to the beginning of the second year. This temporal definition, which inevitably also changes the conception of all other relations of development, does not in fact coincide with the results of the analysis of adults, and is particularly difficult to reconcile with my findings about the girl's lengthy pre-Oedipal attachment to the mother. One way of mitigating this contradiction lies in the observation that in this field we cannot yet distinguish between that which is rigidly established by biological laws and that which is mobile and changeable under the influence of accidental experience. As we have long known with regard to the effect of seduction, other elements – the time of the birth of brothers and sisters, the time of the discovery of sexual difference, the direct observation of sexual intercourse, the encouraging or prohibiting attitude of the parents, and so on – can provoke an acceleration and maturing of child sexual development.

Some authors are inclined to play down the significance of the child's first and most original libidinal impulses in favour of later developmental processes, so that the role of these impulses – *in extremis* – is only to indicate certain directions, while the psychical intensities that follow those paths are supplied by later regressions and reaction-formations; thus, for example, when K. Horney ('Flucht aus der Weiblichkeit' [Flight from Womanhood], *Internationale*

Zeitschrift für Psychoanalyse, XII, 1926) says that we greatly underestimate the girl's primary penis-envy, while the intensity of the later striving towards masculinity should be attributed to a secondary penis-envy, which is used to fend off feminine impulses, particularly the feminine attachment to the father. That does not correspond to my impressions. However certain the presence of later reinforcements produced through regression and reaction-formation may be, however difficult it may be to undertake a relative assessment of the converging components of the libido, I do not think we should ignore the fact that those first libidinal impulses have an intensity of their own which remains greater than all later impulses, and which we may actually call incommensurable. It is certainly correct to say that an opposition exists between attachment to the father and the masculinity complex – it is the general opposition between activity and passivity, masculinity and femininity – but that does not give us the right to assume that one alone is primary, and the other owes its strength only to resistance. And if resistance to femininity occurs so energetically, whence can it derive its force but from the striving for masculinity, which is first manifested in the child's penis-envy and therefore deserves to be named after it?

A similar objection can be made to Jones's conception ('Die erste Entwicklung der weiblichen Sexualität' ['The Early Development of Female Sexuality'], *Internationale Zeitschrift für Psychoanalyse*, VIII, 1927), according to which the phallic stage in girls is more of a secondary protective reaction than a real stage of development. This corresponds neither to dynamic nor to temporal conditions.

(1931)

Notes

1. In the well-known case reported by Ruth Mack Brunswick ('Die Analyse eines Eifersuchtswahnes' ['The Analysis of a Jealous Delusion'], *Internationale Zeitschrift für Psychoanalyse*, XIV, 1928), the illness arises directly out of the pre-Oedipal fixation (on the sister).

2. We may predict that feminists among the men, and our female analysts, too, will not agree with these interpretations. They could hardly fail to object that such theories arise out of the male's 'masculinity complex' and are supposed to serve to create a theoretical justification of his innate tendency to the abasement and suppression of women. But such psychoanalytical argumentation recalls, in this case as so often, Dostoevsky's famous 'two-ended stick'. Opponents will on the one hand find it understandable that the female sex refuses to accept what seems to contract its hotly coveted equality with man. Clearly, the agonistic application of analysis does not resolve the question.
3. In accordance with the wishes of the author, I am correcting her name, which is given in the journal as: A. L. de Gr.
4. 'Zur Entwicklungsgeschichte des Ödipuskomplexes der Frau' ['The Evolution of the Oedipus Complex in Women'], *Internationale Zeitschrift für Psychoanalyse*, XIII, 1927.

"Freud ultimately did more for our understanding of art than any other writer since Aristotle."
—Lionel Trilling

The Joke and Its Relation to the Unconscious
Translated by Joyce Crick
Introduction by John Carey
In a rich collection of puns, witticisms, one-liners, and anecdotes, Freud answers the question "why do we laugh?" *The Joke and Its Relation to the Unconscious* explains how jokes provide immense pleasure by releasing us from our inhibitions and allowing us to express sexual, aggressive, playful, or cynical instincts that would otherwise remain hidden.
ISBN 978-0-14-243744-5

The Psychology of Love
Translated by Shaun Whiteside
Introduction by Jeri Johnson
This volume brings together Freud's illuminating discussions of the ways in which sexuality is always psychosexuality—that there is no sexuality without fantasy, conscious or unconscious. In these papers Freud develops his now famous theories about childhood and the transgressive nature of human desire.
ISBN 978-0-14-243746-9

The Psychopathology of Everyday Life
Translated by Anthea Bell
Introduction by Paul Keegan
Starting with the story of how he once forgot the name of an Italian painter—and how a young acquaintance mangled a quotation from Virgil through fears that his girlfriend might be pregnant—this volume brings together a treasure trove of muddled memories, inadvertent action, and verbal tangles. Freud's dazzling interpretations provide the perfect introduction to psychoanalytic thinking in action.
ISBN 978-0-14-243743-8

The Schreber Case
Translated by Andrew Webber
Introduction by Colin McCabe
In 1903, Judge Daniel Schreber, a highly intelligent and cultured man,

produced a vivid account of his nervous illness dominated by the desire to become a woman, terrifying delusions about his doctor, and a belief in his own special relationship with God. Eight years later, Freud's penetrating insight uncovered the impulses and feelings Schreber had about his father, which underlay his extravagant symptoms.

ISBN 978-0-14-243742-1

Studies in Hysteria
With Joseph Breuer
Translated by Nicola Luckhurst
Introduction by Rachel Bowlby

Hysteria—the tormenting of the body by the troubled mind—is among the most pervasive of human disorders; yet, at the same time, it is the most elusive. Freud's recognition that hysteria stemmed from traumas in the patient's past transformed the way we think about sexuality. *Studies in Hysteria* is one of the founding texts of psychoanalysis, revolutionizing our understanding of love, desire, and the human psyche. As full of compassionate human interest as of scientific insight, these case histories are also remarkable, revelatory works of literature.

ISBN 978-0-14-243749-0

The Uncanny
Translated by David McClintock
Introduction by Hugh Haughton

Freud was fascinated by the mysteries of creativity and the imagination. His insights into the roots of artistic expression in the triangular "family romances" (of father, mother, and infant) that so dominate our early lives reveal the artistry of Freud's own writing. Freud's first exercise in psycho-biography, his celebrated study of Leonardo, brilliantly uses a single memory to reveal the childhood conflicts behind Leonardo's remarkable achievements and his striking eccentricity.

ISBN 978-0-14-243747-6

"The Wolfman" and Other Cases
Translated by Louise Adey Huish
Introduction by Gillian Beer

When a disturbed young Russian man came to Freud for treatment, the analysis of his childhood neuroses—most notably a dream about wolves outside his bedroom window—eventually revealed a deep-seated trauma. It took more than four years to treat him, and the "Wolfman" became one of Freud's most famous cases. This volume also contains other case histories, all of which show us Freud at work, in his own words.

ISBN 978-0-14-243745-2

FOR THE BEST IN PAPERBACKS, LOOK FOR THE